PRAISE FOR

ONE DAY CLOSER

NATIONAL BESTSELLER

"A **gripping** account of what [Stewart] went through on the other side of kidnapping."

Chatelaine

"For all its **moving** detail about a mother's love and ferocious dedication, *One Day Closer* is most **compelling** in the way it makes clear there's no going back."

Maclean's

"Aside from being a love story between a mother who refused to lose hope and her strong-willed daughter, Stewart's book is also an indictment of the Canadian government's handling of the case."

Toronto Star

"A **harrowing**, soul-baring account of [Stewart's] quest to get her daughter."

The Canadian Press

"This book is **impossible to put down.** It is as inspiring as it is bone chilling. . . . *One Day Closer* is an incredible story of hope and joy, grit and gumption. This a five-star roller-coaster ride that will keep you up at night until you've devoured the very last word."

Jann Arden, singer-songwriter and bestselling
author of *Feeding My Mohter*

"A gripping, mother's-eye view of Amanda Lindhout's kidnapping ordeal. . . . For any parent who has ever worried about, advocated for, and deeply loved a child, Lorinda Stewart's honest, lion-hearted account will leave you both stunned and uplifted."

Sara Corbett, co-author of *A House in the Sky*

A MOTHER'S
QUEST TO
BRING HER
KIDNAPPED
DAUGHTER
HOME

ONE
DAY
CLOSER

LORINDA
STEWART

Published by Simon & Schuster

New York   London   Toronto   Sydney   New Delhi

SIMON &
SCHUSTER
CANADA

Simon & Schuster Canada
A Division of Simon & Schuster, Inc.
166 King Street East, Suite 300
Toronto, Ontario M5A 1J3

This Simon & Schuster Canada edition July 2018

SIMON & SCHUSTER CANADA and colophon are trademarks of Simon & Schuster, Inc.

For information about special discounts for bulk purchases, please contact Simon & Schuster Special Sales at 1-800-268-3216 or CustomerService@simonandschuster.ca.

Interior design by Carly Loman

Manufactured in the United States of America

10   9   8   7   6   5   4   3   2   1

Library and Archives Canada Cataloguing in Publication

Stewart, Lorinda, author
    One day closer : a mother's quest to bring her kidnapped daughter home /
    Lorinda Stewart.
Previously published: 2017.
ISBN 978-1-5011-4316-8 (softcover)
    1. Lindhout, Amanda—Kidnapping, 2008. 2. Stewart, Lorinda.
    3. Hostage negotiations. 4. Mothers—Canada—Biography. 5. Hostages—
    Somalia—Biography. I. Title.
HV6604.S662L56 2018 364.15'4092 C2018-900120-8

ISBN 978-1-5011-4318-2
ISBN 978-1-5011-4316-8 (pbk)
ISBN 978-1-5011-4315-1 (ebook)

To my mother and my five children—Mark, Amanda, Nathaniel, Janet, and Tiffany—who have taught me that love has no limits and ultimately it is always love that brings us home. You are my heart.

Janet, although you left this physical world while I was writing this book, love is eternal.

The First Nations man leaned in to my right ear and said, "Your name shall be Motherwind, because you have a Mother's heart, and like the wind you can be very gentle but also very powerful. So powerful that you can change the face of the rock."

Exactly one month after I received the gift of my native name, I would need that force.

—LORINDA STEWART

CONTENTS

PART I

CHAPTER ONE

BEFORE AND AFTER

On the day my daughter Amanda Lindhout was kidnapped by outlaws in Somalia—August 23, 2008—my life split into two parts: Before and After. That was Day 1, the day that catapulted me into a nightmare few parents can begin to imagine. Amanda, at age twenty-seven, was captured in the African country the United Nations has called the most lawless in the world.

In the seven years preceding the day that changed everything, Amanda was an intrepid, brave, spirited world traveler. She loved the intoxicating highs and freedoms of offbeat travel. Not for my daughter the paved roads and postcard sites beloved of tourists. Before going to Somalia, she had already traveled to more than fifty countries.

Amanda's first traveling adventure to Venezuela at the age of nineteen with her boyfriend, Jamie, ignited a seemingly insatiable desire to keep exploring, to see and experience as many countries and cultures as possible. On their next trip, Amanda and Jamie traveled to Thailand, Malaysia, Vietnam, Cambodia, and Laos. Amanda has always been a gifted storyteller, and as she related her travels to me upon returning, I could almost see, feel, and taste my way along with her. I roared with laughter and felt her frustration at the misunderstandings caused by language barriers and cultural differences. I recalled the stack of worn and dog-eared *National Geographic* magazines that she had kept beside her bed when she was young. It made me happy to watch her realizing her dreams of travel.

Shortly after she and Jamie returned from Asia, they broke up. Amanda and I had conversations about how that would change her travels in the future. She was adjusting to living as a single person and sometimes expressed fears of being alone and traveling on her own. This opened a new possibility to both of us. I had more freedom to travel now that my children were all grown, so Amanda and I went on an incredible trip together to Thailand and Malaysia, after which Amanda continued solo into Myanmar and India.

She was scared of the solo part, and I was scared for her, too. After all, I am a mother. Any mother will understand that I worried for Amanda, even as I respected and admired her incredible wanderlust. And I couldn't help but be proud of her tenacity. I didn't know then that Amanda would come to love traveling on her own or that this same tenacity would lead her into dangerous countries and war zones.

After that trip, Amanda's desire for exploration deepened, and she veered into unstable countries dominated by darker realities. Most often she traveled solo, and she sought assignments as a journalist covering war, poverty, and corruption, as she attempted to tell the stories of victims who had no voice. She willingly risked her life to capture the frontline stories she felt our complacent world needed to know about. I admired her for that then, just as I do now.

Over the course of seven years, Amanda established a pattern: she would work two jobs in Calgary as a bar server or waitress, living penuriously, with little social life, until she saved enough for her next trip. She would travel for months until her money ran out, then return to Calgary to repeat the cycle. She had made an art of living frugally, and she could stretch a dime as far as humanly possible, allowing her to travel for longer periods of time.

I often found myself defending her choices when confronted by people who thought she was crazy for risking her life for people half a world away, people she didn't even know. I had come to realize long before that my daughter did not belong to me. She belonged to the world, and God knows the world needs more people like her. I was determined to support the shining light I saw in her.

For my part, during those years, I learned how to remain sane and not become crazed with fear at the "what-ifs." To do so, I had to stand vigilant over my imagination. I tried very hard not think of the risks involved when Amanda was abroad. That was not an easy task, especially when phone calls with her were punctuated by gunfire in the background and laced with her commentary on bombs and mortars exploding nearby or in neighborhoods she had recently visited. I remember her dangerous time in Afghanistan—land of roadside bombs, suicidal terrorists, and the Taliban's contempt for women, expressed in harsh sharia law. After that came Ethiopia and Egypt, then a second stint in Afghanistan, where a Global News team, shocked that as a freelancer she had no defense gear, kindly outfitted her with a flak jacket and helmet while she worked on stories for *Afghan Scene* and *Combat and Survival*. All this time, I forced a running narrative in my head: I would worry only if I knew something bad was actually happening to her—that was nearly impossible for a mother, but I really tried.

Amanda and I had had complicated struggles and many arguments during her teenage years. But when she began traveling, we made a concerted effort to communicate and mend past hurts. Every time she returned from a trip, she would rent a place in Calgary for a while and work to make more money to travel. There were several times that she came home and stayed with me in Canmore. I treasured those visits because when she wasn't working we would spend time together chatting about her last trip or her next one, shopping, cooking, hiking, laughing, drinking wine, and having our own private dance parties. Amanda has always loved to dance. She loves the freedom of it—the movement a way to celebrate life. It was a great comfort to me then that we had become so close. While she was away, phone calls and emails became a lifeline between us, and we made those happen almost daily, depending on the cell and Wi-Fi service in the area she was in.

We kicked off New Year's Eve 2008 by celebrating together in my small basement suite, chanting "2008 is going to be great!" Amanda had just been hired by Press TV for live reporting from within the war zone in Iraq. We were both excited but afraid of what that could mean. In reality, my mind was in panic mode, but I had learned not to share my fears with Amanda. It annoyed her when I worried, and there was no good outcome from it. In the last few hours of 2007, we feasted on our favorite food—cheese fondue, crab legs, and artichokes dripping in garlic butter—and we drank copious amounts of red wine. We watched movies. We laughed. And of course, we danced, feeling optimistic for the future.

Little did I know that only a few months later, my optimism would be crushed. In August 2008, I was living in Balfour in southeastern British Columbia, when events in Somalia, half a world away, became the fixed focus of my life. I had moved to BC to be closer to my sons, Mark, thirty-two, and Nathaniel, twenty-five. I rented a room nearby and worked in a bakery.

A week earlier, Amanda had called me from Kenya. "Mom, I'm going to Nairobi. Nigel is flying to meet me there. Then we're off to Somalia. We're going to collaborate on the story that I've been wanting do for a long time on the war there. He'll be the photographer, and I'll be the writer."

This was interesting news. Amanda had been a late starter as a journalist and was just now beginning to earn credits and commissioned assignments. Amanda had met Nigel Brennan, an Australian photographer, in the winter of 2006. They'd become involved but were no longer together in that way.

"It's a relief to know that you won't be going into Somalia alone," I said. "But won't it be awkward between you and Nigel, given your past history?"

"Oh, Mom," she said. "We've both moved on. In fact, Nigel has a girlfriend. We're just friends now, and this is an important story we need to cover."

"Does his family in Australia know he's doing this story with you?" I asked.

"I don't know. He's an adult making his own decisions."

There it was—that annoyance again when I asked too many questions. "Okay, okay," I said, laying off.

"Just so you know, Mom, once we're in Mogadishu we're hiring armed guards and staying in a secure hotel. That means the hotel is surrounded by armed guards 24/7."

This was a relief to hear, and I thanked her for telling me. "You know I try not to worry, but this news helps. Please," I said, "call me before you go. I love you, Peanut."

"Thanks, Mom. Don't worry, I'll call. I love you too!"

A few days later, Amanda let me know that she'd arrived safely in Nairobi, Kenya, and would soon leave for Somalia. My motherly instincts felt heightened, and I had a foreboding feeling of apprehension about her trip into Somalia. I emailed her: "I woke up crying and thinking about you. I couldn't go back to sleep, so I got up and went out in my kayak. It was my first solo trip. It was amazing! Are you safe? Safer than in Iraq? I love you so much and I miss you like crazy. I'm so very proud of you, Amanda. You inspire me and countless others every day."

I felt uneasy as I waited to hear from Amanda. While awaiting her call, I was busy looking for a new job because I'd quit my job at a bakery. By nature, I'm a very sociable person. Working at night alone in an unbearably hot bakery, then sleeping during the day, was not a good fit for me. I wanted to be of service, perhaps at the local women's shelter. The idea of service is part of who I am. From the earliest age, I always imagined myself in a role helping people and making the world a better, more loving place. I recognized that same compassionate drive in Amanda, and as dangerous as her chosen profession was, I wanted to encourage her. When you have a child committed to pursuing a high-risk lifestyle, danger is an omnipresent part of the package.

On the morning of August 23, my life changed forever. I didn't know it then, but this was Day 1 of an ordeal that would last 460 days. I received a call from Jon Lindhout, Amanda's father and my ex-husband. Jon was irritated because Amanda had spoken to him the night before from Somalia, where she'd been for two days. She had called her father to ask him to send her money through Dahabshiil, an international East African money transfer agency with branches in Canada. When Jon had tried to call her back in the morning for clarification, she had not answered.

"Have you talked to Amanda today?" he asked. "I don't know what she expects me to do when I can't even reach her!"

"No," I said. "I haven't heard from her. In fact, I haven't talked to her since before she went to Mogadishu. You know how she is sometimes. Maybe she's out of service area. Who knows? If she needs money she'll get back to you."

It was a short conversation but enough to niggle at my mind. Amanda had been in Somalia for two days, and she hadn't called me yet? It seemed odd. I felt a little hurt that she had spoken to her father several times but not to me. I couldn't figure it out.

I remembered one instance years earlier when she had been going into Pakistan for the first time and she had called both Jon and me to say that if she died we should know that she was doing exactly what she wanted to do with her life. I expressed my fears and told her that she wasn't being fair to her family. I begged her not to go. She became so angry with me that she cut off all communication for about two weeks. When she finally restored communication, it was with a defiantly triumphant email that declared, "I LOVE PAKISTAN!!!" She told me it was her favorite place to date and the people were among the kindest she had ever met.

But that was then. Now I had no reason to think that she was angry with me.

I wondered what was going on in Mogadishu, and I hoped she was okay. It had been seven months since I had driven Amanda to the airport for this journey. She had gone first to Iraq for her job as a journalist for Press TV, an English-language station financed by the Iranian government. We discussed how biased reports were coming from both sides of the war. Amanda's reports for Press TV were edited for Iranian biases, but articles she sent to the *Red Deer Advocate* in Alberta more clearly reflected her dismay at the United States and its "Green Zone" in Baghdad. A person in the Green Zone could go to Burger King or Starbucks, while those just outside the gates were starving. She was shocked by the reality of the average citizens and what they had suffered and lost. She referred to the 4.5 million orphans as the forgotten victims of war, many of whom were begging on the streets for food. Iraqis were now questioning their newfound "freedom" and they were bitter at the United States for throwing them into a deeper hell than what Saddam Hussein had inflicted upon them. The devastation of the war on Iraqi families was hard for her to swallow.

It was after a few months of being in the thick of the Iraqi war when Amanda called me and told me that she was ready for a change. Her plans would take her to Kenya and then to Somalia. She had talked for months about Somalia, and it bothered her that there was very little news being reported on the war there. I knew very little about Somalia except that the United Nations had deemed it one of the most dangerous countries in the world, though I couldn't imagine that it could possibly be more dangerous than being in the middle of the war raging in Iraq.

Somalia is a sickle-shaped country in the Horn of Africa that stretches along the Arabian Sea. It remains a place where few reporters dare venture. At the time Amanda was there, international humanitarian organizations had withdrawn their aid workers after too many had been killed or kidnapped for ransom. Piracy and kidnapping had become two of the country's main industries. Somalia was one of the poorest countries in the world, in a state of anarchy run by warlords and Al-Shabaab, a terrorist group closely linked to Al-Qaida. That's where my Amanda was.

Jon called me again an hour after we had spoken the first time. Now panic replaced irritation. His brother, Jack, had been contacted by a Vancouver radio announcer who had just seen a news stream from Reuters Africa. The news stream claimed that a Canadian journalist and an Australian photographer—Amanda Lindhout and Nigel Brennan—had "gone missing" in Somalia.

"Turn on the TV!" Jon screamed. "It's all over the news. Amanda and Nigel have gone missing. Oh my God, I don't know what to do!"

Although I felt a rush of adrenaline and weakness in my legs, my first instinct was to try to calm Jon.

"Jon, let's try to remember we don't know for sure what is happening," I said. "'Missing' can mean many things."

I hung up and turned on the TV. I saw Amanda's face passing across the screen. The reports quickly changed from "missing" to "kidnapped at gunpoint." I sat down, got up, paced. Then I started to cry. Suddenly everything felt as though it were occurring in slow motion. I was having a hard time breathing. I was at my friend Glen's house, and I stared at the TV, stunned. Was this really happening? Old photos of Amanda, dug up by various news agencies, streamed past. I checked online. The internet carried the same story: Amanda and Nigel, kidnapped at gunpoint in Somalia, along with their translator, Abdifatah Mohamed Elmi, and two Somali colleagues.

Despite the endless repetition of the news, the reality was slow to sink in: It's a mistake. This can't be happening. But what if it is true? It can't be. Not Amanda. *Noooooo.*

Glen was obviously uncomfortable and did not know what to do for me. I had to get out of there. I had to get back home, so I phoned Debbie Till, who rented space in the same house as I did.

"Debbie! Debbie!" I was wailing now.

"What's going on, Lorinda? Are you okay?"

"I'm at Glen's. Amanda's been kidnapped!"

"Holy fuck! Stay right there and I'll come to get you."

"It's okay, I can drive. Oh my God, Debbie. This can't be happening."

"I have my cell with me, so call me if you need help," Debbie said.

I felt numb as I got into my car. I had driven these roads countless times, but I found myself lost and confused in what became an unfamiliar maze of left and right turns. Glen probably realized that I had gone into a state of shock, because he followed me on his motorbike. When I pulled over to figure out which way to turn, he drove up beside me. "Follow me," he said, and I did.

When we arrived, Debbie was standing at the top of the driveway, waving her arms. I wasn't even out of the car before she had her arms around me. The two of us stood on the back deck, overlooking beautiful Kootenay Lake, while I cried and Debbie smoked. I asked her for a cigarette even though I hadn't smoked in years. I lit it, took one drag, and realized that I couldn't smoke it.

She tried to reassure me that Amanda would be fine. Hadn't I told Debbie story after story about my girl's resourcefulness?

"Amanda will get out of this, too."

I phoned Jon, hoping for more news, hoping that it had all been a mistake and she was fine. The Vancouver radio announcer who had first contacted our family had given Jon the phone number of the Department of Foreign Affairs and International Trade (DFAIT) in Ottawa. At first, the staffers didn't believe he was Amanda's father. They thought he was a reporter looking for a scoop. When he was finally able to verify who he was, he was told only what we already knew: that Amanda and Nigel had "been reported as having been kidnapped at gunpoint." Foreign Affairs then asked Jon to call if *he* heard anything more.

Jon was in a state of high anxiety. "Lorinda," he said, "you can't believe what's happening here. The media has been calling nonstop, asking for a comment or interview. There's even news vans parked outside my house. This is insane. I can't even go out my front door!"

"Jon, I'll head out first thing in the morning. We need to be together for this. Let's not forget that Amanda's been in many sticky situations before, and she's gotten herself out of them, right? This will all be over soon." I was reminding myself as much as I was reminding him. "Boy, she's in trouble when she gets home." I said. "I think we may have to take away her passport after this."

Once I got off the phone with Jon, I called Amanda's best friend, Kelly Barker. She, too, had been inundated by calls from the media and had even given a short interview. Strangely, no one had attempted to contact me, not then and only rarely afterward. That actually worked out for the best later on, when I needed to work under the media's radar.

Next, I called Foreign Affairs myself, hoping for an update, but was told they could not give me any information. Maybe the people there thought I was a reporter, too. I needed to get to Sylvan Lake, where Jon lived, so we could get updates at the same time.

I tried to call Amanda's brothers, Mark and Nathaniel, up in Fort Nelson, British Columbia, where they were working, but my call didn't connect and I assumed they were out of cell phone range, as they often were. I texted them instead: "I've been trying to call you with some news and I need you to call me asap! Amanda has been kidnapped! It's all over the news!"

They didn't check their phones until their first coffee break the next day. They called and put me on speakerphone so both could hear me and ask questions at the same time. By the way their voices were quivering, I knew they were trying not to cry, and my heart went out to them.

They had basically the same questions that Jon and I had: "Are they sure that it was Amanda?" "What's being done?" "What can we do?" I had few answers for them. They wanted to know if Jon and I were okay.

"Should we come down there now, Mom? Do you need us?" they asked. I encouraged them to stay put, to try to stay calm.

"Don't worry," I said. "I'll call you if we get any updates."

Next I called my mom. I hated to burden her with this news, as she was still mourning the loss of my father the previous year. She was momentarily silent, absorbing the surreality of what I was telling her.

"I don't even know what to say, Lorinda. Are you okay? What can I do?"

"Can you please put Amanda and Nigel on every prayer line you know of?"

My mom was a regular churchgoer and was herself a prayer warrior. "Of course. I'll do that right now," she said. Although we saw religion differently, I appreciated all the positive energy that would be focused on Amanda and Nigel.

"Thanks, Mom. Please pray for Jon and me, too. Love you, Mom!"

"I will. I love you, too," she said as her voice broke.

Once at home, I sat on Debbie's couch and stared at the TV screen. A friend had prepared a spaghetti supper, but my stomach was in knots and I couldn't think about food. Debbie generously offered to drive me to Sylvan Lake. "We'll take your car. I'll fly back. That way you'll have your car while you're there."

I didn't sleep much that night. I mostly sat in front of the TV or paced around, trying to figure out what I could or should be doing. I could hear the snoring and breathing of everyone else in the house and was grateful for some quiet time to think.

The next morning, Debbie and I caught the 8 a.m. ferry. From the other side of the lake, it was another eight-hour drive to Sylvan Lake. It's a gorgeous, pine-scented journey through the mountains, but I saw none of it. Debbie, who is quite a funny character at the best of times, tried to keep the conversation light. She reminded me of the first time we had met and she had given me shit for being too noisy. She compared herself to Danny DeVito's mother in the movie *Throw Momma from the Train*, and it made us laugh as it had even then. Laughter was a helpful distraction. Debbie can seem tough at first meeting, but she has a heart of gold and was a loyal friend when I needed her most.

We talked about how we would all be on *Oprah* after Amanda was home. We talked about what we'd wear on her show. We talked about anything and everything but Amanda's kidnapping.

About three hours into our trip, we stopped at Cranbrook for a bite to eat, but I still couldn't stomach any food. Cell phone service is sparse in the mountains, so I took advantage of being able to call Jon to let him know where I was and ask if there were any updates. There were none.

We arrived at Jon's house later in the afternoon, and as we pulled up I couldn't help but admire his green thumb. His house was surrounded by meticulously manicured flower gardens. It was no wonder that he had won the "Communities in Bloom" contest several years in a row.

When Jon opened the door, his eyes were red, his face distraught.

We hugged each other. I could feel him shaking. We were both crying. Jon was unnerved when he realized that Debbie was with me, and
I couldn't understand why he was so agitated. I reminded him why she
was there. He asked to speak with me privately, and the reason for his
panic soon became clear: Royal Canadian Mounted Police (RCMP)
investigators were sitting at his dining table. Three of them—Dave
and Jason from Edmonton and Barry from Red Deer. I was introduced. They explained that this was a private meeting, so we agreed
that Debbie would watch TV downstairs until she left to catch her
flight back home.

Having been married to Jon for seven years, I knew that this situation would cause him a lot of stress, and I wondered how this would
go for us. It was so gut-wrenching to see his anguish that I momentarily forgot that I was in the same boat. In one clear moment, I realized
I needed to get myself together and be strong for all of us.

I joined the investigators at the table. "So," I said, "what do you
need from us? How can we help Amanda?"

I listened carefully as Dave said, "Lorinda, you should know that
this morning, while Jon was in the shower, the kidnappers called and
left a message on his answering machine." I looked at the faces around
the table—tense, grim. They wanted to put us at ease, but they needed
to be direct as well. I looked at Jon. His face was void of color. He
looked as if he might throw up. I'm sure I looked the same.

"We'd like to play that message for you now."

"Okay," I said.

The officers played the message back for me. A heavily accented
male voice announced, "Hello. We have your daughter." The man
identified himself as Adam, then claimed to represent Amanda's kidnappers. He demanded $1.5 million dollars American for her release.
Then he hung up.

Something shifted in that moment as I felt a powerful responsibility set in. I became analytical and found myself focusing on Adam's
tone. I was surprised and relieved that he didn't sound like a monster.
The kidnappers I had seen in the movies sounded much more sinister.

I knew that I needed to operate in this clearheaded, rational mode if I were going to be useful to the RCMP and Amanda.

The three men from the RCMP explained that it was against the Canadian government's policy to pay a ransom to kidnappers; however, our country had had great success in engaging local governments to intervene with kidnappers to secure the release of hostages. Instead of paying ransom money, our government offered aid in the form of food, pharmaceuticals, hospitals, and schools for local communities in exchange for hostages' freedom.

That actually sounded great to me. To imagine that good might come from this horrific situation was something I hadn't dared to hope. I even thought that Amanda would be pleased by that outcome. What I didn't realize at the time was that Somalia had a very small and weak transitional government with very little bargaining power. This would prove to be a daunting challenge.

"Do you know where we can get Amanda's dental records?" Barry asked. "Does she have any distinguishing birthmarks, scars, or tattoos?"

I'd watched enough TV shows to know the sobering reason for these requests, as had Jon.

"You don't think that we'll need them, do you?" he asked.

"No, but we have to be prepared for anything."

Jon knew where to pick up her dental records. I explained that I had an identical tattoo to Amanda's. I pulled my shirtsleeve down a little to reveal a daisy on my shoulder. "Amanda has one just like mine on her ankle," I said. Mother-daughter tattoos had been our way of celebrating her fourteenth and my thirty-ninth birthdays—June 12 and June 13, respectively, 1995. When Amanda had announced that she was getting a tattoo, I'd surprised her by suggesting we both get one.

"Really, Mom? We can both get tattoos?"

"Sure," I said. "Why not? That way, in the future, no matter where we are in the world, we'll have matching tats." We agreed on our favorite flower at the time, a daisy. The investigators seemed to think it had been a sweet gesture, or if they didn't, they did a great job of convincing me they did.

Before the investigators left for the night, they cautioned Jon and me to refuse to talk to the media and to keep their presence confidential from everyone. They would be back the next morning to wiretap Jon's landline, so they could monitor calls from the kidnappers and perhaps trace them. Dave told us that they would be up most of the night developing a plan on how to move forward.

"If the phone rings tonight, you must not answer it. Do you understand?"

"But what if Amanda is trying to call us?" I asked.

"That's possible but not likely at this point. You must trust us. We need a plan in place before we speak to the kidnappers, and we need that wiretap. They will call back, so don't worry about that."

Our investigators had been dropped into a complicated, life-and-death global scenario. I wondered to myself if they had the experience to handle something like this. How many times had they done this before? How many times had they been in similar homes across the country, telling distraught parents how to cope with one of their worst nightmares? As they left for the night, I had a feeling that many phone calls would take place later with the higher-ups as they scrambled to come up with a plan.

I spent the night on the couch in Jon's living room, listening to the phone ring. Four times. Every time it rang, I jumped up and ran over to the phone, my anxiety level rising with the increasing temptation to answer in the hope that Amanda was on the line. But I couldn't answer. Instead I just stood there, staring at the phone. I thought how confused Amanda would be that no one answered. I thought the kidnappers would be puzzled, too, and I worried that it would anger them. But ultimately, I knew that I had to trust the experts, the RCMP. So I went back to bed. I lay there and listened, silently whispering "Amanda, I'm here! Please know that we are going to do everything we need to do to bring you home. We love you. I love you more than you possibly know." The tears started, and soon I was sobbing.

Between fits of agitated sleep, I lifted my spirits by reminding myself of all the times—and there had been many—when Amanda's ingenuity had gotten her out of trouble or someone had shown up at just the right time on her travels to help her. I was certain that this would be the case yet again. I was buoyed with confidence throughout the night as I replayed specific memories, such as the time she was in Bangladesh and an auto rickshaw driver had tried to take her out to the countryside to "meet his family." Amanda had become frightened and demanded that he return her to her hotel. When he had kept going, she started punching him. He turned around and took her back to where she was staying.

On the same trip, she hadn't been able to obtain the exit papers she needed to get out of Bangladesh unless a man vouched for her. When she told me that, I called Interpol, demanding that they help her, but she wasn't pleased with me and told me straight out, "I can take care of myself!" And she did. She contacted a German businessman she had met on the plane, and he arranged to have his armed car escort her out of the country.

In most countries, she had made contacts whom she could call if she needed aid, and there had been times they had helped her. This wasn't even the first time she had been detained. While working for Press TV in Iraq, the car she was traveling in was forced by bandits to stop. She and her colleagues were taken into an empty warehouse for questioning. Frightened because many foreigners had been kidnapped or murdered in similar situations, she had covertly used her cell phone to call a government contact who persuaded the men to let all of them go two hours later. There were so many stories like this throughout her seven years of travels.

Eventually I drifted off to sleep, feeling confident that, just like all her previous experiences, this one would be resolved quickly.

CHAPTER TWO

"YOU ARE THE MOM"

Day 3. At 8 a.m. on August 25, our three investigators arrived as promised, bringing with them a tech specialist from Calgary and another RCMP negotiator from Red Deer. All were in good spirits, laughing and joking while they set up the equipment, creating an air of optimism that I greatly appreciated. Surely, if they were so relaxed, it meant our nightmare would be over quickly. As they discussed where to set up, we decided to use the table in Jon's dining area, which opened into the living room at the back of the house. Strategically it was perfect because anyone coming to the front door could not see into the area with the recording equipment. Within the hour, we were set up and ready to go.

The team went out onto the back deck for a confidential conversation, as they did every time they needed to discuss things. Jon and I stayed inside, watching their animated gestures and trying to guess what they were talking about. A while later, they came back into the house, and Barry approached me.

"Lorinda," he said, "do you think you can speak with me privately for a moment?" I looked over at Jon, then turned back to Barry. Jon and I were in this together, but I was eager to play my part, to do whatever needed to be done.

"Sure," I said. "Of course."

We went to the deck to speak out of earshot.

"Lorinda, last night before you arrived, we asked Jon if he would consider taking on the role of negotiator. He said no, which is understandable given the pressure."

I nodded. Jon and I had spoken about that the night before, and I understood that he was clearly shaken to his core and in a fragile state. I waited to hear why Barry had wanted to speak with me privately.

"Being the negotiator means that you would be the person on the phone with the kidnappers. It's not easy being the person on the end of the line. The kidnappers will try their best to manipulate you, threaten you, and scare you."

He paused, then said, "Lorinda, we want to ask you to take on the role of negotiator. After meeting you, we think that you would be the best person to negotiate on your daughter's behalf. What do you think about that?"

I could feel my heart racing as I considered the gravity of his question. "You really think I could do it?"

"I wouldn't be asking if I didn't think so. One of us will be sitting beside you, guiding you through those difficult conversations. You won't be alone."

I considered what this would mean—that my daughter's life would depend on my ability to find a resolution with the desperate, violent, and unpredictable men who'd kidnapped her.

"Of course I want to, but to be honest with you, I'm absolutely terrified," I admitted. "What if I make a mistake?"

Barry looked me in the eye. "I'm not going to lie to you, Lorinda. It scares me, too, but we will be with you every step of the way to guide you."

I was boosted by Barry's firm confidence in me and his assurance that I would never be left on my own. I agreed.

"Great!" he said, sounding relieved. "Together we can do this. Let's bring Amanda home."

Barry continued by explaining the next step: logistics. Two RCMP negotiators would split twenty-four-hour shifts for ten days, after which time another two negotiators would rotate in. This would

continue until Amanda was released. We would be advocating for
the release of both Amanda and Nigel. At the same time, the RCMP
and the Australian Federal Police (AFP) would set up a joint cell in
Nairobi to negotiate with the kidnappers through on-the-ground
contacts. Canada's Department of Foreign Affairs and International
Trade (DFAIT) and Australia's Department of Foreign Affairs and
Trade (DFAT) would also be involved. Nigel's family would work in
tandem with us from Australia, using a similar setup in Nigel's sister
Nicky's home. In Nigel's case, Nicky would be the negotiator.

"Are you following me?" Barry asked.

"Yes," I said. It was a lot to take in, but I was still running on adrenaline, and everything seemed clear and focused.

"Good," Barry said, escorting me back inside just as the rest of
the team was leaving. He let them know I'd agreed to negotiate, and
everyone seemed pleased. We said our good-byes, and then we filled
Jon in. He was grateful that I'd be stepping into the role.

There was no time to waste. Barry immediately began to explain
how the process would work. The house phone had already been
blocked to all calls other than Somali numbers and had been wired to
a center where every call would be recorded, transcribed, printed, and
sent back to us. He had me sit at the dining table to demonstrate how,
as I answered the phone, the negotiator sitting beside me would put
on earphones to monitor the conversation. He would have a stack of
index cards and a pen beside him. As he or one of the others listened
in, they would write talking notes on the index cards with questions
or points I should make or statements to be repeated for emphasis or
clarification.

"Do you think you can do this?" Barry asked. "Do you think you
can follow these prompts?"

It all sounded quite clear. "Yes," I said. "I can do that." At that point
no one—myself included—really knew the length I was prepared to
go to get my daughter back.

"Okay," Barry continued. "So one of your most important tasks is
going to be getting POLs—proofs of life."

That's when I learned that "proofs of life" were pieces of evidence that confirmed Amanda was alive. I tried to focus on the hope rather than on the threat it implied. I would get a proof by asking the kidnappers a question only Amanda could answer. Barry asked me to start writing up a list of POL questions, which I did:

What surgery did Dad have four years ago?

Back surgery.

What is the name of the restaurant in Sylvan Lake where you used to work?

Chefs.

Where did your mom take you when you were ten?

Disneyland.

Just then, my cell phone rang. I grabbed it and checked the caller ID. "I don't recognize the caller," I said, looking up at Barry. "It's a very long number. Maybe it's Adam." I felt the blood rush to my head. "How did he get my number?"

"It's possible Amanda gave it to him," Barry said.

I was shaking so hard I could barely hold on to the phone. "Should I answer?"

Barry took a deep breath. "Yes, Lorinda," he said. "You can do this. You're going to answer the call. I'll guide you. I'll be right here, listening in."

Since Barry had no way to monitor the call on my cell, he leaned in to me, trying to hear what was being said on the other end of the line. My telephone training had barely begun. I didn't feel ready yet to take a call like this. I had to rely on what I'd seen on TV, along with gut instinct. As calmly as possible, I answered, "Hello?"

"Ah, hello. This is Adam." As on the previous recording, he sounded like a "regular guy," although his strong accent made it hard for me to understand him.

"Thank you, Adam, for calling us back. I can tell by your voice that you're a good man who will look after Amanda," I said. I wanted to appeal right away to whatever humanity this kidnapper might possess.

"Ah, yes, thank you, thank you. I am happy to speak with Amanda's mother," he replied.

Barry was gesturing at me now, pointing at Jon's landline. He wanted me to switch lines so he could record the call.

"Adam, I'm sorry. My cell phone costs too much money to use," I said. "Will you please call me back at Amanda's father's number?"

"Yes, yes, that is fine," he said. Then we hung up.

I didn't have time to think too hard about what had just happened. During our few moments of grace, I seated myself at Jon's phone, while Barry quickly grabbed the earphones. The phone rang shortly afterward. I looked at Barry, and he nodded. I picked up. That's when my real challenge—mental, emotional, and technical—began. I had to communicate with a Somali man who had a heavy accent and only limited English. Often with calls to third-world countries, there's a delay of a few seconds. This means it's hard not to talk over the other person. With this call—along with the hundreds still to come—connections were often weak and would sometimes fail suddenly.

What follows is my first recorded call, on Monday, August 25, 2008.

"Hello, Adam," I said.

"Corina," he answered, confusing my name.

"Thank you . . . thank you for calling me back. Thank you for talking to me today."

"How is your condition? Are you Corina, the mother of Amanda?"

"My name is Lorinda, and I am Amanda's mom."

"Lorinda, yes. I only to tell you that Amanda is very good. She is well. She has said to me greet to my mother. Understand?"

"Yes, yes, I understand. Thank you."

"Secondly, she is very good, and we want from you the ransom only. Understand?"

"Yes, I understand."

"Before this time, we found out that she works with intelligence services."

"Sorry?" I asked. I had no idea what he meant.

"Later, she become a journalist."

"A journalist. Yes, she—"

Adam interrupted. "What we need from you is to get money."

"Okay," I said.

"One and half million or two million dollars. Understand?"

"Yes, yes, I understand that." I thought about the proofs of life that Barry had just educated me on. "Adam, I need to know for sure that Amanda is okay. Can I speak with her?"

"Ah, you cannot speak with her. At this time we do not allow you. But everything you say to me I will get her for you answers. Understand?"

"Yes, I understand. Could I get you to ask Amanda a question for me?"

"Yes."

"She will give you an answer that only I know, so I know that she's okay."

"Okay, you asking me and I should ask, and you will get the answers . . . I said to you we don't want hard or to make ah, any, any . . ." It was hard to hear with the delay. We were both struggling.

"Yeah?" I said.

"Everything you're asking, you should get the answer from her."

"I just need to know that she's okay. I'm her mom, you know? I'm sure you can understand. You have a mom."

"Yes, I am respecting to you what ask her . . . The reason I is calling to you and don't call the father . . ."

"Yeah?"

" . . . is that you are the mom."

"Thank you, thank you so much, Adam. Can you ask Amanda what movie we watched on New Year's Eve?"

"What movie we watch," he repeated.

"On New Year's Eve," I said.

"Okay. What movie did we watch on New Year's Eve?"

"Yeah."

"Okay, thank you very much. Thank you. I should memorize and ask her and we shall get the results tomorrow."

"Okay, what time will you call me tomorrow?"

"At this time. *Inshallah* [If Allah allows]."

"Let me again the question you are asking me. What movies do we watch this year eve?"

Barry slipped me a card prompting me to ask Adam if the kidnapping had been politically motivated.

"Yes, your English is very good, Adam," I said. "Adam, can you tell me why you're doing this? Is this political or—"

"It is political. Because your government, this bad government that we are warring with. Understand?"

"It's for your government?"

"We have understood each other, have to understood at this time."

"Could you please repeat that? I couldn't quite hear you."

"Hmm?" Adam struggled to understand, as did I.

"I couldn't hear what you said."

"The problem of the reason is that we have gotten information that she was working with this government of—"

"Amanda's not working for the government," I said.

"No. She come earlier, she is, ah, journalist, understand."

"Yes."

"But that is all. Thank you for interrupting. I have interrupted you, I think."

"Oh, that is quite, quite all right."

"Okay, thank you very much . . . What we need is, at this time, only is ransom."

"Okay, yes."

"Tomorrow. Tomorrow at this time. Tomorrow at this time I will call you with, with the answer this question first."

Barry cued me to ask him for Adam's phone number.

"Is there a number that I could call you at?"

"Yes, yes, it's a number. But it is on four and ten o'clock a.m. Local Somalia. The number is . . . you have a pen?"

"Yeah, the number is?"

Each digit was given and repeated over and over.

"It is on three hours in the day."

"So it's on three hours."

"Hours, in day."

"Okay," I said. "I understand. It's on three hours a day at ten a.m."

"In the morning. Or for longest, maybe four hours, if Allah allows."

Barry asked me to confirm that Adam was actually in Somalia.

"Okay. And you are calling me from Somalia, right?"

"Yes, I'm calling you Somalia."

"Okay, thank you, thank you so much."

"Thank you so much, Lorinda."

"We are working on getting the money together, but it takes time. Hello? Hello?"

The call had been disconnected. I put down my phone.

Before I had a chance to even process what had just happened, Barry said, "That was fantastic, Lorinda. You're a natural! You handled that like a pro. I'm so proud of you."

I'd handled my first call, with minimal instruction, and instead of the threatening, yelling madman I had expected on the other end of the line, I had found myself talking to a soft-voiced, even friendly human being. I felt really good about that. I felt confident that I could reason with him and he would work with me and not against me. And I had Barry's guidance to count on. We were doing this. *I* was doing this.

Barry and I talked about everything that had happened during the call, and we even laughed together. "They want 1.5 *or* two million dollars. Seriously? They don't know for sure?" Clearly, Adam had no concept of how impossible that was for us to come up with. Neither Jon nor I had anywhere near that kind of money, even if we liquidated every asset we owned. Still, the fact that we had requested our first POL felt like progress. Adam was listening to us. We were negotiating, and tomorrow, when he called back, we would have our first successful POL. Thanks to Barry's index card prompt, we even had a callback number. Maybe that would help the RCMP track this guy. We were a step closer to bringing my daughter home.

However, Barry's enthusiastic tone quickly changed to one of caution. "This is the way most kidnapping cases begin," he warned. "The captors start out sounding reasonable, even friendly, as Adam does, but as time goes on and their demands are not met, the calls may become more threatening, perhaps even desperate and violent. You may have to navigate some bad calls. But we don't need to talk about that right now. We'll cover that soon enough."

Even with Barry's ominous warning, I was feeling optimistic. It's my nature to be positive, and I had no doubt that Amanda would be free before I'd ever have to learn what a bad call entailed.

With the negotiations having begun, Barry wanted to teach me as much as possible before the next call came in.

"Always ask to speak with Amanda. If you can't speak with her, try to get a POL."

He then explained that I should keep Adam on the line as long as possible, for three reasons. First, it would give the RCMP time to attempt to trace the call. Second, I could use the time to gather background information that might help us locate where Amanda and Nigel were being held. And third, it would help to build a rapport with Adam, the most important task for me, as he was our link to Amanda and Nigel.

"Stroke his ego whenever you can, and make him feel like he is going to be your hero. He's more likely to want to help you that way. Don't challenge him at this point. In his mind, you're a woman and an infidel. We have to feel Adam out to know how best to negotiate," he said.

He also explained that rapport was especially important because if I could befriend Adam, it would make it harder for him to hurt Amanda. I flinched at hearing the words "hurt Amanda," but I was determined not to let my mind go there.

Barry then asked me some questions: "Okay, what is our story about Jon? Why is he not on the calls?"

I felt sure that Amanda would tell Adam that her dad was sick. Years before, Jon had had major back surgery and often suffered debilitating pain. Amanda also knew that her dad did not handle stress well, so she would not have expected him to be on the phone with Adam. Barry agreed to this approach.

"Every day we will be in contact with Ottawa and they will send us a list of objectives that you need to convey or questions you can try to get answered. These could be something like 'Are Amanda and Nigel getting lots of water?' If Adam tells you they are sick, you will ask what their symptoms are and what kind of treatment they are receiving. These may be leading questions to give us an idea of where they are being held."

Barry went on. "One of the most important tactics in negotiating is the philosophy of reciprocity. It is human nature that when you are kind to someone or you give someone something, they feel obligated to give something back. That's why charities will send you something like a calendar in the mail because they know the majority of people will feel guilty about receiving it if they don't send money back."

"That's so true," I said. I had been sucked in many times by that technique.

"So we use the same technique here. When you are nice to Adam, he will feel that he must be nice to you—but of course we need to take into account that we are dealing with a kidnapper, so he may not always respond in the way we hope. Another thing that is very important is for us to listen to the background noise, as this may give us other clues as to where Amanda and Nigel are being held captive."

I hadn't considered that before, but it made sense. In the afternoon, to my surprise, we received two more brief calls from Adam. In the first, he gave me what was supposed to be the answer to our POL question.

"Amanda said the movie was *The Fix It*."

I was confused. That wasn't a movie Amanda and I had watched on our last New Year's Eve together. I hadn't even heard of it. We had watched the Disney movie *Ratatouille*.

I asked Adam for a second POL. "What award did Amanda's dad win?"

Adam called right back. "She said Communities in Bloom. He win the prize for his flowers."

"Yes! That's it!" Then, I asked Adam if I could now speak with Amanda.

"At this time, it is not possible. You should prepare only the money." The call ended.

I sat at the table and took a deep breath. It was a huge relief to have the POL.

But what about that first question I'd asked? Why hadn't Amanda given the right answer? Then it dawned on me. "Barry," I said. "I think Amanda was sending me a message. She's telling me to 'Fix It.'"

Amanda, I thought, *I promise you I will.* If only I could have fixed everything right then and there.

•

AFTER THE LAST CALL WITH Adam, I gave Jon an update on everything that was going on. He was relieved that we'd established our first proof of life. I was so grateful that Jon and I had become friends again, even though we'd had a bitter divorce twenty years prior. The RCMP decided that it was best that I stay at Jon's house for the time being. Jon agreed. If Jon and I hadn't been on such good terms, I would have been moved to a hotel.

"You're okay with it? And Perry?" Perry was Jon's longtime partner.

"Of course," he said. "We have to bring Amanda home. Plus, Shanobi loves all the company." Shanobi, Jon's little dog, was a welcome addition to the team during our times of stress. It made our current situation just a little bit easier knowing that Jon and I could count on each other for support.

That evening, Jason, one of the RCMP officers from the day before, showed up at about 7 p.m. to relieve Barry and take the night shift.

"We had three calls from Adam today, and Lorinda handled them like a pro." Barry bragged.

"I knew you could do it, Lorinda," Jason said, patting me on the back.

"Adam isn't nearly as scary as I thought he would be," I said. I was feeling buoyed by all the positive energy. "We're going to bring Amanda home!"

Jason had brought some large sheets of paper with him. On the top of the first sheet, he wrote "Demands" and "$1.5 or $2 million." He taped it up on the wall and said that we would add to it every time there was a new or different demand. He taped up a second sheet with a timeline:

- *Aug 23rd/08, Amanda kidnapped*
- *Aug 25th, 3 phone calls with Adam and 1 POL*

Jason struck me as an exceptionally intelligent guy. He had gone out and bought a copy of the Koran to educate himself on Islam, knowing that Somalia is predominantly a Muslim country. It could be advantageous to know what the Koran said about the treatment of women. He asked a lot of questions about Amanda and our family. He seemed genuinely interested in helping us.

"Amanda sounds like a smart woman," he said after I'd described my girl to him. "She's going to know how to interact with her captors and hopefully win them over."

I agreed wholeheartedly.

That night, Jason made a bed on the floor in the living room, from which he could monitor any incoming calls. I had moved my bags into Jon's guest room, where I would now sleep with an extension phone beside me. If a call came, I would meet Jason at the dining table and get ready to take the call.

I got into bed, feeling exhausted, but I couldn't sleep. I lay there, and instead of thinking about the present, my mind wandered to thoughts of my family, our ups and downs in the past. At Christmas 2007, a mere two weeks before Amanda had left home for Iraq, my family had gathered in my tiny basement suite in Canmore—Amanda,

Nathaniel, and Mark; my mom; and Janet and Tiffany, the First Nations sisters whom I consider my daughters as well. They had called
me Mommy since they were one and three years old, at which time
they had come into my foster care. They'd lived with me on and off
ever since. That Christmas was our first without my dad, Larry. We
were feeling his absence, and my mom was especially sensitive.

Larry Stewart wasn't actually my biological father, but I considered
him my real dad. I was three years old when my biological father left,
and I have no memories of him. He'd never made an effort to be in
my life. When I was four, my mom started dating Larry. His kindness
shone through his eyes. His dark, wavy hair was neatly slicked back
with Brylcreem. I thought he was so handsome and that my mom
should marry him, so one day, much to my mother's embarrassment, I
impatiently asked him, "Why don't you marry my mom?"

I got my answer a few months later, when I was invited to be the
flower girl at their wedding. When I was five, Larry adopted my two
older brothers and me, making him officially our dad. Now, during
our first Christmas without him, a layer of deep sadness wrapped everything. My mother and Amanda had not gotten along much since
Amanda had reached her teens, and that added tension as well. I felt
I was in the middle and they both needed me. My mom's grief was
palpable, and my daughter was going off to a war zone. The tension
between them escalated into a huge argument, making me feel like
I had to choose a side. I was sick over it but felt that my mom was
not being fair. Meanwhile, my other four kids felt distanced from
Amanda because she was away traveling so often and they rarely
saw her. If only we had known the catastrophic event that was coming just around the corner, maybe our Christmas would have been
different.

I lay there after my first day as a negotiator for my kidnapped
daughter, all of these thoughts swirling in my mind. I returned to
the pleasant memories instead, my thoughts circling back to the New
Year's Eve that Amanda and I had had together, just the two of us:
Amanda didn't have much time to prepare for Iraq, as her flight was

to leave on January 4. This time, packing was different from before because she was going to be broadcasting live, so she needed appropriate clothes to wear for TV. We shopped for dress jackets, because it was winter in Baghdad, and, of course, she needed scarves to wrap her head, as required by the culture in some Muslim countries.

I drove Amanda to Calgary International Airport for her flight. There she was, on her way to a war zone, and her siblings and father had not called to say good-bye. They could not understand Amanda's choices, and they were no doubt scared for her, though that didn't always show. We were *all* scared—for her, for ourselves. Good-byes are difficult, even at the best of times. And this was not the best of times.

When Amanda had first started traveling, the whole family would try to go to the airport to see her off, and we'd all be there to greet her when she came home. To have an international traveler in the family was a novelty at first, but with each trip, less of the family was there to greet her. After a while, she'd come back from some exotic place or somewhere currently in the news, and she'd tell her stories of the people she'd met struggling through war and the events she'd witnessed with her own eyes. Her life seemed bigger and bolder than everyone else's in the family. When she was home, she'd ask, "So what have you guys been doing while I was away?"

"Well," one of her siblings would answer, "I got up this morning, went to work, came home, watched TV." I think sometimes they felt their lives were insignificant by comparison. It was sometimes hard for them to relate to her.

As we drove to the airport to send Amanda off to Iraq, she was crying, hurt that her whole family wasn't supporting her. I couldn't understand why myself, and it made me angry. She was going to a war zone, for God's sake. Could everyone at least try to be civil?

That was the last time I saw my daughter, as she waved good-bye and boarded a flight for Baghdad.

Eventually I fell asleep. The next morning, I got up and went out to the living room to find Shanobi, licking Jason's face. "It's a good thing I like dogs," he said, yawning and petting her head.

At 8 a.m., the doorbell rang. Dave and the two newest faces of our RCMP negotiating team greeted us with a smile. "Hi, I'm Irv, and this is Jan."

"Just in time for coffee," Jon said.

Irv had four small clocks with him and began to set each one to a different time zone. These were the times in the different places that would become a part of our lives for the next few months: Sylvan Lake, Ottawa, Australia, and Somalia. We placed them on the counter, visible to us at all times.

The day was a blur of RCMP investigators and negotiators coming and going (all in plainclothes so as not to attract attention). Everyone was raving about how well I had done on the calls the previous day, boosting my confidence even more. All of us were on pins and needles, wondering if and when the phone would ring today.

Because Jon's phone number had been blocked, Jon had to put in a new phone line and get a new phone number. We had to call family and friends to give them the new number and reassure them that we were okay.

•

MEANWHILE, OUR TEAM CONTINUED EDUCATING Jon and me about various important aspects to consider. "The kidnappers are going to watch the news to monitor what is happening," we were told. "We have to be careful to hide our hand. We don't want them to know what we are doing, or that the government is involved. Understand?"

Of course we understood. We could not risk the media selling our story and inadvertently risking Amanda's life. The only other people who were to be privy to our operation were Perry, and Amanda's brothers, Mark and Nathaniel. We were all sworn to secrecy.

Jon and I told everyone not to come to the house for the time being. This was becoming difficult, as friends and neighbors started showing up with food and flowers, and media vans continued cruising by. Family members wanting to console us visited as well. We'd meet them at the front door, and after expressing our gratitude for their concern and taking their gifts, we would explain that we were just not up for company but would reach out to them when we were. That was only the beginning of the story we invented and told everyone so they would not come over to Jon's and see the operation we'd set up there.

Irv left, and Jan stayed for the day shift. Irv came back later for the night shift. No calls came in for the rest of the day.

CHAPTER THREE

THE DEAD DON'T TALK

Day 4. I woke up that morning, still in a state of disbelief. Had my daughter been kidnapped? Was I really being trained by Canada's top RCMP negotiators? This kind of thing happened on the news or in the movies, but it didn't happen to regular people like us.

I hadn't slept well the night before; my mind had been busy pacing through the past. But when my eyes opened, all that was gone. Here I was. The present beckoned. It was where I needed to be. I got out of bed, drank some coffee, and headed for the dining room, where Dan, the newest member of our team, was getting ready for the day.

He looked up from the member logs he was reading through to greet me.

"Good morning, Lorinda. We've got a great team here. We're going to do whatever it takes to bring Amanda home." His voice rang with confidence. "I'm so sorry that you and your family are going through this ordeal," he continued. "I'm a father, and I can't begin to imagine how you're feeling."

I liked him immediately. Actually, I liked everyone I'd met so far. I was confident in our team and believed that Jon and I were in the best hands possible. Together, we would bring Amanda home.

While waiting for more calls from Adam, my negotiators spelled out more details of proper strategy and how I should take calls going

ONE DAY CLOSER 35

forward. I was to maintain a calm, friendly attitude and never show I was ruffled or angry or upset. Could I do that? It would be a monumental task for any mother. But I was determined to do it. I had to.

During every call, I was to secure a new POL and gain as much detailed information as I could, especially about the well-being of Amanda and Nigel: Were they getting enough food and fresh water? Were they safe from flying mortar in Somalia's sectarian battles? I was also instructed to push speaking directly to Amanda. I was to "read" Adam's voice and respond to his mood: Was he angry, growing impatient, trying to confuse or con me? If so, I was to remain neutral and calm, not give in to exasperation or frustration. I was to keep him talking for as long as possible in an attempt to trace his calls and get as much information as I could.

It wasn't long before our strategy was put to the test. On Day 5, August 27, at 11:10 a.m., I received my fourth call from Adam.

After our ritual hellos, he said, "Talk to your daughter." I couldn't believe it. He was going to put Amanda on the phone.

"Amanda?" I said, waiting to hear her voice. My heart was pounding; I already felt the tears welling up in my eyes. But I stopped myself, recalling the conversation with our team the day prior: *She needs to hear your confidence and strength.*

"Mom?"

There she was. I could hear my daughter. Her voice was strong and urgent.

"Amanda, I love you. Sweetheart!"

"Hi, can you hear me?"

"Yes, just speak slowly because sometimes the connection is bad. Amanda—"

"Mom, are you okay?"

"Well, no, not really, Amanda. Are *you* okay? Is your health okay?"

"Yeah, we're okay."

"Good, good. Oh, I'm so happy to hear your voice."

"What's going on at home, Mom? What's going on?" I looked at Dan for guidance. Though we had come up with some objectives for what we needed to get out of Adam, we'd had no idea Amanda would be on the call.

"Well, we're trying to find a way to raise money. I'm here with your dad, and Nathaniel's here, and Mark is coming. We wanted you to know there are thousands of people praying for you, and we love you so much, and we are doing everything we can to try to get the money."

"How much is it?"

I wanted to avoid telling her the amount, because I knew she would be alarmed. "We need to speak more to Adam about that," I said. "Is Nigel okay? Is he there with you?"

"Yes, Nigel's here."

"Okay, good."

"So what's the amount? I have no idea."

Amanda could tell from my voice that I was hiding something, so I knew I had no choice but to tell her. "He has asked for $1.5 million."

"Oh my God!"

"Is Adam there with you, too?"

"No."

Amanda left the phone for a moment. I could hear her explaining things in the background. "My government does not pay money for me. My family is trying to make money. I come from a poor family."

"Amanda?"

The call was disconnected. Our exchange had lasted only a few minutes, but every second had been precious to me. I felt intense relief after the call. I'd heard her voice!

For the duration of the call, I'd been focused on following my instructions. I was assessing the situation, even while I was in it. It was the best proof of life we'd gotten so far. I had spoken with Amanda, and she had sounded okay. She and Nigel were together. This had been a good day.

"You did really well," Dan told me. "Seems like you're a natural." Never in my life had I imagined being a natural at negotiating for my daughter's release.

The next day—August 28, Day 6—Adam called again. Jon and Perry had gone out, leaving me and one of the RCMP negotiators, Jason, to man the phones.

"Hello, Mom," Adam said. "Are you fine?"

Strange as it was to hear, I knew his calling me "Mom" was a good thing. If he related to me as Mom, then it would be harder for him to hurt me or Amanda.

"Your daughter is so frightened, understand? She is saying, 'Our family has no money.' We want her to be happy. We don't want to scare her."

Before I could respond, he told me he was putting Amanda on the line. I waited, heard chirping birds in the background. Then the call was disconnected. Adam called back immediately, now with Amanda. He gave her the phone, and she launched right in.

"Mom, I don't know how long we have to talk, but what's going on with the government in Canada? Are they negotiating?"

I hid the truth. "We haven't heard very much about it."

"But you need to get in touch with the government. Leave it to the government to pay the money, because you guys will never get it."

"I guess I need to ask Adam if it's okay that we get the government involved . . . Amanda?"

The call was disconnected.

We made two more call attempts, but Amanda and I were able to speak only for a few minutes.

"Mom, you need to turn everything over to the government. You need to be in touch with them. The information that we're getting here is that Canada sent, is sending, a diplomat over here."

"How did you get that information?"

Disconnected. Again.

For the whole conversation, I could tell Amanda was doing exactly what I was—both of us going through role-playing for the sake of others listening in. I could hear it in her voice: she had a script and was working her own messages in between those she was told to pass along to me.

Once it was clear this was the end of conversation for the day, Jason said, "Good job, Lorinda. That was a very positive call."

But I didn't need the praise. What I wanted was to focus on Amanda's updates. "Is Canada really sending a diplomat to Somalia?" I asked. It sounded hopeful to me, and I wanted Jason to confirm.

"I don't know," he said. "To be honest, we don't really know much more than you do. To protect their strategies, Ottawa doesn't tell us everything."

What did that mean? I wondered. Either our negotiators really didn't know everything, or they weren't willing to say if they did. They did inform me and Jon that a joint Canadian/Australian cell had been set up in Nairobi to negotiate with the kidnappers, but beyond that, we knew very little.

It seemed the kidnappers now understood that our two families, Nigel's in Australia and ours in Canada, were not wealthy, so they were changing strategies. Now they wanted to squeeze a ransom out of our governments. Of course, I had my own objective: to convince them that there would not be a big payoff. Ours was a double game, in which both sides were playing verbal dodgeball. I trusted Amanda knew I was working to help her, even if she didn't know all the details.

I soon learned the kidnappers weren't the only ones changing strategy. The RCMP felt it was time to reevaluate and adjust its plans, too. A few days later, on September 1, one of our RCMP negotiators, Dave, pulled me aside. "Lorinda, we can't continue to use Jon's home as our operational center. We're realizing that, unfortunately, this could take longer than we had hoped. It's getting harder to keep the media from finding out about our involvement, and we really can't risk that exposure."

My stomach dropped. "What do you mean, *longer*?" I could hear the alarm in my voice. "You heard the last call. Adam is showing signs of humanity and wants to work with me."

But Dave was insistent. "I'm sorry, Lorinda, but we have to be prepared for anything. We've found a house ten minutes from here,

so Jon and Perry can still be actively involved but also have their living space back. We're concerned about you, too—you need space for
yourself. The upstairs in this new house will be for you alone."

I didn't like the idea that this wasn't going to end quickly, but I
realized I really did need some personal space, as did Jon and Perry, so
I agreed. We would move to the new location on September 9.

•

THE DAYS STARTED TO MOVE more slowly, and as we waited for the next
call, I grew impatient. What was happening? Why wasn't Adam calling? The team tried to encourage me—the silence was normal, they
said. Adam and the others were probably formulating their next move,
knowing that a lack of contact would only wear on me and work in
their favor. I had to stay calm, focused, and not let my anxieties take
over. I did my very best.

On September 4, after five days of grueling silence, Adam finally
called.

"Adam, I've been worried about you! I haven't heard from you for
so long."

"At this time," Adam said, "I wanted to connect you to your daughter, your beautiful daughter. I was told that you are beautiful, and that
you are mom. Understand?"

My stomach turned. I didn't like the way he'd said "beautiful
daughter." He continued. "We are worried that you are collecting
money. What we want the money is from your government, understand?"

"Our government has told me that they will not give us money
because they will not pay a ransom, Adam."

"Believe us, they will pay. Understand? They can afford this. But
what we wanted to be, Amanda is our sister like, um, you are like our
mom. Understand? We want her not to be frightened or concerned
about this problem."

Here was a man who was involved in kidnapping my daughter and
who was claiming to have our best interests at heart? It was insane.

I wrote a notecard and passed it to Irv, who was on call with me that day. "Can this really be happening?" I asked.

Irv smiled, shrugged, and wrote his own card: "This is good. You and Amanda are building good rapport."

I took heart in that. I didn't respond to Adam's hypocrisy, not then, not ever. I took solace in his not wanting to harm Amanda. The closer he felt to us, the safer Amanda would be.

Adam continued, "I will connect you and speak to her and we tell her not to take from your families. Understand? That is all. Talk to your daughter."

Irv quickly wrote on another card and slid it to me: "Let's see what other information we can get from him since he's in a good mood."

I tried to keep Adam on the line. "When you get the money, Adam," I asked, "where will you take Amanda and Nigel so they will be safe?"

But Adam didn't take the bait. He told me Amanda was waiting to speak with me and that we would have only a few minutes. He said he couldn't pay for any more minutes on the phone.

"Hi, Mom."

"Oh, Amanda," I said. "I love you! Are you okay?"

"I love you, too. I'm okay."

"Are you getting enough food and exercise?" I tried to extract information about her living conditions and her health.

"We are in a room," she said. "There's not a whole lot of exercise, but we are eating, and everyone has taken very good care of us . . . we have water."

The point of this call was soon apparent. "Listen to me, okay?" Amanda said, her tone changing. "I don't know how long we have. I want to be clear that they do not want your money. I know the government probably won't pay, but we have to try. They are our brothers, and I don't believe that they will kill us. They have told us that they will not. They will release us. We spoke to somebody, Michael, in Nairobi, last night. Of course they want the government to pay. That's the point."

We seemed to be at an impasse: no money was to come from our two families, and our governments were united in their refusal to pay a ransom.

I didn't know who "Michael" in Nairobi was. I looked at Irv with eyebrows raised, wrote a card: "Is this the diplomat?"

"Don't know," he wrote back.

I continued. "I'm waiting for calls from the government, Amanda. We'll see, but they are firm on their stance concerning ransoms."

There was a new strain in Amanda's voice. "I'm having a really hard time here thinking about you guys at home selling everything, trying to get money. I need to know that you won't do that."

There was little I could say. "We're here for both you and Nigel."

"I know, and Nigel knows that, too. How is Dad?"

This was my chance to substantiate our story about Jon's condition, but how was I going to do that without worrying Amanda? "Your dad is . . . you know he doesn't handle stress well, and with his illness, it's very hard for him right now."

"Is he okay?"

I heard the alarm in her voice, and I hated it. But I needed Adam to hear our story confirmed. "He's okay, Amanda. We're all supporting each other on this end."

"Work with Nigel's family," she urged.

"We just want you home so badly!"

"I know. What about—" The line went dead.

I hung up and looked up at Irv. He held two thumbs up in the air.

I knew Amanda had no idea that an RCMP officer was listening to our calls. She was programmed to parrot the kidnappers' demands. But her assurances that her kidnappers would release her and Nigel seemed as though they were coming from her, not from the kidnappers. As I would learn much later, Amanda paid dearly for telling me that. The kidnappers would sometimes taunt her, warning her that they would kill her if they didn't get the money.

At the time, though, I didn't know that, so I chose to believe what she said—that she and Nigel were being reasonably well cared for. I knew she and I were instinctively using the same strategy, which meant building an emotional bond with the captors. In my case, that meant appealing to what I hoped was Adam's better nature. I frequently repeated to him, "You're a good man. I know you're going to protect your sister." I also stroked his ego by praising his English, even though it was often very difficult to understand.

Irv asked me about Amanda's relationship with Nigel, explaining that it was essential that they know as much about Amanda and Nigel as possible. Though I had never met Nigel, Amanda had sent me enthusiastic texts and emails about him from Ethiopia in the winter of 2006: "Mom, I've met this amazing man."

They'd met while staying at a cheap hotel in Addis Ababa. Nigel was a thirty-four-year-old Australian photographer living in London. He was on a three-month assignment to promote Ethiopian aid projects for the International Rescue Committee.

They'd taken a trip together to Ethiopia's Danakil Depression, one of the hottest places on earth. At times, she and Nigel had been so thirsty that they'd drunk out of puddles with camel dung in them. Once, when Nigel had dismounted from his camel to photograph a little girl from the nomadic Afar tribe, the girl's father had challenged him with a gun, yelling in a language they couldn't understand. Amanda placed herself between Nigel and the father and successfully eased the tensions. Later, when Amanda suffered heatstroke, Nigel tenderly cared for her until she recovered.

That trip to Danakil had been a powerful bonding experience for both of them, but there was a terrible falling-out as well. When they initially met, Nigel had not told her that ten months earlier, he had been married to his long-time partner. Instead, he told her that he had been splitting up with his long-time girlfriend. Amanda phoned, brokenhearted and angry, saying she'd cut off all communication with Nigel. She continued her silence even after she'd returned home to Calgary.

By the winter of 2007, however, after Nigel had made a clean break with his wife, Amanda and Nigel agreed to try their relationship again. Amanda planned a stopover in Australia to visit him, while en route to Afghanistan. She wanted to continue her reporting on the war. On a phone call, she told me how she and Nigel were planning to establish a reporting business and that he was going to join her in Afghanistan. It didn't happen, though. Nigel didn't turn up. Amanda felt angry yet again, disappointed and hurt.

But they did mend fences once again after that, in the summer of 2008. While in Nairobi, Amanda was planning a trip to Somalia. She realized that working in this failed state would cost lots of money. She'd need to hire security guards and translators and pay for transportation and bribes. Why not invite Nigel, a comfortable travel companion and friend? He'd always harbored dreams of becoming a war correspondent. Maybe he'd like to share the costs of travel with her?

Nigel arrived in Nairobi on August 16, 2008, for a couple weeks of travel with Amanda. On August 23, only three days into their trip, just outside the Somali capital of Mogadishu, they were captured on their way to report on the plight of displaced persons in a refugee camp. Now two families waited by their phones for life-and-death calls from somewhere in Somalia.

I often wondered what Nigel's family members were thinking and feeling, if we could offer each other help and guidance, but the RCMP negotiators had forbidden us to contact them. The Brennans had been given the same orders by the AFP—they were not to contact us. We were told that any news we shared with each other had the potential to confuse official communications.

On September 3—Day 12 of our ordeal—Geoffrey Brennan, Nigel's dad, broke the silence and called Jon. Before Barry could intercept the call, Jon grabbed the phone, ran into his bedroom, and locked the door. As I would learn later from Jon, Jon had used Facebook to connect with the Brennans and exchange phone numbers. When Jon emerged from his bedroom after the call, Barry was furious and made it known.

The next day, Nigel's sister, Nicky, called. Jon and I were expressly forbidden to answer the phone. She left a message saying that she wanted to touch base. Jon and I rallied, pleading with the RCMP to let us to call her back. But we were denied. We started to feel resentful, but we had to let it go. We had bigger concerns to deal with, after all.

Around that same time, an event occurred which seemed to lift operations inside Jon's house up a notch in importance. We were told that RCMP Inspector Gordon Black, a high-level international negotiator, would be flying in from Ottawa to meet with us. He would be offering guidance and instruction to our family and answering our questions. We were thrilled to hear this, and even the negotiators seemed excited. Amanda's brothers, Mark and Nathaniel, joined us for that meeting.

Everyone from our team was there, as well as a new negotiator from Edmonton named Brad W. Shanobi entertained us all, running around the house dressed in a Hawaiian shirt, her hair pinned up in a sparkly clip. Everyone loved Shanobi and looked forward to her frequent wardrobe changes. She had been Amanda's dog until she started traveling and Jon had become her caretaker. We were all grateful for the way she eased and distracted the palpable tension in the room.

We lined up on Jon's couches, waiting for Inspector Black to arrive. It's odd that I don't remember what he looked like; what I do remember is his powerful presence, the way he radiated confidence and authority.

When he arrived, I was identified as our team's chief negotiator. His piercing eyes took me in. "I hear that you're doing a great job," he said. "But I do want to educate you. As time goes by, the kidnappers' phone calls may get really bad."

I'd heard it before from the RCMP officers, but hearing it from Inspector Black made me feel more nervous.

"At times," he went on, "they simply make it sound like they're hurting the hostages. They may even threaten the hostages before the call, warning them, 'If you don't scream and act frightened on the phone, we really will hurt you.' You must hold yourself together during those calls. You can cry all you want after, but when you're on that phone, you need to hold yourself together. If you seem upset or frightened, the kidnappers will know they manipulated you successfully. If you become angry, they may actually hurt the hostages. After a bad call, even if you're lying on the floor crying, you have to be ready for when that phone rings again. You're going to have to get up, answer it, then listen calmly to what is said."

I nodded, taking in every word. "I understand," I said. But did I? I'd never had a call like that before, and I definitely did not want to experience it. Despite the inspector's warning, I honestly believed that negotiations would never go so badly. Adam was still polite, and everyone seemed so sure the situation would be resolved quickly.

Inspector Black went on to stress what we already knew—that the Canadian government would not pay a ransom. "But," he assured us, "Foreign Affairs has an impeccable record for bringing home hostages. We've never had a single failure in seventeen years." What we didn't learn then or later was who in the Canadian government actually made these decisions.

I was relieved. That was exactly what we needed to hear. I tried to shake the new fear about a "bad call." We were going to be okay.

"I'm going to Australia to speak to the Brennans. It's imperative that neither family acts independently in a way that might jeopardize what the RCMP and AFP and our foreign affairs departments are doing. Be assured that while you continue your negotiations, our joint agency in Nairobi will be working with the government of Somalia." Inspector Black went on to explain that in cases like this, the Canadian government would engage with the government of the country where the captives were being held. In exchange for aid in the form of schools, hospitals, and food, for example, the local government would intervene with the kidnappers to secure the release of the hostages.

Inspector Black also talked to us about POLs. "The best procedure is the one you're now using: to ask a question only Amanda can answer. In a hostage taking in Brazil, the kidnappers showed the captive sitting in a chair, reading the paper of the day. Though they updated the paper every day, the hostage was actually dead and had been frozen. It's from this case and others that we've learned what works for POLs, and I want to assure you that the Mounties are with you to stay. We *will* bring your girl home."

That's when I let myself cry. Soon we were all crying. Even the inspector himself was teary-eyed as he hugged each of us. Inspector Black had one more thing to say: "Mrs. Black, my wife, said to tell you that you couldn't be in better hands."

Despite everything I'd just heard and despite my worst fears, I believed Gordon and Mrs. Black: our girl was coming home.

CHAPTER FOUR

THE WAR ROOM

As the days went by, I felt I had a better sense of how to handle myself on calls and how to move negotiations forward. I was getting anxious to move into the new operational center. It wasn't just a matter of space; Jon and Perry's home had turned into a chaotic headquarters.

Nighttime had become a curiosity for the negotiator sleeping on the couch, as Jon had been a sleepwalker for years. At times he would sleepwalk into the living room in the middle of the night, eyes wide open, and shift furniture or go into the kitchen, turn on the light, and pile up slices of bread—all while completely asleep. Perry seemed to be tormented by nightmares and could be heard yelling and hitting the walls. And I was sleeping on an inflatable rubber bed, which though comfortable enough, squeaked loudly every time I moved. No one was getting much rest, and the lack of sleep was starting to wear on our already fragile nerves.

Our team wanted to know more about my relationship with Jon and Perry. They commented on our amicable friendship, noting how often we laughed, teased, and consoled one another. It was obvious that each of us genuinely cared deeply for the others.

Jon and I met in April 1980, when I started working at Michener Center in Red Deer, Alberta. I was immediately attracted to him, and the feelings were mutual. He was nineteen; I was twenty-three and a single mother of a three-year-old son, Mark. I was separated though not yet divorced, but that didn't stop us from dating. I had recently come out of a particularly unique and traumatic situation with my first husband and was yearning for some normalcy in my own and my son's life. Jon seemed to offer that. We married in April 1981. Amanda was born the following June, and our son Nathaniel was born two years later. It wasn't long into our marriage that I felt like something was wrong. I assumed that it was me, that my previous experiences had damaged me, making me hard to love. We fought often, and both of us were miserable. As I felt Jon withdraw, I became very lonely and bitter, and in 1987 I left the relationship with very little self-esteem intact. We would share custody of Amanda and Nathaniel. Shortly thereafter, Jon met Perry and came out to everyone. For the next couple of years, we battled like bitter enemies, spewing out our hatred on each other and to anyone who would listen. Everyone suffered, most of all our children.

No one, especially me, could have predicted then that one day I would consider Jon and Perry among my dearest friends. It took years of work for the three of us to forgive one another and repair the relationships we thought were lost, but I felt so grateful to have them as we struggled to navigate the kidnapping of our daughter.

On September 9—Day 18—we shifted our technical equipment and personnel to an innocent-looking, three-level white house with maroon trim in a residential area bordering on the railway tracks. We were instructed to use the back door and driveway behind the house so as not to draw any attention. We covered the small windows of the front door with cardboard. The blinds of the living room, which became our workplace, were perpetually drawn. I was told to avoid speaking with the neighbors. Our password for anyone we didn't know who wished to enter was "pink cotton candy," because pink was Amanda's favorite color.

Ottawa referred to this house as the SLOC—Sylvan Lake Operational Centre. It was outfitted with long tables, chairs, and, of course, computers, phones, recording devices, and assorted electronic equipment. We plastered the walls with timelines, demands from the kidnappers, and "speaking boards," which outlined potential scenarios and what my responses should be. For example, if Adam told me that Amanda (or Nigel) was being hurt or tortured: *"You must protect her. She is your sister. I am doing everything I can to get the money."* Another board addressed the "marriage issue" on the chance that Amanda was forced to marry one of her captors: *"You need our consent as her parents. And you need her consent. Her father is sick. He needs to see her."* And if Adam told me they were dead, I was supposed to ask, *"What happened? How can you be sure? Do you have the body/their bodies? You are responsible for returning their bodies to their families."*

They were intense statements to be surrounded by every day, but the speaking boards were there to help me build a sort of muscle memory for moments when I would have to act quickly. The idea was that if one of those horrific events did happen, as devastating as it would be, I would be able to respond constructively, without falling apart.

I knew I had to surround myself with images of hope, too. I was determined to hold tight to my belief that things were going to go smoothly and quickly. I posted photos of Amanda and Nigel that Jon had blown up and printed. I knew there was value in personalizing Amanda, not only to Adam but also to our team who had never met her. I added a poster that said, *Today is one day closer to Amanda and Nigel coming home.* It helped me focus on something more positive than how many days she had been held captive. Much later—after Amanda's release—Kate Snow, an NBC journalist who interviewed Amanda and me for a feature segment on the television show *Dateline*, upon seeing the pictures of the SLOC, said, "This literally looks like a war room."

Jon didn't spend all day in the war room; he would come over for a daily call with Ottawa. "Ottawa" came to mean the person (and there were several) who called daily to update us on what was happening. Ottawa was in charge of all aspects of Amanda's case, and they directed all efforts at the SLOC.

We met some of the people in "the chair" in Ottawa, but they were rotated on a regular basis, and as for who was behind the chair giving directives, we would never know. There was rarely anything of real substance in these calls. We asked questions and got vague answers or none at all. When we were asked by our family and friends how we were holding up, we assured them that the government of Canada was doing everything in its power to secure the release of Amanda and Nigel.

Whichever RCMP officer was at the SLOC with me that day would write a daily log for Ottawa and the incoming negotiators, a log that I was never privy to. I often wondered what they wrote about me. I knew the RCMP needed to monitor both Jon and me to figure out how to manage our relationship with "Ottawa." It was keeping us close to "them" but carefully making sure that "they" were not close to us.

One of the problems we needed to resolve was my lack of income. I still had bills to pay but could no longer work to pay them, as all my time was spent at the SLOC. After discussing the issue with the team, the solution was to pay me as a secret agent. That decision freed me to work full-time for Amanda's release. Of course, at this point, we all expected our operation would be short term.

The secrecy was starting to affect me, though. I found I was isolating myself from the world outside the SLOC. I hid the truth from my family and friends, saying I would continue to live at Jon's until Amanda's release but would be happy to meet them in a coffee shop or restaurant. I reasoned that I needed to get out for a break anyway, so I would time my outings from three in the afternoon until around six at night, careful to protect times when Adam might call. One day my mom called and told me that she was coming over to Jon's. Despite my objections, she was adamant. I grabbed a few things from the SLOC and quickly drove over to Jon's before her arrival to place familiar items where she could see them. After she arrived on his doorstep and settled in, I offered her coffee. Then I realized I had no idea where to look for the sugar. I was relieved that she didn't notice.

For the most part I kept my circle tight, afraid I would slip up on the "facts" of my fabricated life. I was often asked what was happening in our case. My response was always the same—that the government was keeping me and Jon in the loop and that we had total faith in what it was doing. When pressed, I said I couldn't discuss the details of the case. Well-meaning people were starting to suggest that I get a job and normalize my life as much as possible instead of sitting at Jon's, depressed. No one could have guessed the crazy secret life I was living.

Between calls, I spent my time at the SLOC reviewing—and sometimes correcting—the transcripts. Some of Adam's comments were quite confusing, mostly because of my lack of context or because of his broken English. Still, with every conversation, I was tuning in to Adam with such concentration that I was finding it easier and easier to understand him. The same was true for the other team members. But there were still things Adam said that confused all of us at the SLOC.

On September 8—Day 17—I was trying to learn everything I could about Somalia. Irv suggested I watch *Black Hawk Down*, the movie based on a true story that took place in 1993 when the United States sent special forces into Somalia to destabilize the government and take food and humanitarian aid to the starving population using Black Hawk helicopters, which were gunned down. It was upsetting for me to watch the fierceness of the Somali fighters against the US Army.

I was settling in when the phone rang. I hit pause, and Irv and I jumped to the phone. It was Adam. He informed me that a member of Amanda's family who wanted to pay the ransom had contacted him. He reiterated that he and the other kidnappers did not want our money, only money from the government. He repeated his message two more times and told me to stop efforts to raise money.

"I understand, Adam," I said, trying to hide my bafflement. I didn't know who this family member could be.

"That is all. That is all. Ah, and Lorinda, uhm, I am thanking you. I want to tell you this only, and I am thanking you."

"Adam, can I speak with Amanda?"

"Not at this time," he said, and hung up.

I turned to Irv. "Do you know who Adam was talking about?"

Irv shook his head. "No, I don't, but let me see if I can find out through the Ottawa channel."

As I would learn later, a few of the calls from "family" were actually rogue calls from journalists fishing for stories. Others were from self-appointed Somali middlemen trying to claim a percentage of the ransom. We were also harassed by homegrown hucksters seeking to profit from our anguish. Within days of Amanda's kidnapping, my niece, Angie, came upon a website called "Pray for Amanda." Visitors could leave comments, such as "Let's light a candle for Amanda and wish her a safe return." I was aware of the site but hadn't noticed the sidebar, "For more information on how to help, click here."

My niece clicked.

This website advertised coffee cups, T-shirts, bags, and other items with Amanda's picture emblazoned on them. No one had asked for permission to do this. We had not given anyone those photos of Amanda. And the website owners most certainly were not collecting money to help bring Amanda home. I had Angie contact the creator of the website and threaten legal action. It was taken down.

Meanwhile, Jon and I were starting to receive emails and Facebook messages from people who knew people who had "boots on the ground" in Somalia and people for hire. I shared them all with our team, and their response was always the same: ignore them. They continued to remind us how precarious our situation was. We could jeopardize all the hard work being done and even Amanda and Nigel's lives if we interacted with anyone outside of the government's strategies.

On September 16, I was driving to visit my mom in Rocky Mountain House when I received a call from Dave at the SLOC: "We've heard rumors that Al Jazeera will be releasing a video of Amanda and Nigel, and we're waiting for confirmation."

I made it to my mom's, but I had difficulty getting through supper. I couldn't mention anything to her, of course, and I was desperate to get away to watch that video. When I returned to the SLOC, I couldn't find the video online. I called Jon, and fortunately, he'd made a recording of the video from the news and came over to show it to me.

For whatever reason, there was no audio. Amanda was wrapped in the traditional Islamic dress, a hijab, with only her face and hands visible. She was kneeling, with straight back and downcast eyes, projecting strength and calmness. Nigel, now bearded, was sitting cross-legged beside her, in blue jeans and a black shirt with elbow-length sleeves. His eyes were also downcast, his shoulders slumped, and his arms awkwardly pitched forward. They were in a courtyard with potted plants, surrounded by masked gunmen. I analyzed their body language, how they held themselves or looked into the camera. I thought Amanda looked strong, and that encouraged me. Knowing Amanda, I was not surprised by her posture. Nigel, however, appeared to be despondent.

Jon and I watched the footage over and over again, taking in every detail but focusing mostly on Amanda. It felt like an eternity since we had last seen her. I realize it might sound odd that I didn't fall apart at that display of my child in captivity. The truth was, I was glad to actually see her and to have the opportunity to read into what I saw. I'd only heard her on the phone before this, but an image is, as they say, worth a thousand words. I was so well trained by the RCMP by this point that I scoured the screen for information, rather than letting myself respond as Amanda's mother. The tears came later, when I was alone in my room. Jason told me the next day that it was okay, even healthy, to react as Amanda's mom. It didn't mean that I wasn't strong; it only meant I was human.

The following day on CTV News Edmonton, a lip-reader attempted to translate what was being said. Although it was unclear, it seemed that Nigel and Amanda were appealing to their respective governments for their release and also saying that the Canadian and Australian governments were contributing to the destruction of Somalia. Though the RCMP asked Al Jazeera for a copy of the video with the audio, we were told they refused. Our official response to this HT (hostage takers) tactic of releasing this video was no response. I never mentioned it to Adam, nor he to me.

As I would later learn, within a week of Amanda's captivity, she had told her kidnappers that she wanted to become a Muslim. She had to persuade Nigel to follow her lead so the two of them might escape a death sentence. After receiving Korans, Amanda had searched the text for teachings that might save them. She found one: "A believer is not supposed to kill a fellow believer."

During a brief ceremony, Amanda and Nigel accepted Allah as their only God and Muhammed as his prophet. They were given new names: Amina and Noah. Their captors were apparently pleased with their decision to convert, but the conversion did not spare Amanda from being considered one of the "spoils of war," which gave them license to treat her much differently from Nigel because she was a woman.

Though I knew none of this when I watched the Al Jazeera video, I intuited that Amanda would employ bonding strategies to stay safe. I felt proud of her, my daughter, while trying not to think of her vulnerability among that gang of young, gun-toting, desperate men with little regard for women.

The "what if" part of my brain was not useful to me. Neither was the part that indulged in flashbacks to times when I myself had been victimized by men. My confinement in the SLOC, along with frequent restless nights worrying about Amanda, caused me to replay scenarios from my past, which I seldom had before, when life had been normal. I tried to block out the times when I'd been powerless to protect myself, from my grandfather, who had preyed on me when I was young, to times later in life when I had been alone, voiceless, and vulnerable. I knew the devastating and lasting effects of abuse. I never wanted Amanda to know these things.

Instead of being pulled back into the past, I tried to focus on thoughts of my self-possessed daughter. Even as a child, she had been smart, confident, and strong-willed, just as she'd appeared in the Al

Jazeera video. Even now, I assured myself, she would be employing all her ingenuity and experience to keep herself safe. I kept my focus on that idea and on the daily work at the SLOC, which would bring Amanda home. I also drew comfort from the camaraderie of the negotiators, who were becoming trusted friends. During their twelve-hour shifts, they heard the same kidnappers' calls as I did, the same demands, the same underlying threats. Most were parents, but as RCMP officers they were trained to be analytical and objective. But I knew that they were living every parent's worst nightmare along with me.

At first they brought their own lunches, snacks, and dinners to the SLOC, but soon we were sharing dinners like a family, normalizing our strange shared life as much as possible. I was deeply touched by their efforts to create an atmosphere of trust and comfort for me. They learned that I love to cook, so we would take turns cooking or would cook together. Often they would show up with recipes in hand. One of the guys joked that he saw two books in my future, one that would be called *My Life with the RCMP* and the other *Recipes from the SLOC.*

It's an odd thing about life: no matter how dire the circumstances, we still have to shop, cook, eat, and clean up. I read once that circumstances don't make you who you are but instead reveal yourself to you. I was learning a lot about myself, as well as about others. I was learning to protect myself from anyone who projected negativity, fear, or judgment. I didn't need anyone else fueling my imagination—another reason why I saw so few people. No one could understand what I was going through, and I couldn't tell them. The space between us was too often filled with inappropriate speculation or advice. I couldn't correct their statements, explain myself, or tell them things I knew that they did not. Listening to their judgments and misinformation was harder than withdrawing.

The RCMP team welcomed me into their easy circle of friendship. Even off shift, they would send me jokes to boost my spirits. Laughter was so precious. So was optimism. I was grateful for all I could get. I especially appreciated Brad W. from Edmonton, who called me

"Sunshine" because he knew how hard I strove to be upbeat for my family and the team. In one email, he jokingly wrote, "When this is over and you are starring in a movie called *The Negotiator*, try to include us in the tiny credits at the end. Nobody ever reads them, but we can show them to our friends in slow motion and brag."

Other emails from the team offered sympathy and comfort: "I know that you are hurting, but hang in there."

Others expressed fears: "I worry that you are lonely and have retreated into yourself for the safety that comes with isolation."

Friendly talk, as we waited for phone calls, was such an important part of my days. It was especially helpful during anxious periods of drought, when the calls dried up, as happened between September 8 and September 21. I was increasingly agitated as each day crawled by.

"Dan, why, why, why aren't they calling? Do you think something has gone wrong?"

"I'm sorry, Lorinda, but this is how negotiations go. They're unpredictable."

"We have Adam's number. Why can't I call him?"

"We don't do anything unless it's cleared through Ottawa. We don't know what strategies they are using from Nairobi." He tried to give me some solace: "The one thing I can assure you, Lorinda, is that there is always something being done in the efforts to bring Amanda home."

That was good to hear, but I couldn't stand the waiting. I needed this to end. Amanda and Nigel needed this to end. The negotiators would distract me by telling their life stories, and I would end up telling them mine. Happy or unhappy memories, trivial or dramatic, it was much better than brooding. The guys were especially enthralled by my story of becoming Penninah Peace. Given the passage of time, that part of my life had begun to feel more like a fantasy than real, even to me.

In September 1971, when I was fifteen, a yellow school bus pulled into our yard and I was introduced to the Children of God (COG). My family ran out to see why a bus was in our yard, and we watched a stream of laughing, long-haired hippies climb off the bus. My cousin

Brian, whom we had not seen for years, was with them. He had brought the busload to our home to tell us of his conversion to Christianity and to share the gospel with us. At the time we didn't realize that the COG was a cult. We only saw these happy people willing to forsake their materialistic lives to live for God. We'd never seen such happy Christians before; in fact, I don't recall ever connecting being a Christian with happiness.

Many people believe that cults appeal only to homeless, rudderless kids, but that's often not the case. I found it interesting to see the RCMP guys struggle to imagine me as the impressionable young woman I was when I found myself in a cult. When I was sixteen years old, my parents, thrilled to put me in the care of what they thought were good Christians, signed legal documents that handed me over to my "colony shepherd." I was taken away from my family, and over the course of six years, I lived in communes in Nanaimo, British Columbia; Burlington, Vermont; Seattle; Hawaii; and Japan. I was brainwashed to take on the ways of a cult, which meant conforming to a belief system that was strict, unforgiving, and often abusive. I was stripped of my former identity as Lorinda Stewart and given the name Penninah Peace—Penninah being a biblical wife in I Samuel 1:2, and "Peace" because I was told that I had an "aura of calmness." I was taught to solicit donations for the Children of God, to prostitute myself (though I resisted), to fear authority (especially the authority of the cult leaders), and to blindly obey my superiors, despite any contrary thoughts swirling around in my head. When I was pregnant with my second child and he died due to complications within hours of his birth, I believed that it was God's punishment. I was thoroughly brainwashed alongside thousands of other men, women, and children.

On November 18, 1978, the Jonestown Massacre occurred in Guyana, South America. More than nine hundred members of the Peoples Temple, including some three hundred children, committed mass suicide/homicide through ingesting a cyanide-laced, grape-flavored drink. They did so on the orders of US-born James Jones, the founder and leader of the Peoples Temple. Though the Children of God were

not affiliated with the Peoples Temple, the resulting international re-
vulsion toward cults posed a threat to David Berg (known in the cult
as Moses David), the prophet and founder of the Children of God.
He ordered those of us in the COG's rank and file to return to our
families (while continuing to raise money for the COG, of course).
That was my opportunity to escape.

Once I was back home, it was a long struggle to find myself again.
After all, I had missed years of "normal" life away from my family and
friends, only to return to a world that had moved on in my absence.
During my six years in the COG, I never read newspapers, never had
access to a TV, never listened to the radio. Any news I received came
through letters from my parents or from billboards I happened to see.
I had no idea what bands or movies were popular. Last I'd heard, it
was the Monkees, Bobby Sherman, the Moody Blues, and Alice Coo-
per's "School's Out." But once I returned home, I slowly let the old
ways of the cult go and started a new life with my son, Mark, who had
been born when I was in Japan, still in the COG commune. I separated from the man I had married in the group, and we went our own
ways. With time, I found belonging again, and then I married Jon.

That was one of the stories I told my RCMP friends between
phone calls from Somalia.

"Wow," one of the guys kept saying. "It's just so hard to believe,
seeing who you are now."

"Well," I said, making light, "at least the training made me good at
keeping secrets and keeping the blinds drawn."

But remembering that story made me think of Amanda, of the
similarities in our character and our differences. Interestingly, we had
both had wanderlust as young women—the major difference being
that Amanda had channeled hers into journalistic pursuits, whereas
mine had been used against me, to lure me away from my family and
into a cult. Amanda was strong-willed, independent, a fine judge of
character, and not easily swayed from her deeply held convictions. As
I reflected on my own past, I was grateful that Amanda was so determined and resourceful.

Often, when I thought of Amanda, I spoke to her in my mind, sending my words to her as if I were writing them down, little messages of strength and solace to keep her going, to keep her strong. *Amanda, continue to be strong. Know that I will move heaven and earth to bring you home. I just know that it's going to happen soon. You are loved more than you could ever imagine.*

CHAPTER FIVE

"DO THEY BELIEVE . . . WE ARE SKELETON EATERS?"

September 18, Day 27, was a dismal day for me.

That's when Jason sat me down to tell me that all the negotiators I had worked with to date—who felt like family to me—would be replaced by new negotiators in two days' time. I hadn't realized that each RCMP officer had other duties and commitments, as well as being a trained negotiator. I wasn't prepared for that at all. I'd assumed that we would continue to work as a team until the ordeal was over, until Amanda and Nigel were home safe. I was crushed. I had come to trust my team, and I relied on their support. They were the only ones who knew what we lived through every day as we negotiated Amanda's release. We had bonded. Soon they would be gone, and I'd be left to pick up the pieces on my own, forced to explain a common history to a whole bunch of strangers who would take their places in the war room.

"Jason, you can't do this to me! Please! I'm begging you not to let them do this!"

"I'm so sorry, Lorinda, but when Ottawa speaks, we have to do what we are told. You have to hold the faith that they are doing what's best for you and Amanda."

"Fuck Ottawa!" I needed a place to direct the rage, the hurt. "Don't they know that I need you guys?"

I couldn't wait for an answer. I ran upstairs, locked myself in my bedroom, and screamed into my pillow. I felt myself unraveling, and all the tears I had been holding back soaked my pillow.

Eventually I heard a knock on my door.

"What?" I asked. "Who is it?"

"It's Jason," I heard from the other side. "Why don't we go for a walk?"

I took a deep breath, blew my nose, and opened the door. Jason and I wandered down to Sylvan Lake, mostly in silence. The tears wouldn't stop, even though I tried to swallow them. I couldn't help but notice the sympathetic looks from bystanders who had no idea that my daughter had been kidnapped, who had no idea that I was now losing the only people who had been my support and comfort. Somehow their sympathy only added to the injustice of the moment.

It's so unfair that you get to go on with your everyday lives. This thought played over and over in my mind.

Jason and I sat on a bench facing the lake. "Lorinda, we're having a hard time leaving as well. As RCMP officers, we are trained to avoid becoming emotionally involved with cases, but that has proved difficult and even impossible in this case. Please trust me when I say that every new negotiator who comes will have your best interests at heart, just as we have. Ottawa can be a heartless machine, but it's how they get things done. Unfortunately, it's impossible to predict how long negotiations will take, and we have other duties and families that we have to attend to, but we will be supporting you wherever we are."

I tried to listen; there was little I could say in return. The feeling of loss consumed me—loss of Amanda, loss of control over my life, loss of my support team. Loss that I had dared not let myself feel was pouring out of me now in my tears. In a crisis, it's those first faces you see, those first arms that embrace you, onto whom you transfer all your gratitude and hope. And now they were abandoning me.

September 20, one year ago to the day, my father had died, though it felt surreal, like everything from my "before" life. After my morning coffee, I headed back to bed. My family was meeting at the grave site, but I could not bring myself to go. I could not even get out of bed.

I wanted to be there for my mom, but I was devastated and broken, so I never went.

As is the RCMP tradition, there were no emotional good-byes when it was time to go. I promised to keep in contact with most of them via email. It was small comfort as I adjusted to my new reality Now, the new negotiators would rotate in from all over Canada, two at a time, changing every ten days. I went over to Jon's to rant about the changes. He was upset as well. Later, I went to meet my mom and my brother, Dirk, for supper at the Chinese Cafe on Main Street, but I could barely eat. I was so tired and distracted. They told me about the meeting at the grave site, but I couldn't hold on to the threads of the conversation. My mom and Dirk knew only that Amanda had been kidnapped. They still had no idea about the depth of my involvement, but that one fact seemed enough to excuse my behavior.

When I got back to the SLOC, Irv was on night duty.

"Irv," I said, "This is so unfair. It's cruel and inhumane to take my team away. Can't anyone see that?" The anger and sadness of the day snagged at the edges of my voice.

Irv looked at me. "Lorinda, this is incredibly hard for us, too. It's impossible to say how long these negotiations are going to last, and unfortunately we have other families we are responsible for as well."

He and Jason seemed to have similar stances.

Then he smiled. "It's true that no one will measure up to us, but they will sure try."

I went upstairs to try to sleep but couldn't, so I went back downstairs to talk to Irv. That's when the phone rang. It had been eleven days since I had spoken with Adam, and there was his voice on the other end of the line.

"Adam, I have been so worried. How are Amanda and Nigel?"

"They are sick. Both of them. She has a problem with the food, Somali food."

"Do you have medicine for them?"

"I want only to tell you that Amanda needs eyeglasses. I want to ask you how, what numbers does she take?"

"Can you get her some glasses?"

"If we can get the number, they say we can get eye seeing. She can't ignore. We take her hand to reach the panel, understand?"

"Can I speak with Amanda?"

"No, no. You cannot talk until we are getting what we are demanding."

"For me to know that Amanda is okay, I need you to ask her a question for me."

"Obvious question will be answered when we get our money."

I could feel Adam getting impatient with me. He asked about "Marc," who had contacted him from Nairobi. So that was why I hadn't had any calls from Adam. The Nairobi cell was reaching out to Adam as well. Adam did not trust Marc and thought he was lying.

Irv slipped me a card: "Trust Marc."

"Adam, I need you to trust Marc, that he is working for both of our families."

Adam asked me who the man was—what his last name was, what country he was from—but I was stuck. I looked at Irv, waiting for him to slip me another card. But neither of us knew anything about Marc. Crap! Why hadn't Ottawa informed us of the details?

Adam continued, "Oh, oh, you are like my mother. Who I can trust if you lie at me and tell me what I didn't say, how can I trust him? I will trust him only if he bring me the money. Nothing else. That's what I am recommending. You wanted from me, Nigel and Amanda are still alive, still healthy. They are good, I am told, but no one will talk to them until we get what I am demanding."

"I understand," I said. "Thank you for trusting me and taking care of Amanda and Nigel. I am her mother, so you understand that I am worried." I needed Adam to feel I trusted him.

"You are a peaceful woman. Amanda said to me, my mother is peaceful."

"Where is Amanda now?"

"She is south, far from the capital, one hundred and fifty kilometers away."

We finished the call with a promise to speak again the next day, when I would also have Amanda's eye prescription.

I put down the phone. "Damn it, Irv, how can Adam protect her if he's that far away?"

"Remember, Lorinda, we don't know anything for sure. He could just be toying with you."

"And what's that business with Marc?" I asked. I could hear myself getting louder. "It's ridiculous! We should know these things. How can I take calls like this when I don't know everything that's going on? I hope Adam still trusts me."

Irv took a deep breath. "You're right, Lorinda. We should have known more details, but you've built a strong rapport with Adam. He wants to trust you."

I hoped "good rapport" would help me hold on to my team at home, too. The next day I made a frantic phone call to Gordon Black and pleaded with him to not take my team away. The new negotiators wouldn't understand Adam, I reasoned. It had taken us time to become accustomed to his accent, to understand the nuances of the conversation. We couldn't afford to drop the ball. I cried and begged. Gordon told me he would see what he could do. We weren't sure whom he needed to consult with and who, in the end, was making decisions.

Later that morning, Dave and Charmaine, two RCMP officers from Edmonton, showed up for an unexpected meeting. They were accompanied by another woman named Barb, who was introduced to me as a therapist. It was clear that Ottawa had sent them.

"We understand the turmoil you're experiencing, Lorinda," Dave said. "And we want to help. That's why we brought Barb here today. This mission is highly covert, but Barb is with the RCMP, so she can help you with the emotional upheaval caused by Amanda's kidnapping and your feelings of abandonment around our leaving."

Barb stepped forward and handed me her card. "My office is in Calgary. You can make an appointment with me anytime, Lorinda."

I took the card but couldn't look at it. "I have a call scheduled with

Adam tonight. Please let Irv come back to take it with me," I said to Charmaine.

"I'm sorry, Lorinda, but Irv has other duties and two new negotiators are already on their way."

Charmaine, I learned, was the noncommissioned officer of the National Security Enforcement section who was in charge of the SLOC and coordinating the incoming negotiators. She was running the show from her office in Edmonton, under Ottawa's orders, of course. She promised to sensitize each new negotiator to my situation.

"Some of the local negotiators from your team may even take shifts every now and then," she said. I felt somewhat relieved at that possibility, but it wasn't enough to make me feel ready for the change I knew was coming.

Brad M. and Joanne, the new negotiators, arrived at the SLOC around noon. They both looked apprehensive. No doubt they had been told that I wasn't happy. Dave made the introductions: Brad M. was from Vancouver, and Joanne was from Saskatchewan.

I was still defiant about the new plan, so I ignored them, speaking only when necessary. When I did speak, my voice was cold and to the point. They sat at the desk facing away from me, reading the daily logbook and the transcripts, speaking to each other in low tones. I could only assume they were discussing what to do with me.

I turned away and delved into my research. It was my daily habit to scour any news coming out of Somalia. That day, I read about a female Japanese doctor and a Dutch male nurse who had been kidnapped and were being held in Mogadishu. I read an interview with the doctor, in which she was quoted saying she and her colleague were being treated well. That's encouraging, I thought. I hoped Amanda and Nigel were being treated well, too. In the case of the nurse and doctor, their captors were demanding $1 million from the Japanese government after coming down from their initial demand of $3 million. Okay, so negotiations are working, negotiations can work. I continued to read the interview. The doctor apologized for the trouble she had caused to the people of Japan and the company she was working with. Trouble she caused? Those bastards!

I knew I had to limit the time I spent reading the news from Somalia. Brad M. and Joanne had decided that he would take the night shift and Joanne the day shift, so in midafternoon Brad M. went over to the hotel that housed the negotiators. I left around three o'clock, as I did most days, to take a walk. I had come to realize that for my sanity I had to get out into nature pretty much every day. It had been my go-to for years whenever I felt overwhelmed and needed to calm myself. As I walked, I wondered how I would make it through this. I remembered that in my "before" life, I used to meditate, taking time to sit quietly and not think, a practice that had helped keep me grounded. I realized that I needed to take time to meditate again. I needed to practice gratitude by thinking about all the positives in my life. The practice had always helped me feel more optimistic, and I needed all the optimism I could get right now. I had been so consumed by the kidnapping and negotiators that I had barely noticed anything around me. I looked properly then and saw the bold rusts and burnt oranges of the fall leaves, the calm blue of the lake. I felt the warm sun on my face. I felt grateful for the beauty that surrounded me. I walked back to the SLOC, feeling calmer and ready for the next stage.

Brad M. and I had a chat that evening, and with tears in his eyes he assured me that no one could even begin to understand the trauma that was my life at that point.

"Please," he said, "know that we only want to help you bring your daughter home safely and as quickly as possible."

That's when it hit—I suddenly felt ashamed of my indulgent self-pity. This wasn't about me. This was about bringing my daughter home. I switched gears and spent a good deal of energy profusely apologizing to everyone for my behavior. I was so profoundly grateful to anyone who was helping me bring Amanda home safely. As it turned out, most of my negotiators—twenty-four in all—proved to be genuinely concerned about me. They did whatever they could to lift my spirits, and, much to my delight, some of the original team did return for shifts at the SLOC as the crisis dragged on.

Lying in bed that night, I started to feel better about things at the SLOC, which allowed my mind to deal with other problems. I reflected on my last conversation with Adam. His words pained me. In a country as poor as Somalia, Amanda's and Nigel's living conditions were almost certainly squalid. Amanda's need for glasses was very real. She was nearsighted. When she had packed her bags to be a Press TV journalist in Iraq, she had taken her glasses but had counted on wearing contact lenses in front of the TV cameras. When she was kidnapped, she was wearing her contacts and had left her glasses at the hotel. Without lens solution, her contacts would last only a few days. Without contacts or glasses, her vision would be severely compromised. Having been nearsighted and worn glasses my whole life, I knew that not being able to see clearly would have been terrifying in Amanda's situation. She was depending on someone else's eyes to see. I felt sick for her. Then I remembered Adam's comment about taking her hand to lead her to "the panel," which I interpreted as the bathroom. I knew Amanda could see far enough not to need help getting there. So what was going on? Then it hit me: Amanda was using this problem to make them help her. She was using human touch as a bonding strategy. I smiled to myself. Smart girl!

The realization was a good one, but it did mean that this night, like so many others, was spent in restless thought. Sleep would not come. Alone with my thoughts, my biggest challenge was not to entertain my fears. I knew that although it was night for me, it was daytime in Amanda's world, and I wondered what her days looked like. I tried to imagine that she had built some connections to her captors and that they were being kind or at the very least civil. I hoped that she and Nigel were together and that they found some solace and strength in that. Often I spoke to her in my mind: *Amanda, do you know what day it is? Are you getting enough food and water? I take comfort in knowing how strong and courageous you are. You've come through so much throughout your life. You will come through this, too, my girl. I want to hug you so bad it feels unbearable.*

I knew that I had to get some sleep. As each sleepless night went by, I could feel the toll it was taking on my physical, mental, and emotional states. I knew my gratitude practice would help keep my mind from spiraling into negative territory. On that night, and on the many that followed, I practiced gratitude: *I am grateful for knowing that Amanda and Nigel are alive, that Adam is being reasonable, that I am surrounded by caring people who are helping us . . .*

Eventually I fell asleep. I was tired the next morning but slightly more optimistic. Adam didn't call on the twenty-second as promised, but I was ready with Amanda's eye prescription for when he did. On September 24, at 10 a.m., Brad M. and Joanne were both with me at the SLOC for our daily call with Ottawa. On that call, Ottawa decided that I should call Adam, so I did.

"Hello, Adam. It's Mom," I said. I reinforced my role as a mother figure in his life. I immediately told him that I was worried about Amanda and Nigel and asked to speak with Amanda.

"No, I am not with Amanda," Adam said. "Believe me."

I tried for a POL question, but he refused. Then I tried for a POC—proof of care—question.

He reassured me that Amanda and Nigel were being fed. He said they had been given cabbage, lettuce, and other food, as well as water. "You should tell me the number of the glass. Then we shall buy and give her."

After making sure that he had a pen and paper, I tried to explain her prescription, but it proved impossible for him to understand.

Joanne handed me a card. "Ask for his email."

Adam's accent made it difficult, but eventually I got it down. Now we could send him an email with Amanda's prescription. I asked him to promise to visit her and make sure she was okay, then call me after his visit.

"I cannot promise, but I will try," he said.

I pushed again for a call with her.

"The others they always say that it is forbidden to talk to anyone. But I was make it my own fair fight. Lorinda, what they want is money because they are not civilized. They know how to shoot only. They are but I am not, I am on a level university. If the time allows, I shall try to see her, but I don't want to liar you."

"Do they understand, Adam, that if they want money, Amanda and Nigel have to be alive? Sometimes people have to talk and negotiate and it takes time." I could feel that I might be pushing his limits, so I thanked him and told him I knew that he was honorable and I trusted he would protect his sister and brother. "How was Amanda the last time you saw her?" I added.

"She was good. She is beautiful. What about if I marry her?"

I could feel the blood draining from my face. I wondered if this was the mental equivalent of being shot with a stun gun. I glanced at Brad M. and Joanne, whose faces also looked void of color. My eyes went up to the speaking board, where I sought reminders of what to say.

"I need my daughter to come home," I said. "Her father is sick, and we, we need her to come home."

"Allah give him health. We are not curse him, we shall offer bless to him from Allah."

"Adam, you, you have a wife already."

"Yes, but in Islam almost Islams always have two, three, or four wives. It is not forbidden, and she will get what she needs from me."

I was trying to hide the panic creeping up my neck. "But, but, but I need my daughter to come home." I was stuttering, my voice shaking.

"She will come home, but after coming home, not Somalia, I mean. I meant if I can come to Canada."

Brad M. handed me a card. "Ask if he has been to Canada before."

I did as instructed. He told me he had not been to Canada, but he suggested that he knew how to speak Arabic and Italian. Apparently he had learned his English in Mogadishu.

"Ah, you must be a very smart man. Would you like to come to Canada?"

"Yeah, why not?"

My mind was racing. Could we use this information to make a deal with him? "Would you bring your family with you?" I asked.

"It is possible, but I think if I come there, they say to me, oh, Mr. Adam you have victed our daughter. It will be in a court everytime, everyday what happened, for example."

"Adam, court is not important to me. I just want Amanda to come home."

"But still you didn't give answers to give me Amanda to be married. What will happen when she comes home and she needs a man? She will need a man, isn't it?"

"It is Amanda's choice who will be her husband. If you let me talk to her, I will ask her."

"What about if she's says I am ready, I want to stay here Somalia? What shall we do?"

"Her father is very sick, and she needs to come home," I repeated.

"She told me she has a boyfriend in Iraq. I have his number and his name. She wrote me it. Still, I didn't call him."

"Okay." That was news to me. I assumed this was a contact strategy on Amanda's part.

"Let me ask you this," Adam said. "Is this your birthday?"

It was not, but he was not far off. "Oh, it's my son's birthday," I said. "Amanda's brother. Amanda has two brothers." I told him the names of her brothers and how worried they were, how much they loved and missed their sister.

"What about if they see me in Canada, I think they should box me, huh?" he said. "Do they believe that we are killers? That we are hunters? That we are skeleton eaters? What do they believe from us?"

"I tell them that you are a very honorable man," I said. "That you take care of Amanda. That makes them feel a little better. They need and want to see their sister. They are very sad." I was trying to steer the conversation away from marriage. I told Adam that Amanda had gone to Somalia to help his country, to create awareness of the war and the food shortage. Such awareness could result in humanitarian aid for his people.

"We have talked and we give her a diary to write whatever she needs.

But most of the things that she should write of is our victories. She should write more from Adam is if she goes to Canada because she's a really active girl. She's very curious." Adam continued, "Let me say Western countries always helping us with mortars. What I believe in Western countries is bad because there is a Uganda mission, what they call a mission, and last night they bombarded the capital city. Two hundred, they said, at least, mortars. They say, 'We help,' and this help come from the UN. They give UN, and the UN give us mortar and missiles."

"If Amanda knows this truth," I said, "then she can tell your story to the world." I wanted to verify that Amanda really did have a pen and paper. "Does Amanda have a paper and pen so she can write?"

"Yeah, why not? We allow her to write what she wants."

"Thank you for allowing her to write. Thank you very much. Amanda loves to write, and to write your story, too."

"My story," he said. "Adam is a story."

I asked Adam to tell me about his children, and I found out he had two boys aged two years and nine months. That was good to know; it meant I could appeal to his paternal instincts.

Then our conversation shifted to negotiations with Marc in Nairobi.

"Marc did not give us the exact money to pay. He talks talks talks. He talks, and says Canada does not agree, Australia does not agree."

I encouraged him to trust Marc, which was what Ottawa had instructed me to say. But Adam believed that Marc was a broker who wanted a cut of the money and told me I should find another way.

I went back to Amanda's need for glasses. I offered to send a package with her glasses and medicine. He agreed, so I asked for an address to send the package to.

"There is no address. There is no like government to deal. You can understand what is going on in Somalia? War. Four or two or three short planes come and look in Somalia. You should put it to that airplane and then you should tried my phone."

I agree to do as he said. We ended the call.

In total the call lasted a monumental sixty-five minutes. We had been able to source new information on Adam, on Amanda and Nigel's health, and on the negotiations, and create a window to send a parcel. The prospect of sending Amanda glasses and of sending other supplies to both Nigel and Amanda was a heartening breakthrough. The fact that I could hold a friendly conversation for that long was indicative of the personal rapport I had built with Adam.

But the most alarming issue was Adam's marriage proposal. My brain was playing Ping-Pong with the idea. If Adam married her, maybe he could protect her from the "uncivilized thugs" until we could figure out how to get her free. But we might lose her forever if he married her. What if he would not release her? How could we be faced with this level of madness?

The next day, September 25, I emailed Adam the prescription for Amanda's glasses, hoping he could buy them in Mogadishu. In the email, I asked for more details about Nigel's and Amanda's health: "Please, it is very important that Amanda and Nigel get medicine for their sickness. It is very important they drink a lot of water. When you speak with your sister, Amanda, and your brother, Nigel, please ask them what are the symptoms of their sickness. It would mean very much to me if you can print this email and show it to Amanda. Please tell Amanda that her family loves her and we want her to come home." I also added a POL question: "Where does Oma keep her candy?"

I was still having trouble sleeping, and that night was no different. I felt tense and distraught. The tears were ready to erupt at any given moment. Jon and I were very concerned about the new RCMP negotiators arriving every ten days. We worried that as information passed among so many hands, the ball would get dropped. And there was still the concern of understanding Adam's accent. It was very hard for me to understand him, even after all the calls we'd had.

On September 29—Day 38—Charmaine organized a meeting to try to put our minds at ease. She introduced us to Al, an international negotiator who worked with Gordon Black. Craig, who had come from Vancouver Island, and Tony, who had come from New Brunswick, were our two newest negotiators. With Brad M., Joanne, Jon, and myself, eight of us were present at the table. The tension lingered in the air even as the negotiators tried to lighten the mood. Charmaine worked to address our concerns and agreed to put together a documentation package for each of the new negotiators, including a recording of Adam's voice.

Reluctantly, we agreed that that would be helpful.

Jon had his own concerns to voice. He'd been feeling out of the loop since we'd made the move to the SLOC. Although he often joined us for the morning call with Ottawa, he'd been missing the calls from Adam. Charmaine suggested that Jon be given a one-way phone at his home so that he could listen in on incoming calls. Jon seemed happy with that solution.

Jon and I then addressed the issue of being forbidden to speak with the Brennans. Craig, who had just come on board, defended what he saw as not only our right to speak with them but the humanity of it. It was agreed that we could call the Brennans, but we were warned that some members of the Brennan family might be hostile toward us and perhaps, blamed Amanda for Nigel's kidnapping. Al asked us to wait a couple of days before calling, so he could get a sense of how they were feeling.

Then Al talked to us about the package we would all send to Adam. He suggested we write a personal note to Amanda and pack something small that would be meaningful to her. I immediately thought of her little pink teddy bear named Teeny. The Brennans would send items in the same package as well. Everything we sent would be shipped to Nairobi, where the medicine and Amanda's glasses, books, and personal hygiene items would be packed, and shipped to the airport in Mogadishu. Al said that we should be up to date with our vaccinations on the chance that things moved quickly and we were needed in Nairobi. This last comment gave both Jon and me a much-needed boost.

Later that day, as I was checking on the news in Somalia, I read that the fighting and shelling in Mogadishu had escalated, sparking a mass exodus of 18,500 people. I hoped that Adam had been honest—that Amanda and Nigel were not within the city. I worried about what would happen if Adam were killed or forced to leave as well. That day, I also sent a lighthearted email to Brad W. in Edmonton, telling him that no matter how much I misbehaved, the new negotiators just wouldn't leave. I missed my old team, but in all honesty, Brad M. and Joanne were wonderful to me and Jon. Craig and Tony were so kind, thoughtful, and caring that I couldn't be angry anymore and I let it go.

On October 2, Jon and I put in calls to Nigel's sister, Nicky, and his father, Geoff, the two family members who had tried to reach out to us. Craig and Tony were tactful enough to give us privacy as we made our calls.

"Hello, Nicky," I said. "Jon and I are both here. It's so wonderful to finally speak with you!"

Jon chimed in, "Hi, Nicky."

"Jon, Lorinda—I reckoned it was only a matter of time until they bloody well let us talk." It felt good to hear her voice.

Jon asked how they were holding out.

"Mom's really angry and Dad's quite a mess, but we manage them. We're a strong lot. How about you guys?"

We expressed the frustration we'd been feeling at not being allowed to reach out to them. We also said how hopeful we were that the situation would be resolved quickly and we'd both have our family members home.

"Our family is split on our ideas about how to proceed," Nicky confided. Nicky said that Heather and Hamilton, Nigel's mother and brother, wanted decisive, independent action apart from what the AFP and RCMP were providing. They wanted to raise ransom money privately, which both our agencies had forbidden. Jon and I expressed our complete confidence in the Canadian government and reminded Nicky of its track record: no hostage had been lost in the last seventeen years.

Next we talked about Nicky's last call with Nigel, which had been on September 5. He had said the same thing Amanda had: the families must not pay; the ransom had to come from the government. It became clear that Adam was speaking with me far more frequently than he was calling Nicky. I wondered why that would be. This was reinforced later that day, at 1 p.m., when Adam called.

I expressed how worried I was for his safety because of the increased fighting in Mogadishu.

"This is our enjoyment. This is our ordinary life." He had tried, he said, but he couldn't get glasses for Amanda. More important, though, he had a critical problem with the people holding her. "Amanda is, I am worried about because . . . I believe she is alive, but who are waiting for the money, I have a critical problem of them. First they always asking me: Is the money ready? I say there is negotiation, but you can understand that they don't know about negotiations. And that is the problem. The total problem I have here. It is nighttime and I want to sleep and I am thanking you."

Adam sounded genuinely concerned not only for Amanda but for himself. But the gang was losing patience—that much was clear. Oh, shit, I thought to myself. This is not good.

CHAPTER SIX

DEADLY NEWS FROM COSTCO

D ay 40. On October 3, during our morning call from Ottawa, we learned that the Brennans had received a call from Adam. Adam claimed that Amanda and Nigel had been sold to another group within Somalia for $2.5 million. I felt my stomach fall as soon as I heard that news.

"What? How can this be?" I asked. Jon expressed alarm as well.

"Let's not jump to conclusions," Ottawa told us. "This is highly unlikely because no one would spend that much money on two hostages knowing that the odds of getting that money back are next to zero. It's another ploy." I started to breathe again. This made sense, but the whole idea of Amanda and Nigel being sold was a scenario that I hadn't thought about, and it concerned me.

Later in the morning, I read a headline online in *The Economist*: "Somalia. Piracy and much worse. What is to be done about the world's least-governed state?" According to the article, there hadn't been a proper government in Somalia since 1991. The country was too dangerous for foreign charities to operate in, and the same was true for diplomats and journalists. So how was the Canadian government supposed to negotiate the release of Amanda and Nigel when the government in Somalia was almost nonexistent?

A separate article on News24, a South African news source, confirmed that the Japanese doctor and the Dutch nurse I'd learned about before were safe and healthy. In an interview, a local resident, Abdulle Omar, said they looked well. In fact, Omar added, they didn't look like prisoners at all. Tents had been set up for them, and two Somali women were cooking for them. I hoped Amanda and Nigel were living as well. I received an email that made the hope feel more sustainable. Charles Levinson, a journalist who had worked with Amanda in Iraq, wrote to let me know that I could contact him at any time and he would do whatever he could to assist me. He knew of two male journalists who had spent time in captivity, and both had been treated well. He also told me of a woman, also a journalist, named Tina Susman, who had been held captive in Mogadishu for three weeks in the mid-1990s. He would connect us. I had heard Amanda speak of Charles before, and I wondered if he was the "boyfriend" whom Adam had referred to. That brought the tally for the day up to three separate accounts of hostages being treated well. I would stay hopeful, and I would connect with Tina to learn more.

Unfortunately, my fragile hope was threatened three days later, on October 6, when Adam's impatience crystallized into a direct threat. On my call with him, he angrily reported rumors that an Egyptian group was planning to rescue Amanda and Nigel. "They say they will use by force," he warned. This was unsettling. I had no idea what he was talking about or why Egypt would have anything to do with Amanda and Nigel. I looked at Tony, who was the negotiator in the room with me that day, then turned all my attention back to Adam's voice. "We fight each other. I want to tell you that only I am thinking of you." Then he admitted to losing control of his own group. "What we are getting from you is that your government will not pay the money. We need that money. My group, they say they will kill Amanda and Nigel in ten days' time, if they don't get the money. Good-bye."

My stomach turned over, and my face blanched. I was terrified to hear him impose a deadline like that, but I tried to keep the conversation going to get more information. "I'm not sure what you are saying. Are Amanda and Nigel still with you and your group?" I asked.

Adam's voice changed. "Yes." He sounded stressed, and his tone grew rougher. He signaled once again that he wanted to end the call. "Mom, I don't have enough time to talk to you. I inform you only of this message. They say if they don't get the money, they will kill. This is their decision. I am saying good-bye because I do not have enough time."

"When was the last time you saw them?" I asked quickly.

"The call at this time, it is broken. It is like an explosion."

"Adam, please promise that you will care for them and protect them."

"They are swearing that they will kill in ten days' time. What can I do? Good-bye."

And that time he hung up.

As soon as the call ended, the calm voice I'd maintained evaporated, and I was very rattled. The words "kill Amanda and Nigel" sent a chill through me.

I went over to Jon's house after the call. He'd heard everything through the one-way phone. He was crying when I got there, and I found myself reassuring him the way Tony at the SLOC had reassured me after the call. "The thing to remember is, without their captives alive, they have nothing to hold on to. They need to keep Amanda and Nigel safe and well. Let's remember that." I was rattled, but I knew the theory made perfect sense. Jon told me how guilty he felt that he didn't feel strong enough to negotiate, and he thanked me for doing it. "It's okay, Jon," I said. "We all have different roles to play." Once again, I felt glad that we had the relationship we did.

As the calls from Adam became more threatening, the atmosphere in the SLOC changed accordingly. The kidnappers were ramping up the pressure. Tony approached me: "Lorinda, it's probably a good idea to get you prepared for a bad call." I didn't like the sound of that, but I knew it was something I needed to do.

Craig and I practiced what is referred to as a "back-to-back." Two chairs were arranged back to back; I sat on one, and Craig sat on the other. The fact that we couldn't see each other was meant to take away the familiarity we had. It also signaled the seriousness of what we were doing.

Craig then began yelling at me, "I'm going to kill your daughter! Can you hear her screaming?"

My mind went to the speaking board: "She is your sister. You must protect her."

"We want our money now!"

"I need more time! I am trying to do as you ask!"

"Do you think I am lying? I will kill her right now while you listen!"

"If you kill her, you will never get your money."

The room went silent except for the sobbing. Even though it was a "practice" run, all three of us were shaken to our cores.

"I'm so sorry, Lorinda, that was so hard. Let's pray that you'll never be in that position," Craig said as he hugged me. Tony hugged me as well, and I could feel him shaking.

I could not believe that this was my life now.

Afterward, I went for a walk on the beach to try to calm myself, to shake off the trauma of the morning. I took deep breaths to focus my mind. It was October, and the temperature was dropping daily, so the beach was almost deserted. I was grateful for solitude. I noticed all my previous footprints in the sand—the evidence of my anxious daily wandering. As I watched the wind ripple Sylvan Lake, I remembered how my brothers and I had used to play there on the beach, building castles and burying one another in the sand when we were kids. We lived on the North Hill, the outskirts of Red Deer, the poor side of town. We didn't have much materially, but we had acres to lap and a horse named Scout. Weather permitting, I rode Scout almost daily after school, riding bareback until our family could afford a saddle. It was a big deal when we could buy that saddle, and we all took turns learning how to ride with it.

As well as gallivanting in the swamp, my brothers and I ran in the fields and climbed trees. For the most part, my early childhood was the source of wonderful memories, but that changed once I started school. I had trouble understanding the teacher and couldn't make sense of the lessons. This made me feel left out, as other children progressed at school while I was left behind. Nobody—including me—realized that my real problem was not stupidity but the fact that I couldn't hear or see properly. Luckily, my hearing difficulty was caught during a hearing test, and after a simple flushing of my ears, the world sounded a whole lot louder and clearer. As for my eyes, I would sit at my desk, pulling at them, trying to make out the fuzzy hieroglyphics on the blackboard. I assumed all the other kids struggled this way. My mom finally realized I had vision problems when we were in an ice cream store. "Choose a flavor," she said, pointing up at the list on the wall.

"I can't see it," I said.

"You can't read that?"

I shook my head.

Mom took me to the eye doctor, and I returned to school with glasses. As if by magic, a whole new world literally appeared before my eyes. Both Amanda and Mark had inherited my poor eyesight. I felt ill when my thoughts returned to Amanda, to my girl struggling to see while in captivity. I was taking in the beach in solitude, watching the breeze as it made the lake ripple and the sand skip across the beach. Half a world away, what was Amanda struggling to see?

Standing alone on the beach was restorative, but I knew it would take a collective effort to bring Amanda and Nigel home. A couple of days later, during our morning call with Ottawa, we were told that Gordon Black had been to visit the Brennans and they were totally on board now to work with the joint plan created by the RCMP and the AFP. I don't recall any further involvement by Gordon Black in our case, and I figured he'd been called to deal with other international incidents.

It was a relief to hear that the Brennans were now working with us. We understood and supported Ottawa's insistence that our families work with our governments rather than in opposition to them.

Meanwhile, the circle of families who understood our particular struggles was unfortunately growing bigger. Two days later, on October 13, I learned through our morning call that CBC-TV journalist

Mellissa Fung had been kidnapped at gunpoint in Afghanistan the day before. That was shared in confidence, as there was a media blackout to protect her safety. That meant that another family was now undergoing the same torment, the same isolation in secrecy, that we had been thrown into fifty-two days earlier. I was asked not to share the privileged information with anyone outside the SLOC. As I thought about Mellissa and her family, I said a little prayer for them.

Later that day, I read a report from Press TV's correspondent in Mogadishu: "Fifteen Days to Save Journalists in Somalia." According to the article, one of the kidnappers had stated that if $2.5 million were not paid in fifteen days, Amanda and Nigel would be killed. I wondered where they were getting their information. Our deadline, the true deadline, was ten days. I could only guess that something had leaked to the reporter from within Somalia and the details had been wrong.

In bed that night, I lay awake as I always did. I directed my thoughts to Amanda. *Amanda, what are you thinking about these days? Do you know that we have been given a deadline? God, I miss you so much. I remember when you were a little girl and you would lie with your head on my lap and ask me to run my fingers through your hair. What I wouldn't give for that chance right now. I'm sad about everything I took for granted.*

•

ON OCTOBER 15, I RECEIVED an email from Charles, who was still in Iraq. A Canadian diplomat had arrived to pick up Amanda's belongings, which she had left there with the thought that she would return to Iraq after her stint in Somalia. Charles said that he would check on her belongings, and if there was anything left, he would ship them directly to me. Charles was still working on connecting me and Tina via email, but in the meantime he had also been speaking with people associated with kidnappings abroad and passing on their contact information, too. The first question they asked him was whether we had consulted independent hostage experts. He mentioned one family who had trusted and followed the advice given by their government, only to realize that they should have gone with their own instincts. The email closed with his urgent plea that we consider consulting an independent hostage expert.

In my response, I expressed my gratitude for all he was doing. "I have absolute confidence in the Canadian government," I reiterated. "Impeccable seventeen-year record, I'd say that they are experts." I was aware that Amanda had planned to return to Iraq but not that she had left anything behind. When I inquired with Ottawa about having her things shipped to me, I was told that they would be returned to Amanda upon her release or sent to me if she didn't return home. But she *would* return home, I reminded myself.

Amanda's two best girlfriends, Kelly and Jelara, had been asking about the progress in Amanda's case, so I made plans to drive to Calgary to meet with them, knowing that I had to be guarded in everything I said. We met in a lounge close to the airport, and I told them that I was still living at Jon's and we received a call from DFAIT daily. "Trust me when I say that the government is actively involved," I said. "We have one hundred percent confidence in their efforts."

My trip to Calgary had a double purpose. I made an appointment to meet with Barb, the RCMP therapist I'd been introduced to previously. She wasn't exactly sure how to help me because she was used to counseling officers after trauma, not during trauma. She emphasized that I needed to take care of myself—eat healthy and get lots of rest and exercise. She also thought it was helpful that I was practicing meditation and gratitude.

•

OCTOBER 16, DAY 55, was our ten-day deadline. Adam hadn't called throughout the long days previous, which in some ways was a relief to me after the "practice call." I was scared for the phone to ring on Day 55. I didn't know what to expect. But the phone didn't ring that day.

While Adam remained silent, the press found ways to contact us whenever something popped up in the news.

The news from Press TV regarding the alleged fifteen-day

deadline had been picked up by local papers, and the press was reaching out to family members for comment. We asked everyone not to comment in order to protect Amanda and Nigel. I stressed that we couldn't have the media knowing or speculating on what the government was actually doing. Of course, no one else knew what the government was doing, but it made them feel as though they were participating in something secret and important. And they were, more than they could know.

On October 17, Ottawa informed us that David, the newest negotiator in Nairobi, had offered $7,300 to Adam. They weren't clear as to where the money had come from, but I didn't care. The way things were going, we needed to step up our game, and Ottawa was taking that initiative.

Two days later, on October 19, Mark and Nathaniel arrived for a few days and we met at the SLOC with Jon and Perry to belatedly celebrate Nathaniel's birthday. I played the recorded call from September 4 so they could hear Amanda's voice. Nathaniel glowed. "Hearing her voice is one of the best birthday gifts I've ever received," he said. That night Mark stayed at the SLOC and Nathaniel spent the night at his dad's. It was so good to see them both, to have them close.

The next morning, I woke up with a new update from Ottawa. Often, Ottawa would send speaking points for my next call with Adam, and the one I received on October 20 instructed me that if I were threatened again to utilize the principle of reciprocity. We would leverage the $7,300 for more time. I was to tell Adam that the money had come from the sale of my car and that a local businessman— a good Samaritan—might possibly lend us more. And as always, I was to push for proof of life and proof of care.

On October 22, it had been sixteen days and there had still been no call from Adam, so Ottawa decided to switch things up. I would call Adam and catch him off guard when it was daytime in Mogadishu. We agreed to call at 2 a.m. our time. I was not to address the deadline that had passed but instead was supposed to kick up the emotional level by crying. I had trained myself so well to keep my emotions suppressed during calls. Would I have a hard time crying, or would the floodgates open? I knew that could depend on the kind of call I found myself dealing with.

As we set up to make the call, Mark put on the extra headset; Nathaniel would listen in on Jon's one-way phone. I dialed.

"Hello, my friend, Adam. How are you?"

"My friend, I am fine," he said. I could hear his children noisily playing in the background. "I marry Amanda, or I marry you."

If his intention was to throw me, this statement worked. I wouldn't look at Mark to see his reaction. I needed to focus.

I quickly changed the subject. "Adam, I'm very worried. I haven't spoken to Amanda since September 4."

"Amanda is so sick. We don't have eyeglasses here. We talk to Mr. David in Nairobi. They still are not ready to pay the money. They are saying $38,000, and that is nothing."

Though this sum was more than I had expected to hear, I played along. "Adam, the government will not pay. I sold my car so that the money could come over there. You know that Amanda's father is very sick, and his medicine is very expensive. Please accept what is offered. Our families are very poor, and, and please Adam, let me speak to Amanda." My voice began to shake as I felt the tears come.

"All in all, if we get the money, you can speak to Amanda."

"Okay, Adam. I need to know how she is. I need to speak to Amanda. Please . . . I am her mother, and I'm worried. I just, I just need to . . . please . . ."

"Don't worry, Lorinda. You should talk at this time, but this time we are afraid if you talk because we are not getting what we supposed to."

I could feel his discomfort at hearing me cry for the first time.

"Adam, I need to know how she is. Is she, is she still sick?"

"She has illness with her eyes. She is feeling sometimes itch. She sometimes has no appetite for the sight of food. That is what I'm telling you before."

"Is Nigel still sick?"

"Yes. He always has cough allergy."

With the prompting of an index card, I followed up on an earlier suggestion that our families send a medical package. "Is the airport still shut down with fighting? Can we send a package?"

"It is working two weeks or three weeks at this time. You can send anything you want."

We had a long conversation about how the package would be picked up from the airport. At first Adam said it was sufficient to address it by his first name and phone number. Then, after we sparred over whether I would be allowed to speak with Amanda, he returned angrily to the inadequate money he'd been offered. "David and Marc tell us lie, and they become liar man."

I pressed for information about Amanda and Nigel: "When was the last time you spoke to them?"

"Before three week, before two week. They are far away, and I am so busy."

"Are Amanda and Nigel still together?"

"Yes, they are together."

I begged again: "Adam, please allow me to speak with my daughter. She needs to hear my voice. She's my daughter, she's my baby. I don't understand why they punish me. I am trying so hard. Promise me that I can talk to my daughter."

"I will promise to make my last effort to talk, but if they refuse, my group will be hard. I shall try." Adam was scrambling to make me understand that he would allow me, but the group would not. It was causing many problems for him when he tried. We ended the call with his promise to try again.

Mark and Nathaniel were both surprised at how polite he sounded. I was sure they'd had the same movie image that I'd had at the beginning. The boys left that day to return to work in BC. It was hard to say good-bye again. Our support for each other brought so much comfort.

The next afternoon, during my time off, I went shopping. In my hurry and confusion when I had packed a bag to head for Sylvan Lake, two months earlier, I had thrown an odd assortment of clothes together. I hadn't known then how long I would be there. Now I needed some practical clothing. Three of my friends had chipped in and sent me some money to buy something for myself. I decided on a winter coat, gloves, scarf, and boots.

Shopping made me think of Amanda's love of shopping and style. Even when my girl was little, she would ask for big earrings or want to hair spray her bangs straight up. After Jon took her to Disneyland when she was five for a father-daughter trip, he complained that she hadn't wanted to go on the rides, she just wanted to shop. That memory made me laugh out loud. Amanda was a born shopper and I was not, but we'd spent many hours shopping together regardless. How I missed those times.

Amanda's passion for fashion magazines had grown to include a passion for travel magazines. I wasn't surprised about that. She had always been an exceptionally curious child. Until the age of three, she'd insisted on sleeping with every stuffed toy she owned. At three years old, she'd thrown all of the animals out of her bed and replaced them with books, her literary friends. When she was older, she treasured her collection of *National Geographic* magazines, and it wasn't until much later that I realized how the exotic locales featured in those pages fed her hunger not just for travel but for escape.

I thought about one morning when Amanda was eleven. I was headed to her room to wake her for school. I was thinking how lucky I was to have such a wonderful, softhearted, happy daughter. When I opened the door, I found a furious little creature waiting for me. It was as if her hormones and anger had kicked in overnight and suddenly she was a teenager. I had heard similar experiences from other mothers with teenage daughters, but it was different when the story rang true for my own. As I left the store that day, I reflected on how much our relationship had grown and changed from her childhood to her teenage years to now. I missed her so much. And with all my shopping bags in hand, I missed her even more.

•

AFTER THE CALL ON OCTOBER 22, Ottawa decided we would change our strategy and hammer Adam with calls and emails for the next few days during daytime hours in Somalia. This meant that the negotiators—now Joanne, Bob, and me—were getting very tired because we were staying up most of the night. But over the course of the next five days, I called or received calls to and from Adam nine times, sent four emails, and received one email in return.

During those interactions we covered the details of getting a package to Amanda and Nigel. There were no functional post offices or boxes due to the destruction of the war. We would send it to the Mogadishu airport, where it would be picked up. We still didn't have Adam's legal name, so we expected that he would have someone else pick it up from the airport.

I asked Adam what they needed.

"No matter, send it to Mogadishu."

I asked if there was a woman where Amanda was to help her with "woman things." Adam didn't know.

I was concerned when Adam said, "This if I tell you the reality your daughter is very sick, she become dismoral. She is always thinking." It sounded to me like she was depressed.

Adam reiterated how insulted he and the others had been by the small ransom Marc and David in Nairobi had offered. "They are liar men, brokers only wishing to take the gang's money. They are not treating us like a gentleman. They are treating us like thieves," he complained.

Adam had become suspicious of the phone numbers that showed up when I called him; he thought there was a man connecting our calls. I had no idea what he was talking about, but he didn't believe me when I told him that. I urged him to call the phone company or call the number back. As per my instructions, I was relentless in pleading to speak with Amanda, but I was denied. Not by himself, he insisted, but by the gang. I pushed him to promise to protect and take care of his sister and brother, but he couldn't promise at that point. At times he agreed to try, but I thought he was only saying that to stop me from asking. He wanted me to see him as the "good guy" in this, but how could I? He was my daughter's kidnapper, for God's sake! He was colluding with thugs to rob my daughter of her freedom and take everything Jon and I had worked our whole lives for—and more than we could ever dream of having. Was he that clueless about the anguish, the terror, and the 24/7 nightmare that he and the others had cast us into? Despite all those thoughts, I had to continue to tell him that he was a good man, an honorable man.

He responded to the encouragement in ways that were often disturbing and puzzling for me and the negotiators. "Okay," he said, "You are my girlfriend, understand?"

"I thought I was your mom!"

"Yes, you are my mom, but is it really impossible to marry you?"

"Well, I am all the way over here in Canada."

"You should send me a ticket. Then there is not problem."

We concluded that my attempts to flatter and establish rapport with Adam had confused him about the nature of our relationship. Or was he playing the same game I was? I would let him believe whatever he wanted if it would help me bring Amanda home.

The biggest victory of those night calls was that we could now send a package to Amanda and Nigel. I phoned Australia. The Brennans were as excited as we were about the prospect of sending them a parcel. They had been given the same instructions: to include letters from the immediate family and something small that Nigel treasured. The rest of the package would be filled in Nairobi and sent from there.

The two small treasures we sent would not be in the package that was sent into Somalia. They would be given to Amanda and Nigel upon release as a sign that we, their families, had indeed hired these people to collect them and bring them home.

I was exhausted after living on this nocturnal schedule for about a week. On October 28, the negotiators told me that I should take a night off. But I was reluctant to leave the phone. What if Amanda called? I was told that it was not likely at that point because of Adam's firm stance. I begrudgingly agreed and made plans to visit a childhood friend in Calgary, booking a night at a hotel there. I was nervous as I left, feeling awkward outside what had become my protective cocoon at the SLOC. The SLOC was home now—a strange home and one I'd never wanted, but home nonetheless. I had a lovely supper with my friend. I asked her not to ask me what was happening with Amanda. Instead, we caught up on our other kids and reminisced. I left and headed back to the hotel to enjoy the hot tub and cry and cry and cry.

As I was driving back to the SLOC the next afternoon, my friend Conni called my cell. "Oh my God, I just heard the news about Amanda! I'm so sorry. I can't even imagine."

"Conni, what news?" I pulled over. I was shaking so hard that the phone slipped out of my hand. I picked it back up.

"The news about Amanda."

"What are you talking about?"

"You don't know? I shouldn't be the one to tell you."

The tears were streaming down my face.

"For God's sake, tell me what?"

"It's the worst news."

I hung up, and though I could barely see, I managed to dial the SLOC. Fuck! I should never have left.

Brad W. answered the phone. I was sobbing so hard I could hardly breathe. "What happened to Amanda?" I demanded.

"What's wrong? What do you mean?"

I relayed what Conni had told me, but Brad W. hadn't heard any news about Amanda.

"Sit tight," he said. "I'll check with Ottawa and then call you back." When he did, he said that no one could find anything on the news concerning my Amanda or any Amanda for that matter. "Lorinda, are you okay to drive? Do you want me to send a car to pick you up?"

"Just let me sit here for a few minutes. I think I'll be able to get myself home."

"Give me Conni's phone number," Brad W. said. "I'll try to find out what happened."

I did so. Then I waited at the side of the road for more news. And I prayed. *Please, Amanda, be okay. You have to be okay! We have so much to do together. We need you. I need you, Amanda!*

Brad W. called back. "Hello?" I said. "What's going on?"

He told me that things were okay. Then he explained. "It seems that a friend of Conni's was shopping in Costco and overheard some people there talking about the girl in Somalia who had been killed. The friend assumed that it was Amanda and called Conni to tell her."

"So it's not true?"

"No. It's not," Brad W. said. Then he told me the actual news reported out of Somalia had been the story of a thirteen-year-old girl who had been raped by four men. She had been stoned to death for adultery. That was the kind of madness that happened in Somalia—the country where my daughter was being held captive. It was Day 68 of Amanda's captivity. I was relieved it had all been a misunderstanding, but I was also shredded. I wasn't sure how I could go on like this. How could my heart stand any more? I felt so fragile. I lay in bed that night wide awake, totally numb.

The next day, October 30, Day 69, my mom called me with the urgent message that my foster daughter Janet had been rushed to the University of Alberta hospital and was in critical condition. She had a new kidney and hadn't been taking her medications as prescribed. She had been found passed out in a pool of blood. I called the University of Alberta to find out what her condition was. Was she dying? Did I need to come? They told me that they could not confirm either way. Should I go to her or stay by the phone? I looked to Brad W. for answers. He told me I should be okay away from the phone for another couple of days, so I made arrangements to pick Tiffany up at the bus station in Red Deer. She and her new baby, Morris, were coming from the Lethbridge area. When we arrived at the hospital, Janet looked frail and discolored, but she was awake. After a conversation with the nurse, I learned that less than 3 percent of her one existing kidney was functioning and she had the beginnings of cirrhosis of the liver. She would have to be on dialysis again, but she would live. I had taken care of Janet since she was three years old, held her hand through multiple surgeries and setbacks. She was a survivor. It was time for me to go back to the SLOC.

When I arrived, I met my two new in-house negotiators, Elly and Lina. Bob was still there, and before he left for home, he suggested that we practice for another possible "bad scenario" call. He explained that Ottawa was concerned that the group was angry with Adam and might feel that he was not being firm enough with me. It was possible that they might remove him and use another negotiator.

While Bob went into the kitchen, out of sight, Elly and I sat side by side. This was for her practice, too.

Bob began yelling, "I am Abdullah! We want our money now, or I will kill your daughter!"

My eyes went to the speaking board for cues once again. "Where is Adam? Why should I trust you?"

"I don't care if you trust me. I don't care about you! I don't care about your daughter! I am a soldier, and I kill! Give us our money, or your daughter will die a horrible death! You say you love your daughter, then pay us! Maybe you don't love your daughter? Believe me when I say that I would enjoy killing your daughter!"

Elly and I looked at each other, speechless. I was shocked by Bob's viciousness. I knew him only as a gentle and kind man. It was clear that if that kind of call came, I would be reduced to a sobbing, pleading mess. We spent the next couple of hours discussing possible responses to that kind of onslaught. Once the session was over, I walked on the beach, again begging whatever higher power might be listening, *Please, I can take the practice. But don't ever allow that call to come!* I had been so strong and optimistic when this had all begun, but now I felt as though my legs could barely carry me.

Fortunately, on November 2, good news came my way. The sitting chair in Ottawa informed Jon and me that Amanda and Nigel had been seen by a doctor. This was the boost my pulverized soul needed. There was some humanity in the group after all. I didn't know then that it was misinformation (Amanda informed me of the truth upon her return), but at the time, this news served me well.

Shortly after this update, Adam called.

"Hello, Mom. Are you fine?"

Am I fucking fine? You fucking asshole! "Yes, Adam, I am fine. Are you well?"

We went back and forth with the usual questions and answers concerning whether or not I could speak with Amanda. I was denied. Adam told me that the group had invested $6,000 in the care of Amanda and Nigel and now they had no money for food or clean water.

"Your daughter is mentally, morally, and physically sick," Adam said. "She have her eyes become . . . as black. Understand? What I am telling you to you is to pay is that you are the mom and she is my sister. Understand? . . . I swear that of Allah your daughter is sick."

He went on to tell me once again that he swore in the name of Allah that Nigel was so sick he could no longer walk. He continued to swear in the name of Allah a few more times that he was not lying. I replied that there was medication that was coming in the package, as well as glasses for Amanda.

"If they die without food and without health, don't say to me, Adam has blamed." Adam told me that he was onto us and the "agents" we had working in Nairobi. I asked him to work with the "agents," that they were working on behalf of both of our families. The call ended with my plea, once again, for a POL.

"I will try, I will try. Believe me, I will try," Adam said.

After the flurry of calls between the SLOC and Somalia, Ottawa, and Australia, after Adam had agreed to deliver a parcel to my daughter and Nigel, Adam disappeared. He simply stopped answering my emails and calls. I would sit by the phone, watching it, aging a year for every day of silence.

CHAPTER SEVEN

THE MILLION-DOLLAR MISUNDERSTANDING

The first few days of silence from Adam gave me a breather and a little time to gather myself. My car needed winter tires, as we were now in deep snow. I contacted my good friend Gordon Scott in Red Deer, who owned the car dealership where I had purchased my car. I knew Gord from high school, and we had kept in touch over the years.

"I'm so sorry, Lorinda," he said, wrapping me in a hug.

I was glad to see him. As my car was taken in, we sat in his office and caught up on our children and our families. I told him the usual lies—that I was living at Jon's waiting by the phone, on medical leave—but then suddenly I found myself blurting out everything.

"It's okay," he said, reaching across the desk and taking my hand. "You can trust me."

I already knew I could. I felt guilty because I had been sworn to secrecy, but the burden I was carrying was crushing me. It was a short relief. Although I felt his continued support, we didn't communicate much after that.

The isolation and secrecy were creating a huge void of loneliness. Even though I was with negotiators 24/7, I still felt alone in my nightmare. They were there only to do their jobs. I was there to save my daughter. The difference was enormous. Jon's emotional pain was taking a bigger and bigger toll on him. Perry was having trouble coping as well. Mark and Nathaniel were working in British Columbia and doing their best to cope with their own emotions and frustrations about their distance and their inability to help. The negotiators gave me space when they felt I needed it, and then tried to cheer me up.

One day at the SLOC, Elly asked, "Lorinda, will you teach me how to make pies?" They all know that I loved to cook and pies were my specialty, so I agreed. It proved to be fun and a good distraction.

On November 4, the newly appointed minister of foreign affairs, Lawrence Cannon, arranged a call with Jon and me. He was cordial and polite, eager to reassure us that Amanda's case was of top priority to the government of Canada, that we were in the best hands possible working with our appointed team. He ended by telling us that we could contact him at any time with any concerns we might have.

"Wow, can you believe that just happened?" Jon said after the call.

"I really needed that reassurance. I've been feeling so down lately," I confided.

"Amanda's going to come home soon, Lorinda. I just know it."

"By Christmas." I said wishfully. "Wouldn't that be the greatest gift ever?"

We held on to every glimmer of hope for release to come quickly.

On the same day, I emailed Amanda's friend Kelly Barker to tell her that I had been speaking with Lynette, a woman Amanda was very close to.

"Lynette has reminded me that Amanda finds beauty in most everything and everyone," I wrote. "She believes that when Amanda comes home, many doors will open to spread her light."

Kelly had given me a CD to listen to, *Grace* by Snatam Kaur. I told her I loved it. "But song number six always makes me cry. It's so beautiful and reminds me of Amanda. It's almost like a prayer for her, to guide her way home."

I tried to write about something lighter, to imagine some fun. "Kelly, do you think Amanda is playing the 'food game' with Nigel?" Since Kelly and I had both traveled with Amanda, we were familiar with one of Amanda's favorite games while traveling long distances and between meals. She always asked, "If you could have anything to eat right now, what would it be?"

Kelly replied quickly to my email. "I had a chuckle at your question about the food game. Was there ever any doubt? Lol! Chocolate cake and turkey dinner!"

Now I was chuckling. Yes, that was Amanda's most common response. I missed Amanda so much.

Amanda, do you remember when we traveled through Thailand and played the food game? That was such a fun trip, riding around in tuk-tuks and the back of trucks like the locals. The Thai women would point at me and say "mama" and then point at you and say "baby," and we would laugh afterward. It was such a beautiful country. Maybe when you're back we can plan that trip to India? I want to experience that country that has made you fall in love with it. We've talked about it for so long. Let's make it happen. I promise I will make all the turkey dinners and chocolate cake you want when you are home. I will cook you anything you desire. Please come home soon so I can.

A couple days later, on November 6, I was once again sickened when I read about four employees of a French charity group who had been kidnapped during a humanitarian mission in Somalia. Seriously? A humanitarian mission!

As the days slowly ticked by with no contact from Adam, I became anxious again, but the sitting chair in Ottawa promised that there was a lot going on behind the scenes. They couldn't reveal specific information to me, though. "One day, when this is over, we'll all sit down and we'll tell you the rest of the story," the sitting chair said. "In the meantime, trust that Amanda and Nigel are our priority."

Jon and I were sent a list of contents in the care package sent to Adam. The lists for Amanda and Nigel were similar, with some notable differences. They would both receive medications for various potential afflictions, toothbrushes, toothpaste, and floss (a small comfort—Amanda was obsessed with dental hygiene), deodorant, lip balm, lotion, multivitamins, water purification tablets, eye drops, pens, pencils, notebooks, underwear, quiz books, and books to read. Amanda's books were Nelson Mandela's *Long Walk to Freedom*, volumes I and II.

I knew she would appreciate the books because she was an avid reader and these would help her get through. And her glasses! I was so excited that she would soon be able to see clearly. Our letters, one to Amanda and one to Nigel, were in two large brown envelopes and safely packed in amid everything else.

We also sent a care package for Abdifatah, the translator who had been hired by Amanda and Nigel to orchestrate their travels and events while in Mogadishu and who had also been kidnapped. We would later learn that he wasn't being kept with them. His package was a smaller version of the other two—minus the books.

We would find out much later that the driver as well as another Somali guide had been held captive for the first five months, after which they were released. The three men were held in a separate room from Amanda and Nigel. The Nairobi team knew of Abdifatah's imprisonment, but I assumed not that of the other two men, thus only the one extra care package.

A first aid kit was included, along with four stuffed toys for Adam's children: one kangaroo, one koala, one moose, one polar bear. The strategy of reciprocity. Before our family's letters could be sent, they were scrutinized by the RCMP to make sure they didn't contain anything that would be damaging to our cause. Jon had been asked to omit any mention of Perry in an attempt to avoid any cultural offenses born out of their relationship, which he willingly did. He realized that we had to exercise extreme caution.

As a last-minute thought, we included a family shot of Jon, Perry, Mark, Nathaniel, and me that we'd taken on the stairs at the SLOC. We didn't have time to prepare before it was taken. We all looked in rough shape, particularly Jon, who had a black eye. A window blind had accidentally fallen on him that week. I wondered what Amanda would think when she saw it.

On November 8, Mellissa Fung was released after twenty-eight days of captivity. As I sat in the kitchen looking out the window at the snow falling, I imagined how her parents were feeling. I was so happy for them, but I was also jealous. This was Day 78 for us. I spent it listening for details of the terms of Mellissa's release, listening for how she had been treated as a woman in a Muslim country. I wanted reassurance that Amanda's treatment might be humane. I watched Mellissa's face on TV, scrutinizing her expressions. Although there were no signs of physical abuse that I could see, I noticed the fear in her eyes. I immediately felt a maternal urge to hug and comfort her. The media reported that the government of Afghanistan had stepped in to intervene with the kidnappers to secure her release. I was desperately hoping that the Somali government would do the same for us, but from all the reports I had read, it remained small, weak, and ineffectual. In fact, the latest news from Mogadishu was that the fighting had increased.

I asked the RCMP if it might be possible to speak with Mellissa after she had time to recover and was told they would check into it. I heard back months later after repeated requests—unfortunately, I was told, she and her family did not wish to be bothered.

November 11 was Remembrance Day and Mark's birthday. I called and had a chat with him. It would be Christmas before I would see my sons again—unless Amanda came home before then. On the morning of November 13, I was finally able to establish contact with Tina Susman, the Associated Press correspondent who had been kidnapped in Mogadishu in 1994. She had been driving through the capital when armed assailants had captured her. Though the kidnappers had asked for $300,000, then lowered their demands, AP insisted that no ransom had ever been paid. She had been released after twenty days.

In her email, Tina told me about the conditions and treatment she had received while in captivity. I'd asked all kinds of questions, and Tina responded with great candor:

I am quite certain that there are women either living in the compound where Amanda is or that they are being brought in to cook, clean, etc, and to tend to things that men would not be allowed to deal with due to cultural issues. Somali men are pretty traditional and if they are going to have a female in their midst they will want a female to tackle the "female issues" that arise. Another thing to bear in mind: periods often come to a grinding halt under such circumstances. Somali men may not be the nicest group, but the women were always very very kind to me.

She went on to tell me a funny story about how she had received enough boxes of tampons in care packages to last her through menopause. "To this day, I'm sure there is a room in Mogadishu with a bunch of Tampax boxes being used as bookshelves."

Not only had Tina relieved me by answering my questions, she had also given me a good laugh. That was a lot for one email. It helped me to forget, for a few minutes, that I hadn't had any contact with Somalia since November 2—almost two weeks. I hoped there was a woman around to help Amanda and be kind to her. Women understand women, I thought.

Though I hadn't heard from Adam, I did hear from the Nairobi team. Our care package had landed, but Adam had not yet picked it up from the Mogadishu airport. The speculation was that it could be due to the increase in fighting in Mogadishu, or maybe Adam was leery that the package could be traced back to him.

November continued to drag on, and my mind wandered to other thoughts. I missed my friends, my social circle, my former life. I missed normal. I missed my mom. I wished I could tell her the truth, but it was for her own good not to know. She frequently asked what was happening. I had to be careful to avoid an innocent slip. We were close, and I knew that she felt lonely living by herself in her first year of widowhood. Of our family, I was the one who had watched out for her, and I could no longer support her through her grief. She was trying her best to be my support now.

We still met from time to time, always at restaurants or at her home, and I always had to be careful about what I said. I tried to steer the conversation to safe topics. We reminisced about my dad, remembering how he'd had only two dress styles—for work, a beanie-type cap, coveralls, a hankie in his pocket, and steel-toed boots; for social occasions, black cowboy boots, black jeans, a leather belt, snap-up shirts, and a pencil and pad in his pocket. For church, he added a black blazer. He wasn't a talker, and he always said that were it not for my mother, he would have been a hermit and gone to live in the woods by himself. He didn't have much use for people. My mother changed all that. She was the polar opposite and dragged him to many social events and to church. The fact that he went for her was evidence that he loved her deeply. He came to love church as much as she did, and they became involved in many Christian organizations.

In my earliest memory of my mother, I am standing beside her in our bathroom, watching her brush her dark hair and put on makeup. I remember thinking how beautiful she was. I wanted to be like her. She was very social, and she loved to laugh. She was a strong-willed woman with an independent mind.

Sometimes this will, along with her religious beliefs, turned stern and judgmental, and I felt that was especially true when the subject was Amanda. It was still a sore spot for me, but I needed her support more than I needed to prove that she was wrong about Amanda. I was grateful that as soon as she'd heard that Amanda had been kidnapped she'd rallied for me and for her granddaughter and put all of her grievances aside. I was grateful for her ongoing prayers and for all the other people she had asked to pray for me and Amanda. It was good energy. I believed in the power of that good energy. I needed it then more than any other time in my life.

On November 15, I read about two nuns, aged sixty and sixty-seven, who had just been kidnapped on the border of Somalia. No one is safe, anyone is fair game, I thought. I wondered if the Catholic Church paid ransoms.

After reading about the kidnapped nuns, I was feeling pretty down.

Jason hadn't been rotated through the SLOC since September, and I reached out to him by email for his voice of reason. I admitted that I was trying hard to stay upbeat for myself and everyone

else, but I hadn't been doing well lately. I wasn't sleeping any better, which was making me more emotional, and I was desperately
lonely.

"*Christmas is coming,*" I wrote, "*and I can't bear the thought of Amanda
not making it home in time. I can't think about it without crying. Things in
Somalia are not going well. Al-Shabaab is gaining ground and the fighting
has increased. I can't allow fear or sadness to overwhelm me or I'm hooped.
Any advice?*"

Jason wrote back:

Lorinda,

*I can only imagine the daily grind and effort you put into being
up and remaining positive in the face of adversity. Though I am
removed, I think that Amanda and Nigel are in good standing.*

*Christmas is a time that we place far too much aggrandizement
upon. Try not to develop expectations around a time and date that
are arbitrary in nature. Should you build this up as a release date, it
may in turn be perceived by Adam and bolster their position at the
bargaining table. Christmas will come and go whether she's home or
not.*

Take care and know that we are all with you,

Jason

Jason's logic about Christmas made sense, but I was going to have
to sit with it. I still didn't know how I was going to handle it if she
wasn't home by then. Craig and Jim were in the SLOC now, and they
were determined to cheer me up. I very much appreciated that they
made me feel like a normal person, not "a case" they were working.
Craig was from the west coast, Vancouver Island, and brought seafood
that he had personally caught. Jim brought pure maple syrup from the
east coast. Both came armed with recipes. I was starting to joke about

how much weight I was gaining. Craig was a skilled cook, and Jim was giving it everything he had. One morning I woke up to the sound of the smoke alarm. Jim had thought he would surprise me with fresh-baked cinnamon buns, and the sugar was burning. Their kindness was like a warm comforting blanket on a freezing cold day.

Cooking had become a friendly competition among several of the negotiators. We tried to make as much room as possible for food and humor. It was therapeutic for all of us. At times Jon and Perry joined us for supper, and the negotiators always got a kick out of the clothes that their dog, Shanobi, was wearing. She had acquired some new winter coats with fur-trimmed hoods.

Sometimes I felt guilty that I was eating well and laughing while Amanda was suffering. I doubted that she had much food or any moments of laughter, but I remembered that Amanda was a person who grabbed life and lived it to the fullest. She loved to laugh and eat good food. I felt that if she could have talked to us, she would have told us that she didn't want us to emulate her conditions, that we should enjoy these rare times that afforded us a brief reprieve.

On November 20, Jon and I got news that our Nairobi cell, which had been actively engaged with Adam, had ramped up our offer to the kidnappers to an amazing $250,000. Where had the money come from? Jon and I were told it was the gift of a benefactor. Eventually, we discovered the donor was Nigel's aunt Alison, a Canadian living in British Columbia. What endeared Alison to us—and still does—was that she had generously insisted her money be used equally toward Amanda's and Nigel's release. Jon and I were ecstatic. It was a huge amount of money. We could only imagine how big it would seem to the captors. Surely this grand sum would bring our children home.

Sadly, our high hopes were dashed almost as soon as they were raised. The kidnappers turned down the offer flatly. They were still demanding their fantastical $2.5 million. Delegates in Ottawa told us not to worry. They believed the kidnappers would change their minds—they just needed a bit more time. After all, Amanda and Nigel were now being moved often because their captors were afraid of

Al-Shabaab, the extremist Muslim group that had taken over most of southern Somalia. They couldn't afford to wait much longer, we were told, and of course, we wanted more than anything to believe just that.

To help negate my loneliness, I started visiting my daughter Tiffany and my four-month-old grandson, Morris, whom I'd had very little time with since Amanda's kidnapping. Tiffany had been spending time in Red Deer to be close to Janet, who had now been transferred to the Red Deer hospital to recuperate. For self-care, I found that during my free time in the afternoon, I needed to leave the SLOC. I walked, skated on the lake, or visited family. It was easiest to visit Janet and Tiffany because they had their own immediate concerns— Tiffany with being a new mom and Janet with her recuperation—and they didn't often ask about Amanda or me. I joked with Janet while she was on dialysis that she was trapped with me and all my "good advice" now. I missed them, and I soaked up the glorious feeling of holding my first grandbaby. I needed this, and they needed me.

That night, after our visit, I crawled into bed and began my gratitude time. "I'm so grateful for my children and my new little grandson," I began. My gratitudes came easier that night, and for the first time in a long time, I was smiling as I fell asleep. I dreamed about Amanda. I don't remember much about the dream, except that she was home.

On November 23, there was good news from Ottawa. The care package had been picked up. Amanda's glasses, her books, her letters, and the photo of our family! I could see her clutching the picture, crying as she read our words of love and encouragement to be strong. She would probably look at the picture closely and wonder why her dad had a black eye. I felt giddy that she was holding the very papers we had held. It was the closest we had come to touching her in eleven months.

I received an email from another former colleague of Amanda's, Chris Gelken, who was working in Beijing. He checked the wire services at least twice a day to see if there had been any news concerning Amanda. He was very insistent that we hire a private hostage service.

If we didn't, our family should be pressuring France 24, the broadcaster for which Amanda had been freelancing at the time of her kidnapping. "Using freelance journalists is one way the networks can substantially reduce costs, because they work under the assumption that freelance means 'free from responsibility,'" he wrote.

My response was a replica of all my responses on this front: we had absolute confidence in the Canadian government.

On November 28, Adam finally called. I'd been given many objectives from Ottawa: to receive POLs for both Nigel and Amanda (which we hadn't had in thirty-three days); to make sure our medical package had been delivered (which we wanted Adam to confirm); and to get proof of care and establish goodwill by reminding Adam about the toys we'd sent for his children (and praising his good character, as always).

I wasn't to mention the $250,000 unless Adam did, because our Nairobi cell wasn't sure how much influence he still had with the kidnappers holding Amanda and Nigel. If he did broach the subject, I was to reinforce that our governments didn't pay ransoms and to stress that the sum had been raised by our families from selling property.

I began with the usual niceties. "Hello, Adam, my friend. How are you?"

Our line was crackly and intermittent, Adam seemed to be in a good mood. "I am fine, my wife."

Ugh. You idiot. I didn't let my feelings show. Instead, I asked if he'd received the care package.

"Yes, we have pick up from the airport, and we deliver it to Amanda and Nigel."

"Did your children get their presents?"

"Yes, they are very, very happy. They are playing every time."

When I asked if Amanda and Nigel had received the letters in the package, Adam replied, "That I can't confirm."

He then commented, in a puzzled voice, "Amanda said, tell this to my mother: 'When I get out, I want to go to India.' What does that mean?"

What? Was Amanda actually tuning in to my thoughts? I almost felt that she was. I also suspected she was trying to cheer us both up by mentioning the future.

After this brief exchange, the call disconnected. But all was not lost. At least I'd managed to ascertain that our care package had arrived, and I'd received a hopeful message from Amanda. That was all good news. I immediately shared the news with the Brennans, who were as pleased as we were.

What I didn't know then was that our care package, so cautiously conceived by us and our Nairobi cell, had been thoroughly pilfered by the kidnappers before it was delivered to Amanda and Nigel. One of those letters was, quite possibly, why our kidnappers had rejected—and would continue to reject—our $250,000. That simple letter, so lovingly meant, had created a one-million-dollar misunderstanding.

CHAPTER EIGHT

A KNIFE TO THE THROAT

We were headed into the fourth month now. December 1 would be Day 101. I could hardly believe it. Ottawa assured us that things might be going at a snail's pace, but they were going. As I had been told before, the government's first priority was Amanda and Nigel's safety, and it had to proceed with caution. It was hard to argue with that logic, but I wondered how safe were they if they remained in captivity?

I had now lived with eighteen different negotiators. They had been kind and tried very hard to make my life as easy as possible. Most had been visibly moved by our family's circumstances. After they rotated out of the SLOC to go about their regular duties, they slipped out of the loop, so I had taken to writing my own updates, which I emailed to all of them. Every correspondence ended with my mantra: "Today is one day closer to Amanda and Nigel coming home!" Often they responded with encouragement, and some sent jokes to keep my spirits up. These people had become my lifeline to normal, my friends and family in this new absurd reality.

As I continued to scour the news coming out of Somalia, I came across interviews with recently released hostages from a ship that Somali pirates had held for two months. The hostages and pirates had fished together, played cards, shared meals, and swapped stories of home. The captives had been encouraged to go about life on the boat as usual. When they were released, one of the pirates who had become "friends" with one of the hostages asked if he, the hostage, would like to join them, the kidnappers. "Of course, I said no. I was praying every day to be free," the hostage said. A bit of humor and another bit of hope that Amanda was being treated well.

On December 5, I learned from reading the news that the top UN envoy to Somalia had called for all the hostages to be released immediately. "On the eve of Eid, a period of forgiveness, I appeal to all Somalis to help ensure that those hostages being held, both Somalis, and foreigners, are allowed to enjoy their freedom and to return home safe and sound," said the secretary-general's special representative. He noted that releasing the hostages would boost Somalia's image and show that its people deserved respect and confidence. I was not familiar with Eid, so I did more research to get a better understanding of it. In the course of my research, I learned how important charity and gratitude are in the Muslim tradition.

I had so many emotions after all my reading: fear that something might inadvertently happen to Amanda and Nigel or Adam in the warfare surrounding them; but also hope, though small, that the kidnappers would let them go. I was eager to learn how Ottawa was going to respond to these developments.

One response came right to our front door. Jon and I were excited about the arrival of a negotiator who had worked in the Nairobi cell for the past two and a half months. We would have about an hour with him, and we felt that we were finally going to get the inside scoop. Division Intelligence Operations Officer Cal Chrustie looked like a TV personality—tall, handsome, with spiked blond hair, a white smile, and very tanned skin. We sat at the kitchen table with a cup of coffee as he explained that life in Somalia was tumultuous on every level. One day, our team would make progress with someone of influence, only to find everything had changed the next day. Fortunately, many different strategies were in place. The team was working with local Somalis known as TPIs (third-person intermediaries); one person had almost died trying to help us. According to the latest intelligence, Amanda and Nigel were in good health but struggling mentally and emotionally. The Somali elders, who did not want to damage their relationship with the Canadian and Australian governments, had somehow managed to get a message to the kidnappers detailing what constituted acceptable treatment of hostages. But the elders had no way of knowing what Amanda's and Nigel's living conditions were. The Nairobi cell was not sure how important Adam still was in the equation. But Cal advised me to maintain the good rapport we had developed. Finally, he reported, "I'm sorry to say that we think Amanda and Nigel have now been separated. They aren't living in the same quarters." We had been worried for some time that might be the case, but having it confirmed was still upsetting.

The Canadian ambassador to Kenya had been a tremendous support to our team and made Amanda's kidnapping his top priority. "Everyone involved has the most heart and commitment I've ever seen," Cal said with tears in his eyes. "Everybody wants Amanda and Nigel home quickly."

As he was leaving the SLOC to venture out into a snowstorm, he turned around. "Everyone appreciates your family's support and understanding of the complexities of this situation."

To say I felt grateful would undermine the moment. A weight had been lifted off my chest, and I could breathe a little easier. After all the vague calls with Ottawa, after feeling as though Jon and I were being managed, I finally knew the extent of the efforts being made to save my daughter. People were risking their lives. What more could I ask?

I couldn't wait to call the Brennans. Nigel's family had not been feeling confident in the joint strategies of the AFP and RCMP, and I hoped the information would boost their spirits as much as it had boosted ours. I called Nicky, as she was my partner, working negotiations from the Australian side. She was cheery and pleasant to deal with. She was very happy to hear the latest news from Nairobi and said she would pass it on to the rest of the family.

Though the meeting with Cal Chrustie had lifted my spirits, the upcoming holiday season threatened to pull them down. Christmas was everywhere I went when I left the SLOC, and my family was wondering how we would celebrate. Every time I thought about it, I felt angry about our last Christmas and how hard Amanda had cried before she'd boarded the plane to leave. I didn't want to create more pain for my family, but I didn't know if I could make it through the day without some of that anger leaking out.

Jon put up a tree and decorations. "Amanda would want us to be together for Christmas," he said. "It's her favorite holiday." I knew he was right. But I was also thinking that I'd rather take enough sleeping pills to knock myself out until Boxing Day. Because I voiced that at the SLOC, the team suggested that perhaps it would be helpful to see Barb for another therapy session. I didn't see Barb, but during some in-house conversations, I was gently reminded that I had four other children, a grandbaby, and a mother who still needed me, now more than ever. No one could change what had happened last Christmas or that they hadn't called Amanda before she'd left for Iraq. Everyone was living with their own guilt. Wasn't that punishment enough? I knew that was true. I felt bad that I'd ever thought of not being with my family for Christmas. I called Jon, and we arranged to gather at his house for a turkey dinner. Jon would call Mark and Nathaniel, and I would invite my mom, Janet, and Tiffany. It was all set.

While our family holiday plans moved along smoothly, negotiations seemed to be at a standstill. On December 13, I woke up frustrated that we were in a holding pattern again, waiting by the phone. I grabbed a coffee and said good morning to Brad M. He and Joanne were rotating through again, and he was on day duty with me. A few weeks before, I had put up a poster with three headings: *Days in Captivity*; *Days Since Last POL*; *Days Since My Last Contact with HT's* (hostage takers). Each day, I changed the numbers. With a sigh, I changed the number yet again. *Days in Captivity: 113*.

Brad M. and I were chatting about Christmas plans when the phone rang. I glanced at the time, almost noon. Normally Adam would call earlier because it was nighttime in Somalia. I waited until Brad M. had the earphones on and gave me the thumbs-up. Then I picked up the phone.

"Hello?"

"Yes . . . ah, Lorinda. We should call you after, after thirty minutes. My friend has said to me that you should talk to Amanda, but we have little time. You should speak but with limited time. Good-bye."

"Adam, thank you very much. I—"

The line went dead.

I looked at Brad M., and he shrugged. Adam's voice had sounded urgent. My heart was racing.

Less than five minutes later, the phone rang again.

"Hello, Adam?" I could hear men yelling in the background.

"We want to talk, and Amanda, and then it is a little time. Don't waste our time, and don't waste your time! It is a little time, understand?"

I was shocked by Adam's angry tone. He had never spoken to me like that before. My stomach started churning.

"I understand." As I was waiting, I could still hear the voices of angry Somali men yelling. I was starting to shake. Then I heard breathing and sobbing.

"Momma."

"Amanda, Amanda, I love you! Amanda, how are you?"

"I know, I know. Mom, listen. Listen to me, okay . . . really closely, okay?" Her voice sounded so small and pleading, like that of a small child.

"I'm listening, hon."

"If, if you guys don't pay," Amanda was crying, "one million dollars for me, by one week, they will kill me. Okay. Tonight they have brought me out to kill me." She stopped short again, sobbing. "But they have given me one more chance, to call you guys."

"Amanda, stay strong, hon." I couldn't stop myself from crying. "We're doing everything we can."

"Mom, listen to me. We have . . . one week, okay? And I don't, I feel so awful . . . I can't believe they're doing this, but I hate that I'm doing this to you guys."

"Amanda, Amanda, please don't worry about us." I tried to control my voice and speak over the sounds of her sobbing. We were both crying. "Amanda, we love you. You need to stay strong."

"I know, I . . . is there any way that you guys will be able to . . . to pay them in one week?"

"Amanda, we're trying to do everything we can to get money together for you because the government won't pay. We've gone to the bank—"

Click.

I hung up the phone. I looked at Brad M. Tears were streaming down his face. "I'm so sorry, Lorinda," he said.

"We need to call Jon," I said.

One million dollars . . .

One week . . .

One more chance . . .

I leaned forward with my face in my hands and cried until I felt Brad M.'s hand on my shoulder. "Should we call Jon now?" he asked.

Jon picked up when we called, but all we could hear was sobbing. He had heard the entire call on his one-way phone.

"Jon, please come over," I said.

Within minutes, he was at the door. We held each other, bawling without restraint. We sat down at the table, unable to speak. Brad M. made us coffee and called Joanne over for support. A while later, still in shock, I dressed up extra warm—as temperatures were dipping into the minus thirties—and went down to the lake. I kept hearing Amanda's voice in my head, *Momma*, the fear so palpable. I felt so fucking helpless I wanted to scream. I began walking hard and fast, cursing Adam and the kidnappers, swearing out loud, pushing my way through the snow until I tired myself out. I started to think about what might happen next. To Amanda, to me. I understood the strategy that Adam was using, but how did one know when kidnappers would make good on their threats? I couldn't bear to think how terrifying this was for my girl. I would find out later that while we had been on that call, the kidnappers had been holding a serrated knife to Amanda's throat.

I had reached the skating rink, and as I looked at the ice, it occurred to me that if you change the molecular structure of water by freezing it, you can do the impossible: you literally can walk on water. My mind was racing. If I were to survive this and continue to be useful to Amanda, I needed to change my thinking. Amanda and I were tough women, steel magnolias. We were going to get through this. Life had prepared us for this; we had already come through so much. It had made us strong and resilient. We were both positive thinkers, and that had already saved us in many situations. My fingers and toes were numb from the cold, so I went into a coffee shop to warm up with a hot chocolate, and on the table I noticed a flyer with a quote from Louis Nizer: "I know of no higher fortitude than stubbornness in the face of overwhelming odds."

My whole life I had been accused of being stubborn, and I knew firsthand how stubborn my daughter could be. It wasn't something I had always appreciated—until now. On my phone, I googled the meaning of "fortitude." Then I headed for home.

Although it was only 5 p.m., it was already pitch dark outside, but I had the streetlights to guide me. Brad M. and Joanne looked apprehensively at me as I came through the door. I shed all the layers. Joanne had made supper, but I had something to do before I ate. I went into the war room, picked up a poster board, grabbed a felt-tipped marker, and wrote: *FORTITUDE: the strength of mind that enables one to meet danger or bear pain or adversity with courage.*

I taped the poster to the wall.

That night, alone in my room, I summoned Amanda:

Amanda, we're going to survive this. I will never, ever stop fighting for your freedom. I'm so sorry for the fear and pain you have had to experience. I know that you're stronger than they think you are, and so am I. I can't wait until you're back home. We have so much shopping to do and so much wine to drink and so many dance parties to have. I will never give up. I promise.

I lay down and listened to my favorite song from the CD Kelly had sent, my pillow wet with tears.

Thank you for the negotiators who are working to free Amanda.
Thank you for Amanda's fortitude.
Thank you for all my children.
Thank you for Jon.
Thank you for my voice, so that I can talk to Adam.
Thank you for my ears, so that I can hear what he says and respond
    in a useful manner.
Thank you . . . thank you . . . thank you . . .

In the morning, I asked the negotiators if Nigel and Nicky had been subjected to the same terror tactic as I had during my recent call, but they had not. The Brennans had been informed of what had happened so they could be as prepared, as anyone can be, for that possibility. Why, I wondered, had the pressure been ramped up for us but not the Brennans? I hoped they would never have to endure an emotional assault like we had. I sent out an update to the former SLOC members. Immediately sympathetic, encouraging, and logical emails came back to me:

"I hope we did a good enough job preparing you for that call. I don't know of anyone I have met who would have handled it any better than you . . ."

"You're doing a fantastic job. Although this was a difficult call for you, the POL is a huge positive."

"Remind yourself of Gord Black's record—he's batting a thousand."

"Fortify yourself with the knowledge that you are actively working to free Amanda. It is our fears and emotions that terrorists prey upon."

"Now you can change two of those numbers! Days since last POL—0! Days since last contact with HTs—0!"

"By being strong, you are helping Amanda in the long run."

The support I felt from the negotiators lifted my spirits. I would even go so far as to say I felt loved, though they would probably say "cared for." According to their job description, they weren't supposed to feel either.

As a reflection of my resolve, when one o'clock came around, I went into Red Deer to shop. I needed to be ready for Amanda when she came home. I bought flannel PJs, socks, perfume, hair products, dental products, and sweets. She loved candy, and I was pretty sure that I had picked up all her favorites. I didn't enter the clothing realm, though, because Amanda was very particular about her style. I also bought four shades of pink wrapping paper. With three full bags, I went home to wrap.

I didn't know what Brad M. and Joanne were thinking, but I was pretty sure they preferred me frantically wrapping gifts as opposed to being the crying mess I had been earlier. After everything was wrapped, I imagined putting up the Christmas tree, no matter the time of year Amanda came home. I imagined her face lighting up as she unwrapped her gifts, the smell of turkey wafting through the air as we toasted with our glasses of wine. And of course, a dance party would follow. I was getting so excited for Amanda's homecoming that I reached out to Amanda's friends Kelly and Jelara in an email:

> Let's plan a "pink" homecoming party for Amanda! I don't know when she's coming home, but SHE IS COMING HOME! I have a bag of pink balloons we can fill with helium, we can make a banner that says "The Power of Pink." How about a pink piñata filled with her favorite candy? Pink cotton candy?

They joined in my enthusiasm, but they were also a little suspicious that maybe I "knew something" and couldn't tell. I assured them that the only thing I "knew" was that Amanda was coming home at some point and we needed to be ready. In the new year, we decided, we would meet at Kelly's house and invite a small group of Amanda's most trustworthy friends to plan the party. It would be our secret.

My friend Sue from Canmore had been emailing me and really wanted me to come for a visit. It had been hard to brush her off and make excuses for not meeting with her, but I couldn't leave the SLOC to drive to Canmore. It was a five-hour drive round-trip. She thought I was living at Jon's, sitting by the phone, so she couldn't understand why I couldn't leave and come down for a night. I couldn't invite her to "Jon's house," either. She was one of my closest friends, and I desperately wanted to see her. The fact that she kept reaching out to me made me feel that I hadn't been forgotten, that I still mattered to someone from my former life. Although I couldn't visit easily with friends or tell them the truth, I was deeply hurt that many had not tried to keep in touch.

•

ADAM WASN'T GETTING IN TOUCH, either. Our deadline date of December 20 was approaching, and there had been no calls from him. Jon and I were trying our best to remember that it was "in their best interest to keep Amanda and Nigel alive." We watched the world around us in Christmas mode, buying gifts, listening to holiday music, putting up trees and decorations, some happy, some miserable, and we envied them. If they only knew how good their lives were.

One day before the deadline, on December 19, we were heartened to hear from Ottawa that something positive was going on "over there" and team Nairobi was "cautiously optimistic." There was no other information they could give us. *Please, please, please: let it be Amanda and Nigel's release! Please!*

And then our deadline date was here. Amanda and Nigel had lived through two deadlines already, but the threat hovering over us this time was more extreme, and it seemed to be directed only at Amanda. Jon came over for the morning call from Ottawa and stayed for most of the day. We paced, we talked, we tried to keep our minds and conversations on positive things. I couldn't bring myself to leave for my daily outing. I needed to be by the phone. The silence from Somalia was a relief as well as a stressor. As long as we didn't hear anything, we could believe that Amanda was alive.

Later in the afternoon I emailed another update to my team that we had received no calls but we believed that Amanda was okay. I updated them on the latest news I'd received from Nicky. It seemed that the Brennans' already strained relationship with the AFP had been stretched to the breaking point. Without warning, they had been told that their operational headquarters was being moved to a distant site, meaning their only connection with events in Somalia would be via computer. Though the new site was supposed to be manned around the clock, the Brennans learned that a pleading message from Nigel had gone to voice mail. When the AFP wouldn't allow them to return the call, a couple of the Brennans had threatened to go to the media.

Both of our families had been repeatedly warned that publicity would only make the kidnappers greedier, expecting some kind of payoff from a big public audience. Though Jon and I sometimes shared the Brennans' frustration over the lack of results, our loyalty remained, as ever, with the Canadian government. We were relieved when the Brennans agreed to hold off on their threats to change course.

The next morning, Nicky emailed me: "I have to admit I'm still pretty unhappy with the Federal Police. I'm absolutely furious at their behavior and support, or lack of, so profoundly affects us and I believe endangers the lives of Amanda and Nigel!" She was exhausted and feeling completely unsupported. She ended the email with her dream, which was the same as mine: "I am thinking a little holiday on a tropical Island in a safe country after all this is over."

I immediately responded with sympathy for the way they felt they had been treated. We were so fortunate in our relationship with Ottawa and the RCMP. They would never treat us like that. I reminded her of the positive information we had received from Cal Chrustie. We were still 100 percent on board with what our government was doing.

On December 23, Brad M. and Joanne were rotating out for the holidays, but as they were leaving, they handed me a large present wrapped in festive Christmas paper. "What's this?" I asked.

"Open it," they said.

I unwrapped a beautiful pair of snowshoes for my afternoon outings. With tears, we hugged each other good-bye.

"Let's hope that the next time we see each other, it will be at Amanda's homecoming," I said. We had just weathered an extremely tough ten days together, and I was so grateful to have had them.

I had not yet met the next negotiator, Gil, who had volunteered to come over Christmas and New Year's. The second negotiator slot would be filled by local officers, who would take turns to split up the holidays. Gil had studied up on every bit of information he could get his hands on concerning our case. He was teary right from the start. He explained that he had asked his family's permission to come out to be with us over Christmas. "I am here with their blessings," Gil said. He had a daughter the same age as Amanda.

To accommodate everyone's holiday plans, we met on Christmas Eve for our holiday meal. As I looked around the table at my loved ones, I felt weary and sad but also grateful. After dinner, the star of the evening was my grandson, Morris, now five months old. He was just learning to roll over, and he became the focal point of our attention and a distraction from the void of Amanda's absence. Before everyone left, my mom brought out a pink candle encased in a glass house with gold trim. She lit the candle. We held hands in a circle as she prayed for Amanda and Nigel. My knees started to buckle. I couldn't hold back the tears any longer.

That night, I remembered Christmases past, and I sent my thoughts out to Amanda, wherever she was.

Amanda, do you remember the Christmas when you were ten, when I surprised you with a trip to Disneyland? I remember how you cried because there were only four gifts under the tree that year, and you told me, "Mommy, it's okay, I know we're poor and how hard you try." When I got home from work on Christmas Eve, I was so excited that I told you kids you had to open the largest present with all three of your names on the tag. In the box was a gift balloon with four tickets to Disneyland. I was jumping up and down, screaming "We're going to Disneyland!" Mark looked at me and said, "Yeah, right, Mom. No way!" It took me a few minutes before you believed me. The three remaining gifts you guys opened on Christmas Day were hundred-dollar bills for each of you to spend. I hope that memory gives you joy today.

Another memorable Christmas was the one after you and Jamie returned from Asia. I think it was in February, and I put the tree up again and cooked a turkey dinner. You thought Barbie was the most beautiful doll when you were growing up, and that year I gave you a collectable Barbie. You cried.

Please, Amanda. Come home. We need more Christmases.

•

ON CHRISTMAS DAY, JON, PERRY, and Nathaniel came over to the SLOC to join Mark, Gil, and myself. There were no decorations, as per my wish. We enjoyed a quiet day visiting, eating leftovers, and drinking wine. On New Year's Eve, hundreds of people who were following the "Let's Pray for Amanda" site on Facebook lit a candle for Amanda and Nigel. I saw many pictures of the blue and pink candles on the site—one for Amanda and one for Nigel.

There had been no calls between Christmas and New Year's Day. We greeted 2009 the only way we could, as the year we would bring Amanda home.

CHAPTER NINE

GUARD THE SECRET

We Played a Lot of Chess" was the headline on January 5 when a *Telegraph* correspondent, Colin Freeman, and his Spanish photographer, José Cendón, were freed after five weeks of being held hostage under the watch of heavily armed Somali captors.

José Cendón described their living situation: "We were staying in open caves. . . . The place was okay, we didn't have room service but almost, they would actually bring us tea in bed in the morning. We played a lot of chess on a homemade board. . . . Our kidnappers were actually decent. . . . We ate mainly rice, boiled goat meat, sometimes spaghetti and a kind of bread baked on ashes to which they would sometimes add some sauce. . . . I never felt that my life was in danger." Cendón said he was not at liberty to discuss all the modalities of his release, but security forces in Somalia said a ransom had been paid.

I always had mixed emotions after reading articles like this. Of course I was happy they had been released after only five weeks, and happy that they were treated well. But I realized "only five weeks" and "treated well" were relative concepts. I clung to every positive experience I read in the hope that Amanda was experiencing some form of kindness and being given adequate amounts of food and clean water.

To MY HORROR, THE VERY next day, I read about a Chinese seaman who had spent 202 days on a ship taken by Somali pirates. He said that the crew members had been beaten often, but the most terrifying time had been when a shipmate had been murdered after the vessel's owner had refused to pay a ransom. Following the murder, the owner had paid the ransom and the other crew members had been freed.

"Shit!" I said aloud as I was reading the article.

Emil was beside me, catching up on the secret RCMP daily log. "What's wrong?"

"This scares the hell of me, Emil."

He reviewed the article himself. "Remember what you always say about staying positive and visualizing Amanda and Nigel safe? Nothing good will come from imagining the worst-case scenarios, Lorinda."

He was right. I excused myself and went upstairs to my room, where I tried to meditate, hoping for a few minutes of peace. My mind kept circling back to the article: "murdered because the owner refused to pay the ransom." I had been having trouble meditating since Amanda's kidnapping; I couldn't turn off my imagination. I had been able to achieve only fleeting moments of serenity. Every nerve in my body was vibrating, and I yearned for relief. The constant stress was exhausting. I couldn't begin to imagine what it was like for Amanda.

•

THE INCOMING NEWS WAS INCREASINGLY discouraging on all fronts. On January 8, during our call with Ottawa, I was told that the "something" that the Nairobi cell had been "cautiously optimistic about" had slowed down. They were still uncertain about how involved Adam was with the gang holding Amanda and Nigel hostage. Per their intel, Amanda and Nigel were being moved often. The hostage takers were described as very dangerous, skittish, and uncivilized, and they trusted no one. Better to move slowly and safely than try to push them.

Later in the day, I read about the release of the Japanese doctor and Dutch nurse after three months in captivity. They had been threatened with execution during their last month in captivity. The organization they worked for stressed that there had been no ransom paid for their freedom. I didn't trust that; there were already reports of a $3 million ransom payment.

My mind ping-ponged through uncertainties: Why is everyone being released before Amanda and Nigel? It appears to be because ransoms are being paid. Should I continue to trust Ottawa? They have an impeccable record. They promised. Do I have any choice? They're the experts, I'm not.

The onslaught of troubling news made me feel claustrophobic, stuck in my own head. I had been thinking a lot about widening my circle of trust to include Kelly, Amanda's best friend. I felt as though she could be an additional support and add a valuable perspective for me. She had traveled numerous times with Amanda and knew her well. I asked her to meet me for lunch at the Rusty Pelican in Red Deer to discuss the "Pink Party." I was free from the phone for the time being while the Nairobi cell was negotiating. Even if Adam called, I wouldn't be allowed to answer as it could interfere with the cell's current strategy. What that strategy was, I had no idea; I had to continue developing my own strategy.

I watched Kelly as she came toward the table, removing her coat and hat, her blond hair reflecting the winter sun coming through the window. She was smiling, as she always did when she saw me. I was a little nervous to share the big secret with her, but I felt fully confident that she was trustworthy. I had not and would not let the RCMP know that I was confiding in her. I stood up, and we hugged each other. It felt as though I were hugging a little part of Amanda.

We sat down and began to talk. "I have a lot to tell you," I said. "But the first thing I need to know is that whatever I tell you will be kept a secret."

Kelly's brow furrowed and she leaned forward. "Lorinda, yes. Of course."

After that, I slowly unraveled to Kelly the spiral of secrets at the center of my covert life. When I was done, she looked at me, shocked but calm. "Thank you for trusting me, Lorinda," she said.

We talked things through some more, and I answered some of her questions. We briefly discussed the "Pink Party" and agreed to meet at her house the following weekend to make the plans. She would invite a couple of Amanda's closest friends. I felt good about confiding in Kelly, and I knew I could trust her to keep our secret. Her support would mean a lot in the coming months.

Later in the week, on January 14, Adam emailed me:

SUBJECT: DANGER IS COMING SOON TO AMANDA AND NIGEL IF YOU DON'T PAY THE RANSOM WE WANT!!!!!. . . .

Hello mum Lorinda

Hello Mam iam very sorry that Amanda is still in our han. Mam really I love you but I want to tell you your government's ambassador in Djibuti is searching from awong place. and that is, he came to elder Somali man in Djibuti saying your tribe is 'Duduble' in Somalia ubducted Amanda & Nigel in Somalia and we have 250 000 Dollar. So that i want to tell you that iam not (part of) 'Duduble' tribe and we may not accept 250,000 Dolar ever, we want 2.5 Million Dollars.
   David, Reece and Marc, yuor ambassadors tod that you are intellegence service no matter please don't call me again if you don't have for me the monney (2.5 million Dollars).

Have a good day

Adam

The email was confusing, but it also revealed elements of what the Nairobi cell had been up to. At first I doubted that Adam had written the email—in my experience his English was better than that—but then again, only Adam would have said he loved me. I knew that David, Reece, and Marc were part of the Nairobi cell negotiating for Amanda's release. I wanted to find out more. I got in touch with Ottawa, but they wouldn't reveal any further information as to what the Nairobi cell was doing.

I googled "Djibuti" and saw that Djibouti was a very small country bordering the very northern tip of Somalia. "Duduble" I understood to be a Somali clan.

I forwarded this email to Nicky to share with Nigel's family. The Brennans were still struggling with their government's involvement and were discussing ideas "outside the box." This was concerning to the RCMP and the AFP. Nicky and Geoff had both given me and Jon their reassurances that they would not do anything without our consent. I couldn't blame them, as I was also starting to entertain my own thoughts "outside the box" as days, weeks, and now months passed without Amanda's release. It was impossible not to wonder if there were another faster way to go about this. But I continued to reaffirm my belief in Ottawa.

On January 16, we learned from Ottawa that Adbifatah Elmi and the two colleagues who had been kidnapped along with Amanda and Nigel had been released. They had been blindfolded in the night and driven to an empty market in the capital city of Mogadishu, where they had been dropped off. As reported by the Canadian Press, Elmi claimed that the three of them had been separated from Amanda and Nigel from the beginning and he had no idea where they were being kept.

All day I hunted the headlines for further details, but there was little more. Reporters Without Borders, a Paris-based international nonprofit, said in a news release:

> **Our concern about [Amanda's and Nigel's] fate is as strong as ever given the growing instability in Mogadishu. All the actors**

should combine their efforts in order to obtain their release as
soon as possible.

At the same time, the National Union of Somali Journalists was calling on the Somali government to secure the safe release of Amanda and Nigel. There was a picture online of a group of members holding large signs demanding their release. It made me feel better knowing that even in Somalia, there were people rooting for them.

•

I WAS GRATEFUL TO SEE a community of people rooting for them at home, too. This boosted me with the hope I needed to carry on. The next weekend, I drove to Kelly's house in Calgary to plan the Pink Party. I was excited that we were planning for Amanda's homecoming. Kelly, Amanda's friends Jelara and Dara, and I drank wine and ate snacks while we constructed a ten-foot banner: "WELCOME HOME AMANDA." The letters were in shades of pink. We had pink balloons, a pink piñata, and lots of candy, and Perry had bought a metallic pink Christmas tree. Kelly would buy pink champagne, and Dara volunteered to make cupcakes when the day finally came. Cupcakes were one of Amanda's favorite indulgences. Oh, and a chocolate cake in the shape of a purse. Amanda loved purses.

As I drove back to the SLOC at the end of the day, I imagined what the Pink Party would be like. I could see Amanda's smiling face surrounded by all of her family and friends, drinking, dancing, and laughing. Maybe a disco ball with pink spotlights? Would that be too much pink? Is it possible to have too much pink for Amanda? Amanda will need a pink dress.

Before I went to bed that night, I wrote an update to my team. After sharing the news of Elmi's release, I wrote:

147 days of waiting. Though I have never doubted that
she'll come home, I miss her terribly and wonder how she's

holding up. 5 months in captivity is unimaginable for anyone
but especially for someone who can't even stay in a county
for 5 months let alone in a room. In saying that, I never
forget how strong my girl is. She is amazing! Today is one
day closer to Amanda coming home!

A few days later, on January 26, my mother's birthday, I saw an article online, published by *Metro Edmonton*: "Ransom for Alta. Journalist Falls to $100K." The article cited a Somali press freedom agency claiming that the ransom demand for Amanda had dropped dramatically to $100,000 but that it also wasn't known if she was still alive. For the love of God, I thought. If she was dead, would they drop the ransom demand?

I knew for a fact that the ransom hadn't been lowered, and I was outraged that an Edmonton source had published this false news. Where in the world was the information coming from? We currently had $250,000 on the table, and it was being refused. But of course, no media were privy to what we were doing. Jon and I were told not to worry about the article; if ignored, it would go away.

But the articles didn't go away. Neither did Adam. That same morning, the first call came at 10 a.m. I looked at Brad W., who had rotated back in, and he shook his head. I was not to answer the call. "Remember, Lorinda, the strategy is to force the kidnappers to negotiate with the Nairobi team."

I was already teary. I hadn't slept much in days. The second call came at 10:15. I started pacing close to the phone, and now I was crying outright. I hadn't spoken to Amanda or Adam in weeks. The third call came on the heels of the second one. I begged to answer it. Brad W. walked over and placed his hand gently on my arm. "No, you know that you can't."

I retreated to my room until I was cried out and then went downstairs to grab my coat. I felt smothered. I needed fresh air, I needed to walk. Fuck, I needed my daughter to be home. Brad W. had already been on the phone to Ottawa to let them know what had happened.

When I opened the door to leave, he asked me to give him my cell phone.

"Why?"

"You're extremely upset, Lorinda, and if you were going to do something irrational like call Adam, it would be now. This takes away the temptation. Ottawa has advised me to keep your phone here while you're out."

"Are fucking kidding me?" I yelled. I threw the phone at him and slammed the door on my way out.

I walked to the drugstore and bought some sleeping pills. Up until now, I had refused to take anything to help me sleep because if Adam called during the night I would need to be able to wake up and be sharp. But now I desperately needed at least one good night's sleep to cope with the craziness. Even if the phone rang, I wouldn't be allowed to answer, so it was a good time to take sleeping pills.

When I came back to the SLOC, Brad W. tried to cheer me up. I felt guilty that I had blown up at him like that. Like it or not, Ottawa was running the show. And even if I didn't like how they ran it, they were trying to save Amanda.

That night, I went up to my room and took two sleeping pills before climbing into bed. As I waited for them to kick in, I struggled with finding things to be grateful for. *I am grateful for . . . my toes, my . . . bed, my . . .*

Over the next four days, the phone rang eight more times, twice from numbers that we didn't recognize. Brad W. remained on "day duty" with me. I was frazzled, crying, pacing, screaming, begging to answer, but the answer was always no. If Ottawa knew why we were receiving this flurry of calls, they were not admitting to it.

"What if Amanda escaped and she's trying to call me?" I asked.

"If that was her calling, she would leave a message, Lorinda. Trust Ottawa. Trust the Nairobi team. We're not doing this to be mean; we're doing it for Amanda. Stay strong for Amanda."

I had every reason to stay strong—for me, for my family, and for Amanda. I searched for news that would help me stay strong.

There was one light, though very dim, that came in the form of an announcement on January 31. Somalia had elected a new president, Sharif Sheikh Ahmed. Could that be a step toward peace in war-torn Somalia? I wondered. Maybe President Sharif would work with Ottawa and help us rescue Amanda and Nigel. *Please, please, please.*

I still was not allowed to pick up the phone. I decided that if I couldn't communicate with Adam, I had to communicate with someone. I sat down at my computer to write an update for the rest of the team. I wrote to vent about the eleven calls I had not been allowed to answer, to tell them how angry I was about the mistrust evident in taking my cell phone away. Writing felt good, so I kept going:

> Since the beginning, I've had so little information. I know I've been emotional and anxious. When I hear that phone ring, it's hard because Adam has been my link to Amanda. I feel like Amanda could possibly be by the phone as I'm sure the next step will be another bad call. I've wondered if she feels I've abandoned her. I wish I could comfort her. It's been 164 days and I'm sad, I miss her so much! My heart hurts more than you can imagine. So I cry. Sometimes I just need to. I will not do anything you have told me not to, like sneak out and call Adam. I don't want anybody's pity. I just need your understanding.

I signed off with "What doesn't kill me, makes me stronger. It also makes me anxious, bitchy, and vulnerable. . . . But nobody wants to see that embroidered on a pillowcase. One day closer!"

The responses I received gave me a needed boost.

"Amanda will be proud of you for what you are doing!"

"Lorinda, I know I speak for everyone who has met you; you are our HERO."

"Together we will bring her home!"

I felt so lucky to have my team for support when I really needed it. A few days later, on February 6, Abdifatah was interviewed for

Maclean's magazine about his release. "Allah saved me. I can't explain it to you, how this happened. Please don't ask me anything more about that." He said his mind was still shackled and that he had been held in a dark room. "I am very worried for my colleagues. I wish that they will be free." When he was questioned about Amanda and Nigel's whereabouts, he said, "I tried to find out, but my guards told me, 'Don't ask us that question.' I am very sorry. I am very sorry."

An unnamed security consultant specializing in Somalia weighed in on Abdifatah's story with his own observations. "The situation remains too dangerous for even the bravest aid organizations," he pointed out. CARE had shut down its operations, and the UN World Food Programme threatened to abandon the country after two of its local workers had been killed earlier that month. "What the Canadian government is doing to secure Lindhout's release is unclear." Well, yes, that much was true—it was a total secret, and even to an insider like me, things were unclear.

Foreign Affairs in Ottawa refused to comment on the situation. Instead, it released statements about pursuing "all appropriate channels." But the consultant had some free advice for Canada's diplomats and decision makers on the matter of Amanda and Nigel's ransom: "I think $100,000 is the best deal they're going to get. At the end of the day, everybody pays."

There it was again: $100,000. If only that would be enough. That sum was popping up in the local media, and family and friends began questioning me and Jon. Although we told them it wasn't true, we couldn't tell them how we knew that.

That same morning, Ottawa revealed to us that they were investigating a rumor about Amanda and Nigel. Apparently, both of them had tried to escape their captors on January 26. The story was all over the media. I felt the alarm seeping in.

Jon and I peppered Ottawa with questions: Was it true? Had they been seen together? Who could confirm it? How had they looked? Where were they now? But Ottawa could neither confirm nor deny the statement. "Sit tight," we were told.

But I couldn't. I couldn't just sit there any longer, so I continued my barrage of questions. "What about all the calls starting on January 26? *Eleven* in total. Maybe Amanda was trying to call me," I said. The panic turned to a solid lump in my throat as I said the words out loud.

The sitting chair in Ottawa responded, "If Amanda escaped and called, she would have left you a message. Right? We don't believe that it was her. It could very well be another ploy."

I tried to see their point, but my gut was telling me something different. I couldn't stop myself from imagining all the reasons she hadn't or couldn't leave a message. I knew I had to rein in my imagination or it would be the end of me.

As soon as I was off the call, I powered up my computer and read the reports of Amanda and Nigel's alleged escape. Reporters Without Borders agreed with Ottawa, saying that the source was "absolutely not reliable, it could be manipulation, once again, like the fifteen-day deadline." I read on and discovered two more reports that appeared to confirm their escape. Daud Abdi Daud, the executive director of a Somali journalists' group, wrote that the pair "came close to being killed" on January 26. Daud reported that they had escaped in Mogadishu and had run to the shelter of a mosque, where they appealed to the holy men for protection. He claimed that two gunmen had fired shots inside the mosque and that Amanda and Nigel had been forced outside, where they had been shoved into a car. Daud wrote that Nigel had been hit with the stock of an AK-47 assault rifle. I felt instantly nauseated. But I kept reading.

Another witness claimed that Amanda had tried to throw herself from the car and escape but had not succeeded. Daud quoted the mullah, one of the holy men in the mosque, who had been reading the holy book: "We have no religion here, as we were not able to save the people asked safety. Allah and us!"

The details seemed too specific to be made up. My stomach was turning in on itself. Was it possible that Daud Abdi Daud was the "unreliable source" referred to by Reporters Without Borders? Although Daud wrote that he didn't know if Amanda and Nigel were alive, I refused to believe anything other than that she was and that she was coming home.

Jon called me later in the afternoon, and we talked through all of the swirling and worrying rumors.

"Let's try to stay positive," he said, a welcome reminder. "Hey, I have an idea," he went on. "What if we put together a package for the Brennans? You know, to strengthen our bond with them. We could send pictures of our family, some postcards to show them where we live, that kind of thing. Maybe a letter, too."

It was a great idea, and I said so. Both of our families were reeling from the rumors. We needed to keep hope strong. I told Jon I would pop by shortly so that we could get started. I stopped at the grocery store on the way to his house, and while I was in line the woman in front of me turned my way and started yelling "I can't believe that you would let your daughter rot over there because you can't pay $100,000. You are disgusting!"

Everyone in the store turned to look at me. I could feel my face burn with embarrassment. I dropped everything I was holding in my arms and fled. By the time I reached the car, tears were running down my cheeks.

In the days that followed, more angry articles, comments, and emails surfaced:

"If [Amanda's] parents don't want the money raised for her release, then it will not get raised. It's easy, cheap and simple to set up a non-profit organization, (takes about a week). People could donate to it."

"Her parents have chosen to listen to the Canadian government and do nothing but remain silent."

Nothing, absolutely nothing about any of that was fair. But Jon and I couldn't say anything to exonerate ourselves.

A couple of days later, we learned that at least some of the reports surfacing from Somalia were true. Ottawa confirmed that Amanda and Nigel had tried to escape, only to be recaptured. Ottawa believed that they were both alive. The kidnappers wanted money, and without Amanda and Nigel alive, they would not get any. That statement was worn and overused, but it remained a lifeline, and not just to me. Nathaniel and Mark called often, desperate for any crumbs of information. Mark called me one day, crying so hard he could hardly breathe. He didn't know how to handle the anguish any longer. I could hear Nathaniel in the background; he was crying, too. I told them we all needed to seek out positive support, whether through friends or professional counseling services. But they also needed to vigiliantly guard the secret of what my role was.

"I know without a shadow of a doubt that Amanda is coming home," I said.

"Really, Mom? You know that for sure?"

"I do," I said. And because I meant it, we could all go on.

CHAPTER TEN

GOING ROGUE

We were halfway through February, and the silence was unbearable. No calls to or from Adam, and even if he did call, I would be restrained from answering. Ottawa confirmed that Amanda and Nigel were alive and the Nairobi team was working hard for their release. Once again, Ottawa could not tell us *how* they knew that Amanda and Nigel were alive or *what kinds* of strategies they were implementing. On that same call I was informed that due to lack of resources, I would now have only one negotiator working with me during the day. I was still not allowed to answer the phone, so there was no justification to keep two negotiators on-site at the SLOC.

The Brennans' relationship with the AFP seemed to be beyond repair. Nicky sent me an email outlining private fundraising options their family had put together. They had contacted Colin Freeman, the British citizen recently released from captivity.

"Have you contacted him yet?" Nicky asked.

We had not. In my response to her, I shared Ottawa's most recent updates and reminders. I encouraged the Brennans to keep their eye on the bigger picture and asked them to hold off on taking any action.

Jon and I had been warned that anything done outside of the current strategy could potentially cost Amanda and Nigel their lives. We were also told that if we went outside Ottawa's parameters and contacted other sources, the operation would be dropped. We were both tired, and privately, we started to question if the Brennans might be right. We asked Ottawa about raising money above the $250,000 currently on the table. The Canadian government did not pay ransoms, we were reminded once again. That sum was from a family member and justifiable as "expenses."

As Jon and I pushed for more answers, Ottawa said that if they ran out of options they would tell us, but they still had unused strategies and believed that they were going to bring Amanda and Nigel home. "Run out of options?" I had to wonder: What the hell did that mean?

I continued to scour the internet for my own answers. I read article after article, and every one reported the same thing: "There is still no word about Canadian journalist Amanda Lindhout and Australian photographer Nigel Brennan." A couple of days later, I found an article about Amanda in the *Calgary Herald*: "Alberta Journalist's Release May Hinge on Somali Regime." The article stated that the moderate Islamist president was trying to rally support, and if the new government survived, it might bode well for the release of Amanda and Nigel. "The enormous collective pressure from the international community is to free any westerner being held hostage, and that pressure would become so intense that I think the moderate government would do whatever it could to work with this group, whoever it is, to get the person released," said David Shinn, an expert on the Horn of Africa at Washington University in Washington, D.C.

The article went on to say that the captors had six months of bills piled up, which could prompt a release, or Amanda and Nigel could potentially be handed over to Al-Shabaab to be used as "bargaining chips" by the extremist group opposed to the new government. "The fact that it's been six months means that something's wrong with the process," said Chris Voss, the former FBI negotiator on international kidnappings, adding that the prospects were still "very good" if the motive was ransom.

Jon and I felt as though we were floundering with no information or calls for more than a month. But on March 3, during our morning call with Ottawa, we were told that an on-the-ground TPI (third-party intermediary) had confirmed that Amanda and Nigel were alive and being treated well. They were allowed to exercise on a regular basis. Amanda had sprained her ankle while exercising and was being given ice and medication. Nigel had been given medication for a minor ailment. Both were allowed books to read and writing material. They were allowed to wash their clothes once a week. They were given two meals a day. Their diet consisted of *mufo* (a Somali cake), *angelo* (bean soup), spaghetti, rice, lemons, and mangos. Proof of life and proof of care! I was so relieved, I cried for joy.

•

AT NIGHT I STILL COULDN'T sleep, even with the use of drugstore sleeping pills. The phone calls with Adam had been my lifeline to Amanda, but now they had been taken from me. I felt impotent, and I needed to do something. I was not alone in my urge to act. That afternoon, Nathaniel called.

"I'm sick of this!" he yelled. "I can't stand sitting around doing nothing. I'm going to call the media. We need to get the money to free Amanda."

His call caught me off guard, and I tried to calm him with all the reasons that were being used to calm me and Jon. He wasn't convinced. I looked at Paul, who was listening in.

"Invite him here," he mouthed.

"Nathaniel," I said, "trust us and hold off on doing anything. Jon, Perry, and I could use a visit from you. Why don't you and Mark drive out tomorrow and stay for a couple days?"

He agreed.

Negotiating first with Adam, then with the RCMP and Ottawa and the Brennans—and now with my distraught sons—was starting to strip my reserves. That night I had a complete meltdown on Paul and ordered him to leave the SLOC.

It was time to see the therapist, Barb, again. I needed help, because I knew that if I fell apart, it would have a domino effect on everyone around me. I needed to be strong, and Amanda needed me in one piece.

When I made it down to see Barb, she advised, "It's okay, Lorinda. Your reactions are normal in what is an extremely abnormal situation. Eat, rest, meditate, exercise. And get out of the SLOC and visit people with normal lives."

Nathaniel and Mark arrived soon after, and I found the strength to reassure them once more. We had to be united to keep going. We had to place our trust in the government. We were moving forward, even if it didn't always look that way.

Kelly was good at keeping in touch, and she emailed me on her birthday to tell me how much she missed Amanda. "I keep thinking of the time Amanda steamed me a chocolate cake on Mount Everest because they didn't have any stoves. Lol! I wonder if she knows it's my birthday?"

Of course she did, I thought and hoped.

Living in the confinement of the SLOC hadn't been conducive to putting any effort into my appearance. I had stopped caring and bothering with any makeup, but I realized that those might also be signs of the depression that was starting to sink in. That morning I decided that it might make me feel better to put on a little makeup and dress in something that made me feel good. I got ready and went downstairs for a cup of coffee.

I changed the Post-it note on the calendar to Day 204. I'd never believed that we would see a number this high. As I was sitting in the kitchen, watching birds flit through the branches of the tree outside, the phone started ringing. Whatever the Nairobi team was up to, the kidnappers thought they would make better progress by contacting me. Bob was the negotiator that day. He was sitting in the war room, already shaking his head "no."

I took a deep breath. The phone rang repeatedly, back-to-back calls. By the time the third call went unanswered, my eye makeup was running down my cheeks in two black trails and dripping onto my lap. "Please," I said. "That could be Amanda." Maybe she had escaped again. I continued begging as Bob reminded me that we had to make the hostage takers deal with Nairobi.

I was forced to sit through seven unanswered calls. It was excruciating.

I screamed at Bob, "You have no idea what you're asking of me! How can you do this to a mother?" Bob was doing what his job required of him, but he was obviously shaken and saddened. It could not have been easy for him to tell me no.

Three days later, my cell phone rang. I recognized the number as one from Somalia. That was strange. I showed Bob the number. We had never used my cell phone to call Adam because it had not been set up for interception. Once again I obeyed orders and did not answer my cell. In total, ten calls came through, and on the eleventh, a message was left. Bob and I listened to it together.

"Give me a call. This is Amanda, okay. I'm calling from Somalia. You have to call me back on this number. This is the final time I'm going to be able to speak to you, so you must call me back as soon as you get this message, okay?" She sounded strong and calm.

I shot a look at Bob, "*See*? It was Amanda! She's going to think I have abandoned her, Bob! I cannot let that happen."

Then the intercept line started ringing. Bob stood between me and the phone.

"Lorinda, you can't answer. I'll call Ottawa and ask if you can call back, I promise. We don't know what's happening, but she has not said that she has escaped, so she's still in captivity. Lorinda, please."

There were four more calls, bringing the total up to sixteen unanswered calls.

Even as the phone was still ringing, Bob was on the house phone to Ottawa. He had made me promise that I would not answer the "kidnappers' phone." It was all I could do to sit and stare at the phone, willing it to send a message to Amanda.

I'm here, Amanda. I have not abandoned you, and I promise I never will. Ever.

Bob hung up. "What, Bob?" I yelled, not waiting for him to speak. "For fuck' sake, what did they say? I need to call her back!"

"They can't make that decision at this moment, but they will get back to us soon. They have to confer with the Nairobi team to see if they know what's happening and then with the AFP. Everyone has to be on the same page."

I must have looked and sounded like a raging lunatic, but I didn't care. The F-word and every other swear word I knew flew out of my mouth. I was wildly pacing between the kitchen and the war room. Bob looked as though he wished he were anywhere but where he was. I wanted to overturn tables and throw things. I wanted to rage and vent. Instead I sat down and felt the helplessness compress inside me as I waited, yet again, for Ottawa to call back. The sitting chair did eventually call. Ottawa had a "gut feeling" that I should return Amanda's call.

I was shaking as I dialed the number. It was an unfamiliar number, not Adam's this time, so I was worried that it could be another "bad call" but maybe with a new, more violent thug on the other end of the line.

"Hello?" It was her.

"Amanda!"

"Mom, we have one minute, okay. Listen to me. You have to tell me how much money have you guys prepared." She sounded commanding and urgent.

"Amanda, listen, please—"

"Mom, there's a gun to my head."

"Amanda, we are doing everything we can do. Trust me on this."

"Mom, how much money have you guys prepared?"

"Amanda, please believe me that we're doing everything we can."

"Absolutely, I believe you. I know that. Okay, listen, I'm here with people that have a gun to my head, and I need to know how much money you guys have, and I need to know if you guys are going to be able to pay the money and you have to answer me. Mom, this is the last time I'm going to be able to call you. I love you so much. I love you. I'm so sorry I went to Somalia."

"Amanda, I—"

"Mom, you have to—"

"I love you too, Amanda. The government will not pay." We were talking over each other as we both tried to get our scripted messages across.

"I know that," Amanda said. "How much money do you guys—"

Bob was pointing to his index card: "Work with Nairobi." I was to work on blind faith. Again.

"Trust me," I said, mustering up conviction. "They need to talk to the people in Nairobi because they are in control. They are the ones working on this, Amanda."

"I—Mom, how much money can you give these guys? Mom, you have to listen to me, okay? You have to understand really clearly. These people aren't joking. These people are tired of this and they are going to kill me. Okay? They are going to kill me in a matter of days."

"Amanda, trust me. They already know, and they need to deal with Nairobi. Please trust me on this."

"Mom, I'm sitting here, and I need . . . Mom, Mom, Mom, I'm sitting here with guys with guns. I need to know how much money. If the money is going to be paid or not, okay?"

"Amanda, it's all in Nairobi. They need to speak with the people in Nairobi. Amanda, please, please know that we love you and are doing everything we can."

"Mom, we need to get the money together. Sell Dad's house, sell Oma's and Opa's house, sell Nigel's house in Australia. Do whatever you guys need to do to get the money over here." I could hear her crying now.

"Amanda . . ."

"Mom, they are going to kill me!"

"I promise you, Amanda. Tell them to deal with Nairobi."

There was no response, just Amanda crying harder.

"Amanda, know that we love you and stay strong. They have nothing to gain by killing you."

It was unfathomable to keep repeating what was on the fucking index card while my mind was on fire with images of a gun to my daughter's head, while I listened to her pleading for her life. But

Ottawa had expressly said that I was not to say anything about money. I could only tell the kidnappers to deal with Nairobi. Poor Amanda had no idea why I was being so evasive. She went on to tell me to work with Nigel's family because they had more means than we did. I promised her that we were working together, both families working as one.

"There is a week, a matter of days. Okay? They might even kill me tonight."

"No, no, Amanda. They will not kill you tonight. They have nothing to gain. They will get no money." I tried to throw her the rope of hope that had been saving me through all of these calls.

"It's not about gaining anything. You don't understand, Mom. Mike is the problem. Mike is causing a lot of problems. Mike is making everybody really angry here as well. Mike is making these people talk about killing us. I don't know what his strategy is, but it's not working, because it's making everybody really angry and nervous and they—they want you to know that Mike is a really big problem. Okay? The money needs to get here. Mom, can you tell me anything I can tell these people to make them feel better about how much money you have?"

I grabbed an index card. "Mike?" I wrote and slid the card to Bob, who shrugged, raising his eyebrows. Neither of us had any idea who that was.

"I will tell them that Mike is causing big problems."

"Work with Nigel's family." She knew full well that Jon and I had very little financially between us. "Mom, it's been seven months! They don't want it to be another week. They are absolutely tired of it. They want it now!"

"Amanda, please trust me, please trust me."

"Okay, okay. Mom, I know that. Listen, I love you! Tell Dad I love him, too, and I'm so sorry."

"I love you, Amanda."

"See you, Mom. Good-bye"

"I love you."

As soon as the call went dead, I yelled, "Who the hell is Mike?"

Bob switched seats to get to the house phone to call Ottawa.

"Is he with our Nairobi team?" I demanded. "He needs to stop whatever he's doing immediately. They had a gun to her head, Bob!"

"I know, Lorinda. I know. Let's see what we can find out." He put the phone on speaker as we relayed the details of the call to Ottawa. Ottawa didn't know who "Mike" was, but he was definitely not working with the Nairobi team. I was promised that they would find out and get back to us. It occurred to me then: Where was Adam in all of this? Where was he, and why was he out of the picture now?

It took three long days to get an answer from the sitting chair in Ottawa as to who the hell this Mike was. We were told by Ottawa that Mike F. had been hired by members of the Brennan family to go into Somalia to rescue Nigel. We were also told that because of Mike's involvement, Nairobi's current strategy, which had been looking very hopeful, was now slowed down. Ottawa couldn't assess the full extent of the damage done, but it was possible that their plan had to be scrapped.

I couldn't believe what I was hearing. "No, this can't be," I said. "I'm going to call the Brennans and get to the bottom of this."

I was asked to wait until I calmed down. "We can use this opportunity to find out as much as possible about Mike and where exactly the Brennans are at," Bob said. "But only if you stay calm. We need to work as a team, Lorinda. And you have the capability, if you choose, to get everyone back on the same page. Remember: Amanda asked you to work with Nigel's family as one."

A pretty big demand in a moment when I was only seeing red. *They had a gun to her head, for God's sake!*

After a series of calls to various family members and no pickups, I finally reached Simon, Nicky's husband. He was very apologetic and told me that the family had been split over getting Mike (or Mick, as they called him), a private security contractor, involved. Most of the family was unaware of the plan. He said that the family members who had gotten Mike involved were very emotional and refused to listen to anyone else in the family. He agreed that it was irrational and that we needed to work together.

Shortly after that conversation, Nigel's brother, Hamilton, called me. We were both defensive, but I did my best to stay calm. He explained that they were sick of sitting on their hands and he had no faith in either of our governments. I gave him the shortened version of what Amanda had said about Mike, and I played a short clip of the recording in which Amanda had told me that there were guns to her head and that the kidnappers would kill her. When I asked him how he would feel if they killed her because of his actions, he replied that he would just have to live with it. I almost choked.

"Well, maybe *you* could live with it, but could Nigel? How do you think he would feel?"

"I guess he'd bloody well hate my guts."

Bob was frantically pointing to his card: "Stay calm."

I kept reasoning with Hamilton. I reminded him that Nigel's life was also threatened by Mike's actions. By the end of the call, Hamilton agreed to tell Mike to stop whatever he was doing. He was apologetic now and told me that we should work together, not against each other. Nicky was the next to call me. She made it clear that the rest of the family had been against employing Mike and unaware that Hamilton and Heather had gone ahead on their own.

That was quite a lot for one day, and I think Bob felt the same. The next day, he suggested that it would be good for me to get out for a bit. "You deserve a quiet day to yourself," he said. As I was getting ready to leave, the phone rang. So much for the quiet day. I was back on the "no answer" program. Bob shook his head. I wasn't allowed to answer the call. Instead, we listened as Amanda left a message on the recording system: "Mom, you have to know this. It's the question of my life and depends on Nairobi and Mike. You need to know that Mike has told these guys multiple times to go ahead and kill me. And Mike has said that it was me that made Nigel come to Somalia, so go ahead and kill me. So if the question of my life depends on Nairobi, then my life is finished, because Mike has made such a problem here."

Click. That was it. After the promises I'd received the day before; I was stunned. I was sure the Brennans hadn't told this guy to say something so threatening about Amanda. Maybe something was getting lost in translation? Whatever was going on, this had to stop—fast. Before Bob and I could even discuss the call, the phone rang again and went to voice mail. It was another message from Amanda: "You have to call me back immediately, when you get this message. It's really important. I have something very important to tell you, so as soon as you get this message. You have to call me back tonight. Okay, Mom, I need to speak to you."

Click.

"Bob, this is fucking killing me. I am going to call her back! I don't care what anybody says!"

"I understand, Lorinda." He knew that no one was going to stop me this time. "Just let me call Ottawa first."

After his call to Ottawa, he asked me to wait for a few more minutes. They were going to send me speaking points. They came through email. I was supposed to discredit Mike, using the following directives as my ammunition:

- Does not speak for either families
- He has no money
- He is an opportunist trying to take advantage of the situation
- Nairobi speaks for both families
- Their number is xxxxxxxxx
- If they don't answer, leave a message
- Ask about Nigel. Where is he? Can you speak with him?

Then there was one added message directed to me:

- Only one call back—NO more calls answered after that!
- If beating etc.—hang up phone

I sent out a silent plea to the universe: *Please, no bad call. Please no "beating etc."*

When Bob and I were set up, I dialed the phone and a male voice answered. It was not Adam.

"Hello, can I speak to Amanda?" I heard shuffling as the phone was passed.

"Mom, I don't have long. You have to listen to what I'm saying and take it seriously."

"Okay, Amanda. I have some important information for you, too."

"Mom, we have three minutes. I have been told that Mike is telling these guys that he has nothing to do with me. That he is taking care of Nigel."

"Amanda, now I need to you to tell them that Mike does not speak for either Nigel's family or your family. He has no money to offer them. He is trying to take advantage of the situation. He does not speak for either of us."

"Mike doesn't?" She sounded surprised by this news.

"No."

"They want to speak with somebody different. They don't want to speak with Mike."

"Amanda, I—"

"Mom, Mom, I, I, I can't hear you."

The call kept cutting out, and we couldn't understand each other, so I hung up and called back. "Hello? Hello? Hello?" But I could hear only a male voice echoing the same response.

"I need to speak with Amanda," I demanded, and after a few fraught seconds I could hear her voice again.

"Mom, the line is not good, so speak slowly and very clearly."

I thought the kidnappers must be listening and that was her way of telling me they needed to hear and understand what I was saying.

"Mom, do you understand what I am saying about Mike?"

"Yes, Amanda. I need you to tell them that Mike is working on his own. He is not—I repeat—*not* working for us."

Amanda was speaking to someone else there with her. "Mike is not working for them—for his family or my family. Okay?" Then she spoke to me again. "So they need to speak to somebody in Nairobi? They need to speak to somebody else?"

"Yes!" I said. "Yes, I have a phone number for you."

She turned from the phone again to deliver the message; then as I gave her the phone number she wrote it down and asked, "Who are they speaking to?"

"The people in Nairobi working for us. Ah, Amanda, it's very important that if they don't answer, to leave a message." Once again I didn't have a name, so I tried to be vague without sounding as though I was withholding any information.

"Okay? These are the people working for Nigel and me?"

"Yes, they are."

"Who is Mike?"

"Mike's trying . . . Tell them that Mike has no money."

"Mom, hold on a second. I'm putting you on speakerphone. Okay, go ahead."

"Mike does not speak for our family. Mike does not speak for Nigel's family. Mike has no money."

"But these other people have the money? Mom? The people in Nairobi?" Amanda asked.

"Yes, please connect with them."

"Okay, so we have the number and those are the people with the money and those are the people working for me and Nigel?"

"Yes, they are, Amanda. Oh, and I need to know if Nigel's okay. Is he with you?"

"We have been separated, but I know he's okay. We're in the same house. I haven't spoken to him for a few months, but he's okay."

"Okay, good. Amanda, I love you. We love . . . Hello?"

The line clicked.

I let out a sigh of relief. We shared the news with Ottawa, which then shared it with Nairobi. I immediately called Nicky, and the sigh of relief echoed through the Brennan family and the AFP, too. Finally, Amanda knew that I had not abandoned her; her government and her family were actively working for her release. It was still early in the afternoon, but I went into the kitchen, poured a glass of wine, and toasted Bob as I melted into the couch.

The day was not over. At 2:45 in the afternoon, the intercept line rang. It was a call from Australia. Bob popped on the headphones. I picked up the phone. Heather Brennan tore into me. She was angry that everything was taking too long and angry at me for sticking to my belief in the government. I told her that I understood how she felt, but she insisted I would never understand how she felt.

Bob handed me a card. "Stay calm, let her vent."

She told me that she hadn't heard Nigel's voice since his last recorded call on September 5, while I had spoken to Amanda three times since then. She didn't believe that he was alive. She would believe it only when she heard his voice for herself. She scolded me for attacking Hamilton and for making him cry by forcing him to listen to Amanda's voice message. She said I should have spoken to her instead.

I could feel my face turning red, and Bob could see it. He quickly scribbled: "Bigger picture, Lorinda!" Then, on another card: "Need to work together."

Heather demanded that I apologize to Hamilton. I couldn't believe my ears. I looked at Bob. He handed me a card that said, "Agree to apologize." Then he pointed back at the other cards.

I shot Bob a look as though he were the enemy, but I heard myself saying, "Okay, Heather. I will call Hamilton and apologize."

Blue, gray, and black were the colors of the air in the room after I hung up the phone. Bob acknowledged how difficult that call must have been for me and praised me for holding myself together so well. He rationalized my agreement to apologize to Hamilton. It would get our families back on track for the sake of Amanda and Nigel.

After giving myself time to calm down, I called Hamilton and apologized for upsetting him. To my surprise, he broke down weeping. "I never intended for Amanda to get hurt. We just want Nigel to come home. It's just so hard!"

Yes. It was so hard. It was hard for all of us. Our call ended. Rage singed the blue-black air around me. I poured another glass of wine and then another.

At 211 degrees, water is hot. At 212 degrees, it boils. With boiling water comes steam. And with steam, you can power a train.

CHAPTER ELEVEN

SMOKE AND RUMORS

On April 1, my niece emailed me, "I hope the latest news isn't true?!" I didn't have a clue what she might be referring to, so I immediately checked another email from one of Amanda's friends. In it she asked if it was true that Amanda was pregnant. *Amanda pregnant???*

She included a link to an article written by David Axe on a blog called "War Is Boring." In it, he claimed he'd received an "unconfirmed" report of Amanda's pregnancy from a "trusted" Somali contact.

I went numb. This had to be a hoax. Maybe it was a ploy by the kidnappers to seek leverage for their cause? I immediately called Jon to ask if he'd heard the rumor. He hadn't but said he would be right over. While I was waiting for Jon to arrive, I cruised the internet for more news. I came across the headline "Somalia: Abducted Canadian Journalist Is Pregnant." My stomach dropped as I read on: "Amanda Lindhout, a Canadian journalist who was abducted . . . about eight months ago is reportedly pregnant after she was apparently raped by her abductors. . . . Some reports suggest that one of the abductors made Amanda as his wife."

Jon arrived within minutes. He was in full panic mode.

"Lorinda. What if it's true? Poor Amanda!"

Jon had not read about the possibility of rape or forced marriage, and I was not going to tell him about my recent internet search. If this was true, how would Amanda cope? It was too much for my brain to compute or my heart to bear. I could feel the stress-overload alarm starting to go off in my brain. How much more could Amanda, Jon, or I take? A baby? Another life at risk? Could it be Nigel's child? The other possible scenarios were deeply troubling. At that point, it was all speculation, but my stomach was churning. I reminded myself that if I didn't know it for a fact, there was a chance it wasn't true, and that was where I needed to live at the moment.

Ottawa had not heard any pregnancy rumor but expressed their concern, adding that unfortunately, in Amanda's situation, anything could happen A marriage or baby was a possibility. They promised they would find out as much as they could as quickly as possible and get back to us. Jon left for home, feeling distraught. We waited for answers as we battled our imaginations.

I decided to email David Axe directly. I was angry that he was posting something that was not confirmed and accused him of being not only unprofessional but cruel to the people who loved Amanda. If he had any helpful information, I asked him to pass it on to me or the Canadian government. "Our family is asking you to remove this information unless it is confirmed."

He emailed back, "I am a journalist, not a spy for the Canadian government, nor your private investigator. So, no, I will not be removing my post. . . . I understand that you're worried and scared. I too want Amanda and Nigel freed." He wrote a few lines about his hope that bringing awareness to Amanda's and Nigel's situation would increase their odds of coming home. "Reporting in Somalia, and press issues in Somalia, is my job. And it's a job I'm wholly dedicated to," he wrote.

The Brennans had also heard the rumors and reached out to us with their hope that they were not true. The possibility of it being Nigel's baby also came up, but none of us wanted to entertain anything further. They expressed extreme frustration about a call from Nigel that had gone to voice mail on the line that the AFP had removed from their home. They speculated that no one had been monitoring the line during the Easter holidays. The message had clearly been scripted. Nigel had said that they were running out of food, time was running out, and Mike was causing a lot of problems. I couldn't blame them if they felt that the AFP had dropped the ball. I would have been upset, too.

The AFP had left them on their own months earlier, while we still had the in-house support of the RCMP. But I could feel that things were shifting for us as well. With only one negotiator, and talk of no one being available after April 19, I was wondering if the SLOC would be closed, but I was too scared to ask on the chance that it could be true. The pregnancy rumor left me in a fragile state. I couldn't imagine losing my support team as well.

A couple days later, Ottawa informed us that according to their latest information, Amanda was not pregnant. I felt like someone who had been held under water, resurfacing to take my first full breath of air. *Thank you, thank you, thank you.* Ottawa would not tell us how they had obtained that information, but I was still relieved. They had also consulted Somali experts, who said that rape was not condoned by the Koran. Of course, that was far from comforting, but I hoped for Amanda's sake that her captors' belief system would protect her from this form of violation.

For sanity's sake, I had to stop thinking about the rumors. But shortly after the pregnancy rumor, Jon and I had a surprise of an entirely different kind: we received a letter addressed to us and to Geoff and Heather Brennan, with copies sent to the Canadian and Australian High Commissions in Nairobi.

Dated April 4, it was personally signed by the prime minister of Somalia's Transitional Federal Government (TFG):

To the Families of Nigel Brennan and Amanda Lindhout,

On behalf of Republic of Somalia, I am writing to express my sympathies to you in this trying time. My government views kidnapping as despicable, criminal acts, against Islam and

repugnant to the people of Somalia. Putting an end to kidnapping
in Somalia and freeing of the men and women in captivity are
one of my government's priorities. I want to assure you that my
government is doing every thing possible and working closely with
all appropriate authorities in order to bring about the safe release of
Nigel and Amanda.

Omar Abdirashid Ali Sharmarke

Of course, this was good news, but how good exactly? Prime Minister Sharmarke had studied political science at Carleton University, in Ottawa. He had dual Canadian-Somali citizenship. When he had been selected as prime minister, he had pledged to unify Somalia, but he was opposed by the terrorist group Al-Shabaab. Might he be able to intervene with the kidnappers on behalf of Amanda and Nigel? Or was his letter just a piece of paper to hang in some obscure corner of a den? I appreciated that he had reached out to us, but at the same time I knew that his government had little effective power.

Throughout April, the calls and messages on my Somali line continued. Sometimes it was a male voice: "Amanda wants to speak to you. Please call."

Sometimes it was Amanda: "Mom, this is the last time I'm going to be able to call you, okay? So if you can, just try calling back. These guys have talked to someone in Nairobi, and this woman says there is $250,000 and they can either take it or kill me. And you need to know that they have taken that decision today, and that decision is not to take the money unless there is a million dollars for me."

Another time: "Mom, this is Amanda. I don't know why you didn't call back the other day because it's making a big problem because they think you don't care."

It was unbearable to hear Amanda say that. She must be wondering why the hell I wasn't answering or calling back and what kind of game we were playing. Though I knew it was emotional blackmail, my heart ached every time I heard her voice utter such words, and it took every bit of self-control to stop myself from picking up the phone. At one point, the negotiator on duty that day told me that if I tried to answer the phone he would rip it out of the wall. That comment hurt and puzzled me. I had pretty much been a model cooperative agent.

Following relentless appeals to Ottawa to allow me to answer the phone or call Amanda back—at least so she would know that I had not abandoned her—Ottawa began giving us a bit more information. I felt it was their way to keep us from going rogue. The Nairobi cell was working a strategy with TPI 19, a third-party intermediary. They referred to him by number because they couldn't disclose his name. It looked as though they were making progress daily. That really could be the key, and my interference could not only sabotage their efforts but put TPI 19 in danger.

Meanwhile, Jon and I were receiving more frustrated emails from the Brennans. They were impatient and expressed their desire to become directly involved in negotiations by hiring "a third party with Somali contacts." They were eager for both families to raise money to cover the costs of both a private negotiator and the ransom. Who was the "third party" they had in mind? I didn't know.

In a long phone call with the Brennans, Jon was told about a Dutch geologist who had spent forty years in Somalia but now lived in Kenya. He apparently knew how the country worked and had spoken with the RCMP in the past. Meanwhile, there was also some talk about Mike as a potential resource again, this time working transparently with the AFP and the RCMP. This was worrisome for us, but they promised not to authorize any action without informing Jon and me. They were no longer willing to "agree to disagree" about the best approach to negotiations. We questioned the records of successful releases by Mike and the Dutch geologist friend. Neither had any experience in hostage release situations.

Jon and I were frustrated and also thinking outside the parameters set for us by Ottawa, but we kept going back to the proven statistics of the Canadian government's impeccable record. I asked Kelly to weigh in with her thoughts, and she agreed with Jon and me. The Brennans made it clear that they would be moving ahead with private funding—with or without us. Ottawa asked that I send the Brennans an email requesting that they wait until TPI 19 had a chance to follow through on their strategy in order to protect his life.

Soon after, my faith in Ottawa suffered a severe blow. I had been cut off from negotiations ever since the "bad call" on December 13. I'd had misgivings before, of course, but increasingly, I was concerned about having so little information about their strategies out of Nairobi. In mid-March, the jokes and encouraging emails I used to receive from RCMP team members had started to trickle off. Was this a directive from the top? I didn't know. The clearest sign of change, though, was when I learned that no negotiators were available to work with me at the SLOC. I was left there alone and instructed not to answer the Somali phone no matter what. What did this mean? Was this it? Was the SLOC closing down? How could that be, when Amanda still wasn't home safe?

On April 15, I contacted Charmaine, the RCMP officer in charge of sending negotiators to the SLOC, for answers via email:

> It's 1:40 in the morning and I can't sleep. I am asking you to pass this email to whoever "up there" makes decisions about what happens from here. I understand the lack of resources, but I'm concerned because there's been 29 calls since March 14 so how can you justify having no one here? I have co-operated and done everything that's been asked of me. It's only fair that that someone lets me know what's next! Things are worse than they've ever been with the current pregnancy rumors and I am being abandoned. For 8 months we have put 100% faith in Ottawa. Most of it being blind faith! I guess I don't know if I'm just fucked up or if I'm being fucked!
> I need some answers!

Charmaine visited me at the SLOC a few days later on April 20, with the answers I had asked for. "We are shutting this place down. You should start looking for somewhere else to live."

Day 45 in my war room at the SLOC (Sylvan Lake Operational Centre). When Adam called, I never knew what to expect, so all around me I had posters with questions to ask and answers to give. It was hard to imagine some of the scenarios, but being prepared and keeping calm on the phone was key to keeping Amanda alive and bringing her home.

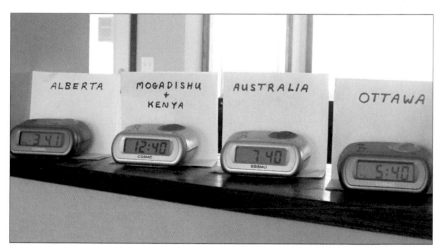

These clocks were an important part of the war room as we were in frequent communication with Nigel's family in Australia, the Canadian government in Ottawa, and the hostage takers.

Behind me you can see some of the proof of life (POL) questions we had ready to ask Amanda, the calendar I started to track how many days had gone by, and pictures of Amanda and Nigel. I knew I needed to see Amanda's face every day, to encourage me and the whole negotiating team to never give up.

This photo of Jon (with a black eye from a falling window blind), Shanobi (Jon's dog) carried by Perry, and (back, left to right) Mark, me, and Nathaniel was included in the care package we sent to Amanda in November 2008. I'm holding Teeny, Amanda's pink teddy bear.

From left to right: Tiffany, Nathaniel, Amanda, Jamie, Janet, and me.

By the end of 2008, I had already heard so many rumors and received terrifying deadlines from the hostage takers. I found solace in thinking of earlier, happier Christmases. These photos were taken after Jamie and Amanda returned from their trip to Asia and I gave Amanda a collectible Barbie. Behind Amanda are her grandparents Larry and Jean Stewart.

Members of the National Union of Somali Journalists, holding signs demanding the release of Amanda and Nigel. After five months of negotiations, I was encouraged to see support was still strong at home and abroad.

238 · DAYS IN CAPTIVITY

11 · DAYS SINCE LAST POL

27 · DAYS SINCE MY LAST (speaking to) CONTACT WITH HT

60

04/18/2009

This picture was taken at a particularly rough time in the negotiations. Two days later, I was informed that the government was shutting down the SLOC.

06/09/2009

At the time of this photo, I was operating alone out of the SLOC. Soon I would be relocating to Canmore to work with John Chase, an international crisis specialist, to bring Amanda and Nigel home.

This was my war room. In the top right corner, you can see the bottom of the poster with my mantra in pink: "Today is one day closer to Amanda and Nigel coming home." As you can see from my calendar, the photo was taken 280 days into their captivity, just over half of the total time they would spend in captivity.

These are photos from my life before Amanda was kidnapped. Here, Amanda and I are taking a break from our logging job during the summer of 2004.

A snapshot from a hiking trip in Lake Louise.

11/14/2009

Here I am with Nicky, JC, and Geoff, waiting in Nairobi at Tribe Hotel to hear from Ed, Shaun, and Nur, who had just arrived in Mogadishu. Unfortunately, unexpected delays caused us to recall our team, but they would try again eleven days later.

Armed guards on patrol outside the Sahafi Hotel in Somalia, where Amanda and Nigel stayed for their first night of freedom after over a year in captivity. *Reuters / Mowliid Ibdi.*

Amanda and Nigel in Prime Minister Omar Abdirashid Ali Sharmarke's office the morning after they were released. *Reuters / Handout.*

Amanda and Ed with Teeny, Amanda's pink bear, on the plane leaving Mogadishu for Nairobi. In just a few hours, I would see my daughter for the first time since January 4, 2008.

Jon, Amanda, and I flew out of Nairobi on December 7, 2009. I was finally bringing my daughter home.

Six years after Amanda's release, the RCMP arrested Ali Omar Ader and charged him in connection with Amanda's hostage-taking. They called us, coincidentally, on Amanda's birthday, June 12, to tell us the news. *The Canadian Press / Patrick Doyle.*

One of the things that got me through Amanda's captivity was talking with others who had been kidnapped or who had had loved ones abducted. Now Amanda and I share our story in the hopes that we can help others who go through similar hardships. *National Speakers Bureau (both photos).*

From left to right: Mark, Amanda, me, and Nathaniel on a trip to the Rockies. *Tanya Foubert.*

After Amanda came home, she wanted to show her gratitude by giving back to others in need, and so she began the Global Enrichment Foundation, which empowers Somali girls through education. In 2011, my brave daughter returned to Somalia to visit these school girls. She continues to inspire me with her capacity for forgiveness and hope. The Globe and Mail / *Peter Power.*

Amanda and I in India in 2016. This was a country that Amanda had fallen in love with on one of her many travels, and it had been my dream to go back with her when she was freed.

I was shocked and outraged. "But why?" I asked.

"The lack of progress no longer justifies our expense."

"You mean that after being told I must be guided in everything and never make a move on my own, now I'm supposed to do *everything* on my own? Or nothing at all? What about Amanda? We've had a total of twenty-nine calls since March 14, which I've been forbidden to answer."

"You are not being abandoned, nor is Amanda. The team in Nairobi will persist with their strategies, and Ottawa will continue to give you daily updates."

"How long do I have before the SLOC closes?"

"June 1. That gives you about five weeks."

"I have nowhere to live. You know I gave up my rental months ago and I will have no income. I still need to negotiate for Amanda. What is going to happen to us?"

"You'll find a place, and if need be you can always apply for social assistance. Maybe it's time to start looking for a job and start normalizing your life."

"Normalizing my life? Are you kidding me? My daughter is kidnapped! How will I be able to continue negotiating for Amanda?"

"We'll figure that out as we go forward. For now, the Nairobi team is handling everything."

I had believed so completely in Ottawa and the RCMP, and now, suddenly, both my support network and my home were being dismantled while Amanda remained in captivity. Always, I had been assured that we were on the right track. "Lorinda, we have strategies in operation. We're so close. Trust us. We'll bring your daughter home." Gordon Black had promised us!

But Ottawa hadn't brought Amanda home, and now they were closing the SLOC. Not only that, but my entire financial livelihood had shifted since Amanda was kidnapped. For nine months, I'd been living in a bubble, isolated from friends and family, and soon I wouldn't even have a place to live. Before the SLOC had been created, I couldn't have imagined living and working with twenty-four Mounties. Now I couldn't imagine living without them—their kindness, their support, their reassurances. I felt that I was being stripped of my RCMP family as well as technical assistance. I'd been the tent post holding up my real family—Jon, Perry, Mark and Nathaniel, my mom—and now I was scared, really scared, that I would fall down and bring them with me. Who was going to help me up?

Feeling stressed to the breaking point, I did what I would never have done before this ax fell across my neck: I replied to a message from an old friend, Grace Baxter, whom I had lost contact with years prior. She was living in Sylvan Lake now, as well. Grace and I had met years earlier, when our kids were small. We had spent a lot of time together until she moved to Mexico, and then our contact had trick-led to a stop over the years. She heard about Amanda's kidnapping and reached out to me through Facebook. Feeling very much alone, I agreed to meet her for a coffee. After we caught up on the years that had passed, I asked her, "Grace, can you keep a secret if I show you something?"

I drove her to the SLOC, then walked her through the back door into the front room with its graphs and pictures and directives and posters. She was shocked and speechless. After taking it all in, she burst out crying. She was appalled by the secret life I'd been living for months and my upcoming loss when I told her the base was soon closing.

•

After considering the options of where I would move, I decided to go back to Canmore. The location would be good for Amanda when she came home, as it would put us close to family and friends and was an hour away from Calgary and various medical facilities should she need them. Amanda had loved Canmore when I had lived there before, and the beautiful surroundings and small-town friendliness would provide us with the support I imagined we would need.

I reached out to my friend Sue Robertson in Canmore and asked her if she would help me look for a place. When I visited her to check various housing options, I asked her the same question I'd asked Grace: "Can you keep a secret?" I told her about my life and work with the SLOC. I told her about the Brennans' plan to fund-raise and how Jon and I had been so torn because of Ottawa's reasonings, their threats of abandoning rescue efforts for Amanda, and, of course, their track record. "I'm going to be so fucking mad if I have to start fund-raising from scratch to bring Amanda home when I could have been doing that eight months ago."

Sue looked at me, her face filled with shock. "Lorinda, I can't believe the secret you've been living with," she said. Finally she understood why I hadn't been able to come down and visit her. "I had a picture of you in my mind, sitting by the phone at Jon's house, paralyzed by depression. I just had no idea."

Since I had lost my support team in the RCMP, I knew that I would need to build my own trustworthy network of strong confidants. Now with Kelly, Grace, and Sue on board, I was starting to feel better. They were strong women who were willing to walk through the fire with me. With renewed strength, I confronted the rumors that were festering online. The media had latched onto the rumor of Amanda's pregnancy. I began to write emails to various outlets, hoping to squash the gossip and unsubstantiated reports.

After my tearful good-bye to Emil, my last negotiator, on April 19, the SLOC was cold and lonely. So much of my communication was through email now. I sent out an update to my former RCMP team, letting them know I was deeply disappointed but that I did not blame them for any of Ottawa's decisions. My gratitude for the time they had supported me would never be forgotten. I wasn't sure how many of them would even think about me, but should they think of me, I didn't want them to worry about me. "**I am strong and will find my way through this until Amanda is home. One day closer!**" A handful of replies came back to me, and a few Mounties kept in touch with me throughout. Later, I learned that Ottawa had given the directive to all members who had been involved with the SLOC that they were to cut all ties with Jon and me. Most of them did.

As April turned to May, I spent more time away from the SLOC, actively looking for a place to rent in Canmore. It became clear there was nothing available for June 1, so I asked for a one-month extension, which I was granted so long as I was out by July 1. Still not sure how I would financially support myself while working for Amanda's freedom, I went to my mother. In 2007, while my father had been dying of cancer, I had financially supported my parents and paid all their bills. They had wanted to pay me back in the future, whenever my mom sold the house. I hated to ask her now because I knew she was struggling financially. I still couldn't tell her the truth about my secret life, so I told her that I needed some space and my own place. She was okay with that and was happy to help. She went to the bank and borrowed $10,000 against her mortgage. Although I shared custody of Amanda and Nathaniel with Jon, I had raised five kids without a partner. I didn't have much to put aside, so that nest egg would have to keep me afloat until Amanda was released. I didn't know how long that would be, but I would make it work. Saving Amanda was more important to me than anything else. I knew I would always find a way to live in the future, but I knew that I could not live with myself if I didn't get Amanda home.

On May 5, while still living at the SLOC, I came across an article online, translated from a source in Mogadishu. The headline read, "Somalia Is Pregnant Canadian Reporter Kidnapped and Reduced to Sex Slave." A local reporter claimed to have seen Amanda and Nigel after their brief escape to the mosque. He reported that Amanda "had the belly." The fact that this was denied by another source in the same article did little to comfort me. The article was filled with horrific details, and once again I felt blindsided. I consulted the sitting chair in Ottawa and asked for an assessment. "I'd put both reports at fifty/fifty," I was told. That was 50 percent higher than the last time I'd asked. My concerns only deepened.

Amanda, I wish I knew what is going on and how to best help you. I hope that none of this is true, but if it is, we'll figure it out. I promise you that we're going to bring you home and we'll fix whatever we need to fix.

I wanted to toss those rumors into the same garbage can as the one claiming that Amanda and Nigel wanted to stay in Somalia because they were planning a book and a film. I much preferred another rumor circulating on the internet—the one where Amanda was teaching English to Somali kids and Nigel was playing soccer with them.

I regularly had dreams about Amanda; it hurt to wake up and leave her. It was so incredibly sad to wake up to the reality that she had been gone for so long and I was facing another day without her. Often in my dreams, I was telling her that I was so sorry. Once awake, I continued to apologize to her. *Amanda, please forgive me that it's taking so long. I feel like I'm letting you down. I am here waiting for you, longing to hug you and see your smile again. I am so sad that I can hardly bear it.*

Ottawa was still insisting that closing the SLOC didn't mean they were abandoning their rescue efforts. Strategies were still in play, now hampered by the savage fighting in and around Mogadishu. The year before, the Canadian government had secured seven hostage releases, along with another five the following year. These had included the recent negotiated release of the Canadian diplomat Robert Fowler and his colleague Louis Guay, kidnapped by Al-Qaeda in Mali. According to reports, the releases had taken longer than the RCMP would have liked—*four months*. We were now up to nine months.

Both the Canadian and Australian governments continually told our families that they could not negotiate with kidnappers for sums over $250,000, our current offer, which had been refused. At that arbitrary cutoff point, "justifiable expenses" turned into the taboo R-word—ransom—and neither country paid ransoms.

While Jon and I mulled over what to do, we had a small boost when we read an article in *The Globe and Mail*. Abdifatah Mohamed Elmi, the released captive who had been with Amanda, had moved to Nairobi, where he finally felt safe to speak about his captivity. He stated that although he had been kept in a separate room from Amanda and Nigel, there had been times when they passed each other in doorways, but they had been forbidden to speak. "Amanda, she was the most brave girl of us five. She started the first connection of us. Since we were so afraid to be killed, she started to sign. She said to me, 'Don't worry, we'll go out. Stay strong.'"

Jon and I were proud of our daughter, and we weren't surprised by her strength and positive attitude. Those characteristics had always been part of who she was. I hoped that would still be the case.

We continued to come across more rumors. Toward the end of May, there was a flurry of reports in the media announcing that all negotiations for Amanda had come to a halt. Ottawa let us know that nothing could be further from the truth.

A few days later, to everyone's surprise, Amanda's and Nigel's voices were broadcast on the major Canadian radio stations, pleading for help from their governments. In an interview set up by the kidnappers with a Mogadishu-based *American Free Press* journalist, both Amanda and Nigel said they could not answer any questions. It was obvious that they were reading from a script. They said that their situation was dire, they were very sick, and they were shackled in chains. There was a severe lack of food. Amanda said that if she was not freed, she would surely die there. It was very hard for me to listen to, but it was a proof of life. I thought about Heather Brennan. At least she now had proof of life as well. Small blessings, but I counted them regardless.

There were more reports of Amanda's pregnancy popping up. We now read online that Amanda had given birth to a baby boy and named him Osama. It went on to say that she was "very contented with her marriage to one of her captors you can't imagine how they exchange laughter and smiles. . . . Amanda is gleefully . . . performing her feminine work such as washing, cooking and cleaning the house. Amanda wears a big black veil . . . and is now learning the Holy Koran." Denial became my only defense against the "baby" rumors. It was the only way my heart and brain could continue to function.

It was hard to imagine her "glee" after another call by Amanda was broadcast on a Canadian radio station. I was driving the first time I heard it played. In that call, it was only Amanda, her words once again scripted: "They are going to kill me. Work together with Nigel's family. Sell everything. Just get the money." Her words played over and over in my mind, and they began to sound like a directive: *sell . . . sell . . . money . . . money.*

The phone call initiated another media storm. Jon was enraged CTV had shown footage of his home, including a close-up of his front-room blinds. After that, his doorbell and phone rang incessantly. I was worried. We knew Amanda's captors would be watching, and seeing Jon's home would only feed their belief that her family had money. Their concept of wealth, based on their own lives in Somalia, one of the poorest countries in the world, was much different from ours. It was unlikely they had any knowledge of the mortgages and debts we carried.

By then Jon was battling serious depression, and I was trying to wrap my head around all the upcoming changes in my life and trying to find a place to call home. Jon and I had asked what Ottawa's plan was for when Amanda was released. They said she would immediately be taken for medical care, possibly to Germany. She would be debriefed, and someone from the Canadian Consulate would fly back with her. We asked if we could fly to Germany following her release, but we were told we wouldn't be allowed to be there because Amanda would need to be debriefed and because she might not want to see us right away. We would have to wait to see her when she arrived back home.

"Like hell we won't be there. After all this time, just let them try to stop us!" I said to Jon. We agreed. Emails zipped back and forth as they tried to explain their logic to two heartbroken, desperate parents. We were not having it. We would be there when she was released.

On June 12, Amanda's twenty-eighth birthday, I drove to Babycakes Cupcakery in Red Deer and ordered two chocolate cupcakes with pink icing—one for me and one for Amanda. I told the ladies serving me that it was Amanda's birthday and this was my way of celebrating it for both of us because the next day would be my birthday. They wouldn't accept payment, and as they hugged me, we all cried. I left with their promise that when she returned, we would once again be treated to free cupcakes.

Happy birthday, Amanda. I know it's not happy, but I know that you're alive, and that means there is hope. Hope for a whole life ahead of you. I wonder if you know it's your birthday? You are one of the most precious gifts life has given me. When you come home, we're going to eat as many cupcakes as we want. I picked the "Diva" cupcake because it reminds me of you. Next year we'll do it properly. Cheers! I love and miss you so much.

•

I HAD FOUND AND SECURED a tiny basement suite in Canmore for July 1. The countdown to the closing of this chapter in my life was lonely and sad. Jon and Perry had almost completely withdrawn from their social lives, and I knew they were dreading my departure. As I closed the door of the SLOC for the last time on Day 313, I wept as I headed for a future I wasn't sure about. But as I got closer to Canmore, I felt an unexpected freedom about leaving the SLOC and the RCMP. I felt a twinge of excitement and optimism that what lay ahead was going to be okay.

PART II

CHAPTER TWELVE

STARTING OVER

D ay 340. July 28, 2009, would prove to be the turning point in our saga. That was the day Jon and I met with the international crisis specialist whom the Brennans were suggesting we hire. They believed this to be the only hope for rescuing Amanda and Nigel. We were both apprehensive but hopeful, desperately wanting to do the right thing.

Jon and I had sent numerous requests to speak with Lawrence Cannon, the minister of foreign affairs, hoping to get clarification on what exactly the government's role would be if we chose to go with a private security company. Would it abandon us completely? We didn't know. It had been eleven months, and we needed answers. The response from Cannon's office: "As this is the holidays and the House is not in session, it is possible that he is out of town." It was the first time that I realized that the House of Commons takes two full months of holiday, July and August. Are you kidding me? My daughter, a Canadian citizen, is kidnapped and has been held for eleven months, and God knows what other calamities are happening, but the House of Commons is on holiday? I was outraged. Our government had left us on our own, and we were facing a new and harsh reality. What other choice did we have but to take matters into our own hands?

On July 19, Jon had sent an email to our contact at DFAIT while

Minister Cannon was on vacation, letting them know that we were on our way to Vancouver to meet with a private security company.

Jon and I flew to Vancouver two days before the scheduled meeting so we could connect with Nigel's sister, Nicky Bonney, and his sister-in-law, Kellie Brennan, who were flying in from Australia. Another important member of both teams was Nigel's aunt Alison, the Canadian benefactor who had donated $250,000 toward the release for both Amanda and Nigel. Alison lived on Vancouver Island, so it was a short jaunt for her to meet us in Vancouver. Our aim was to see if we could forge a united front to bring our loved ones home.

The hugs and tears we exchanged were genuine, despite our past disagreements. Nicky, who was deeply tanned with short brown hair, looked so much like Nigel it was startling. Over dinner that night, we exchanged stories about Nigel and Amanda. We laughed and cried. Meeting the women behind the voices and emails of the last eleven months was wonderful.

The next day—Sunday, July 26—all five of us met with RCMP officers Marion Lamothe and Larry Tremblay from Ottawa and Cal Chrustie from Vancouver at the RCMP Vancouver headquarters. We wanted answers. Alison believed, as we did, that the RCMP might still be useful to us even though it would no longer be spearheading negotiations if we chose to go with a private security company.

We had a tough, honest exchange with the RCMP representatives that day. They admitted that a huge argument had taken place among the negotiators as to whether they should opt out of our case. Some said there were still viable strategies that hadn't been tried; others said that it had been too long with too little progress. On a whiteboard, they drew out their timeline and outlined the strategies they had employed month by month. It was obvious that much planning and action had taken place but nothing had moved us closer to Amanda and Nigel's release.

Marion confirmed that $250,000 was an unimpeachable threshold in kidnapping negotiations, requiring the government to bow out.

They could not raise the cap, we were told, because that would impact all future hostage negotiations.

Ottawa would keep an ear to the ground in Nairobi to "monitor" the ongoing situation. We weren't sure exactly what that meant. For the RCMP, security trumped information sharing. The team assured us that if they found an opportunity to help in other ways going forward, they would do so.

"Due to lack of progress in this case, you need to look at other options," they concluded. They were aware we had a meeting with a private security company scheduled for the next day.

I turned to Jon after the meeting was over, eager to discuss what this all meant. "I guess we got our answer, Jon," I said. "They really are bowing out."

"I have to believe that this is for the best, Lorinda."

"It's pretty scary though."

"I know."

It had been obvious since the SLOC had been deserted in May that this door was closing. Earlier in the month, I had already begun researching and inquiring about the legalities of a "special" bank account for ransom money. The bank manager, although shocked by my request, was anxious to help. Another woman with previous banking experience said she would help in any way possible, including helping me find a trustee should we open that "special" account. I had decided it would be named "The Pink Account." I had a list of people waiting for me to give them the go-ahead to start fundraising. I felt empowered. My mantra, "Today is one day closer to Amanda and Nigel coming home," felt more real to me now than it had in months. I had not shared any of this information with the Brennans or Ottawa; I wanted to wait until Jon and I had made a firm decision based on these meetings.

July 28—our big day—was upon us. Kelly had flown in from Calgary to join us for this meeting. Alison had returned to her home on Vancouver Island. John Chase was the specialist the Brennans wanted to hire. He was head of Kidnap and Release (K & R) for Andrew Kain Enterprises (AKE), a private UK crisis response company. Chase had been born in Canada but lived in London. He had sixteen years of experience and more than one thousand case days behind him. He had worked rescue cases in danger zones all over the world, including in Somalia. He had also trained ABC, NBC, and CBC journalists working in those tumultuous places.

We met in a hotel conference room. In his forties, Chase was a handsome man. He reminded me of James Bond. He exuded both confidence and modesty. "I'm sorry this has happened to you," he said as he shook our hands.

During the first forty-five minutes of the meeting, we took turns filling Chase in on what had transpired to date and what our fears and frustrations were.

"I've seen many families in this same situation. I don't want you to worry. We'll get Amanda and Nigel home. This is how I see it happening."

He gave us each a printed copy of his company's publication "Mechanics of a Kidnapping": Snatch/hit (kidnapping of a victim), Contact (with the hostage takers), Demand, POLs, Initial Offer, Counter Offers and Threats, Agreement, Final POLs, Drop, and Release.

It mirrored what I'd been through already with the RCMP, except that we had never gotten past the middle of the list. Both of our families knew what it was like to be mired in the "Counter Offers and Threats" phase. It was encouraging to know that there was another path to follow, one that had been well worn by global fixers such as Chase, one that ended with hope.

"All security companies follow these steps," he explained. "And just to be clear, this kidnapping is all about the money. Despite the emotions at play, try to think of this as a business transaction." He continued, "The average land-based resolution of a kidnapping takes about ninety days, roughly three months. While I know this is Day 340 for you, you're going to have to think of this as Day 1."

Three months? We've been trusting Ottawa for the last eleven months, and Amanda could have been free in three? I was incensed and felt sick to my stomach. Amanda and Nigel had been suffering—

God only knows what. Amanda could be pregnant or have a child, and now I was hearing we had to start again from Day 1?

Chase's educated guess was that the kidnappers would settle for around $600,000 for the release of both Amanda and Nigel. "This negotiation may take some time because we don't know exactly what has been offered previously or to whom it has been offered. Private security companies are obliged to share their notes, but governments are not, for security reasons. We'll have to start from scratch. In fact, previous government involvement should be regarded as a setback."

Nicky and Kellie were quick to jump in with their criticisms of the AFP and the Australian government, and I couldn't blame them. But for my part, I felt protective toward the RCMP negotiators who had worked by my side.

"Our negotiators were committed to us one hundred percent," I said, "and I will not bad-mouth them. Let's start moving forward from here and get those kids home!"

Chase nodded in agreement, then provided us with his first piece of concrete direction: "You need to set up a crisis management team [CMT] including both families. I will meet with the CMT daily via Skype, and together we will decide on each step to take. Each one of you will actively be involved and have a voice in the decision-making. There will be complete transparency. No more secret missions that you know nothing about."

This news felt like a cool river compared to the drought of information to date. I could feel the relief of all those sitting there as they absorbed the empowering task that had been handed to us. Although Chase told us to think carefully about our next move, there was nothing more for us to consider at the end of the meeting. We were going to hire John Chase. We would meet tomorrow to discuss the details.

After John Chase left, we confronted some of the details. The cost of hiring Chase and AKE was staggering. It would fluctuate according to various scenarios, but in the end we would pay $2,604 Canadian per day. In most kidnapping scenarios, AKE would have been hired by a corporation, for instance by a news outlet whose journalists had been kidnapped. Corporations had insurance to cover the costs. With us, it was the Brennans and the Lindhout/Stewart families footing all the bills. There was no insurance money. It was on our shoulders.

We agreed that each family would pay half of the entire costs accumulated between bills and ransom. Alison had assured us that her financial gift of $250,000, first offered to our governments, could be used for a ransom negotiated by AKE, so that was a start. She made it clear that half of the amount was to go toward Amanda's release. Alison's gift, especially for Amanda, a person she had never met, touched Jon and I deeply. Our bond with Alison would remain strong throughout the negotiations and afterward.

Before this meeting, Chase told me that he had worked to facilitate the rescue of Mellissa Fung from her kidnappers in Afghanistan. Chase checked with the Fungs first, then put me in touch with Mellissa, who sent me warm, supportive emails. Previously, when I had asked the RCMP to arrange contact with Mellissa and her parents, I'd been told they did not wish to be bothered. Now Mellissa told me that she herself had reached out to the RCMP to say she would like to contact us and had been told that we did not want to be bothered. I was once again outraged and immediately sent an email to Ottawa demanding to know why we had all been lied to. I received no response.

Faced with that blatant lie, Jon and I began to question what other lies we might have been fed. After our unwavering allegiance to Ottawa, we began to realize the extent to which we had been skillfully managed through promises, lies, and the philosophy of reciprocity. It was a kick in the gut. I felt like a fool when I thought about the months of unnecessary suffering for Amanda and Nigel.

Three months on average for a release! Charles Levinson and Chris Gelken had advised me to contact outside agencies. The Brennans had been right to pressure us to raise the ransom and cut loose from our governments. But unfortunately, when they had involved people like Mike and others, it caused interference and huge amounts of stress and delays. Finally we were all on the same page with a reputable agency with proven statistics. The optimism we all felt was vibrating through the room.

That very afternoon, John Chase had arranged a meeting for us with Mellissa's parents, who lived in Vancouver. They were full of praise for Chase and AKE but spoke with bitterness about the RCMP. I was beginning to understand.

That night my gratitude came easily as I reflected on the day, until my mind started punching me with regret and guilt. In my mind's eye, I reached out to Amanda. *Amanda, I am so sorry. I hope that one day you'll find it in yourself to forgive me for my stupidity. I just didn't know. They promised, and I believed them. I'm so sorry for the months of needless suffering because of my decisions.*

The weight of guilt I felt in that moment was crushing. How could I have not known? What I did know right now was that I was going to have to shift my focus to what I could do instead of what I'd failed to do. Guilt and regret would siphon off my strength and energy. There would be plenty of time for that later. Now I needed all my resolve to get Amanda home.

The next morning, we met at Chase's mother's home. As we sat on her back deck on that very hot day, she and his two daughters graciously served us cold drinks while we elected our crisis management team. Nicky and Kellie would represent Nigel, with Nicky's husband, Simon, as an alternate; Jon and I would represent Amanda, with Amanda's friend Kelly Barker as our alternate. To avoid a confusion of names, Kellie Brennan would now be Kel (to distinguish her from Amanda's best friend, Kelly), and John Chase would be JC (to distinguish him from Amanda's dad, Jon). We laughed. "JC" seemed appropriate for the miracle we were expecting from both John Chase and Jesus Christ.

As we went over the details to be sorted, JC said that his office in London would send us the appropriate paperwork to be read and signed as quickly as possible. He said that in light of the length of time Amanda and Nigel had already been in captivity, there was no time to waste. We would begin immediately. The paperwork could wait a few days.

The next order of business was setting up the crisis management team. JC informed us that a family member virtually never serves as the negotiator, but in this case, I had been trained by expert negotiators and had built a solid rapport with Adam. Even though it had been months since my last interaction with Adam, he had consistently preferred to speak with me. Everyone agreed that I should continue in the role on behalf of both families. JC commented that since meeting me the day before, he could tell that I would serve well because I was a "formidable force." I took that as a compliment. My whole life, the one word that people had used to define me was "nice." "Formidable" sounded more like someone who could negotiate a hostage release.

Nicky would take the role of chairperson for the Skype meetings, while Jon and Kel would serve as deputies. Kelly would sit on all Skype calls and have a voice in decisions, while Nicky's husband, Simon, would serve as an alternate if needed. We were all happy with the progress we had made, and we were ready to start working.

·

WE THOUGHT WE WERE DONE for the day. After the meeting, Jon decided to do some sightseeing on his own, and I went out shopping and walking around with Nicky and Kel. That afternoon, while I was hanging out with them, I started receiving calls from Somalia on my cell phone. I didn't recognize the number, so I let them go to voice mail. When I picked up the message, the caller identified himself as Osman Emalie. "I have news about your daughter, please call."

Since our team had not yet completed its transition to working with AKE, I asked the RCMP for permission to call Osman back from my hotel room. I knew that the calls would be costly, and I needed to confirm that the costs would be covered. Permission was granted. Ottawa was curious to know what was happening as well. Kel taped our conversation and later put it on disc.

I questioned Osman: "Do you know Adam? Do you know where Amanda and Nigel are being held?"

After answering yes to both of those, he said, "If you pay me, I can get you a video of your daughter and Nigel."

That was the giveaway; I realized that Osman was yet another Somali opportunist trying to cash in on our suffering.

"I will only speak with Adam concerning Amanda and Nigel."

"The kidnappers want me to tell you that if the money isn't paid before Ramadan, one week away, your daughter will be slaughtered like a goat."

The instant visual and proceeding wave of nausea were all I needed to hang up on him.

I was still shaking from his comment while Nicky, Kel, and I came to a consensus that Osman must know something but was probably not part of the gang. After they left my room, I started to cry. How many other mothers, I wondered, heard threats like that about their children? I knew that anything could happen to Amanda and there wasn't a damn thing I could do to protect her. The residual trauma from that threat would stay with me for years to come.

The next day, I received a text from Adam: "They want to be paid by Ramadan or else you will see!!!?"

CHAPTER THIRTEEN

LIES AND COUNTERLIES

When Jon and I returned to Calgary, he headed for his home in Sylvan Lake, while I returned to Canmore. I bought a handheld recorder to tape calls with Adam, though by now I'd refused so many of his calls that I wondered how we would move forward. I had answered his text by directing him to my email so I could get set up at home. The plan was for me to reestablish contact with him, record our phone calls on my handheld device, then download them for AKE to transcribe for the others on our team.

The first practical challenge for our crisis management team was to set up our Skype schedule—not so easy when dealing with four time zones. When it was 7 a.m. for Jon and me in Alberta, it was 2 p.m. for JC in London; 12 a.m. the following day for Nicky and Kel in Australia. And—never far from our minds—5 p.m. in Somalia.

Because of that sleep-robbing timetable, we kept our daily calls reasonably short, supplemented with supportive, informative emails. JC conducted our Skype sessions with calm reassurance, even in the toughest circumstances. When we asked questions, he had logical answers. We were incredibly grateful to have our views respected, to participate in decision-making, and to be given full knowledge of advances we were making or hitches we encountered. Because we could see the result of each action, positive or negative, consensus was usually straightforward. We also received a daily written report from JC, summarizing our last communication with the kidnappers, assessing its significance, and recommending our next action. Accompanying that, we received transcripts of every call.

I sent my first email to Adam (who now called himself "Adan"). I followed my CMT instructions, stressing the solidarity of our two families, and made it clear that we were acting on our own accord, not with our governments:

> Hello Adan. This is Lorinda, Amanda's mother. It has been a long time since we have spoken. December 13. We have trusted others in Nairobi to speak for us, and now we are here 11 months later, and you still have my beautiful daughter, Amanda, and her friend, Nigel. I have spoken with Nigel's family, and we agree from now on I should speak with only you. There have been other Somalis who try to ask me for money. I trust you, Adan. And I believe that you trust me.
>
> Adan, your people have broken my heart. I miss my daughter so much. There are no words for my pain. You know that Amanda's father is very sick and he wishes to see her again. Nigel's family feels the same way for him.
>
> We wish to make a deal. Can you open a hush email account? It is more secure, and government people cannot read what we write. I also think that they are listening to our phone calls.
>
> Adan, I hope that your family is well. You know that we are alone in this now, with no help from our governments or anybody else—it is just our two families. We are not wealthy, but whatever money we have, we will give everything for the love and safe return of our children. Tell us how we can get them home with us, Adan? Thank you, Adan.
>
> Lorinda

We were encouraged when Adan replied the same day, though his words were angry, jumbled and threatening:

> What we believe is that Amanda and Nigel were walking together for ther government's rights aside of intellegence services, to mislead us is worth to us!!!!
>
> all in all I respected your speech for many times but at this time is the time of killing when we reach Ramadan.
>
> Mam Amanda really ilove you because you respect me every time. But i will hate you if i lost 2 million dolars in two weeks, then you will hate me. by mr. Adan.

Still trying to keep Osman's threat out of my mind, I replied the next day, August 1, making all the points decided upon by the CMT:

> Greetings Adan,
>
> 1) You know that Amanda and Nigel are not working for either of their governments (Australia or Canada). They are both young journalists who want to let the world know how the Somali people are suffering. They wanted to tell the story so the rest of the world would send medical supplies and food to your country. They are both humanitarians.
>
> 2) We are ordinary families who have no idea how kidnappings and ransoms work. I'm sorry, but before the governments told us they were the only ones who could help us to get Amanda and Nigel home safe. We also trusted others to speak for us. We now know that this is not true and we feel that they have tricked us. Our Governments have warned us that we are not allowed to speak with you (or anyone in Somalia) and that is why we need to do this secretly. We know they are trying to listen in to our phone calls. We have begged our

Governments to help us pay the ransom but they refuse. In the Countries of Canada and Australia it is illegal to pay a ransom. I don't care because I will gladly go to jail to have Amanda and Nigel come home.

3) I know now that the only way to solve this is for the families to take charge and only speak with you. I trust and respect you, Adan. Nigel's family speaks with us every day so we can solve this with you. This takes a little longer because Nigel's family is in Australia, we are in Canada, and you are in Somalia.

4) How can we solve this? We also want Amanda and Nigel home before Ramadan, but $2m is an impossible amount for our families. We could never hope to see that amount in our entire lifetimes. You must help us reach an agreement on the amount that we can pay. Amanda and Nigel do not work for a big company that has insurance to pay for them if they are kidnapped. This means that they are alone and only have their families to help them now.

5) Our families have worked hard for almost a year now getting together as much money as we possibly can. Nigel's family works for farmers on sugarcane farms in Australia. Amanda's father is very ill as you know, and has not been able to work for many years. His medicines are very expensive. You are a father, Adan, and I'm sure that the other kidnappers have families. Please look into your hearts for us!

6) We have sold 2 houses, sold farming machinery, sold cars and have borrowed money from family and friends to get all the money we could. We have managed to get together $281,000 US dollars. This is a huge amount

of money for our families. You must realize this is more
money than we could hope to see in our lifetime. You
are an intelligent man. You know that the banks are
collapsing and the weak economy is crashing. It has
been very hard for us to get bank loans and sell things
because nobody has money to buy things.

7) Adan, please, you must help us to get everybody to
    accept this huge amount of money so we can bring this
    sad time to an end before Ramadan. What will you gain
    by killing Amanda and Nigel? Nothing! I think that Allah
    will look kindly on all of us to come to this agreement.

Regards, Lorinda

Adan replied the next day, insisting that he knew the Canadian and
Australian real estate markets and rehashing old dealings with our
governments. This included a reference to the recently elected Somali president, Sharif Sheikh Ahmed, and to an Adan Madowe, whom
we later confirmed was actually Adan Madobe, who briefly served as
president of Somalia before Sharif Sheikh Ahmed.

Adan complained about a "Mr. Willium," whom we took to be
the Dutch geology professor Hamilton Brennan had set into play as
a go-between before JC took over. Mr. Willium would continue to
annoy us all, especially John Chase, because he refused to butt out.

Adan also repeated his threats concerning Ramadan:

Realy i can understand and i knew that ahouse locates in
Canada is not sold a little money, a house in Canada and
Australia is worth $700,000 or 7 million "that is one house only."

    you knew that before Sh, Sharif come a president your
ampasador come some sources there $200,000 we refuse!,
then Adan Madowe $800,000 we refuse!, i don't know
agoverment!: either Asutralia, Canada or Somalia!!.

Lorinda still i respect you and i afraid that Amanda and
Nigel shoul dy (go to doomisday) a hunger!!!!??. becouse
we were fasilitating till a year and i afraid if they come home
to be some-how mad becouse what we can give is Tea and
Bread in all day and some times Sorrgham with a little of oil.

If our negotiation is to tell what was before 8months
iam not ready talking starting at this time and I woul tell Mr.
Willium not to call me you Lorinda, Ham. Mr, Adan.

I wrote Adan a return email on August 3, in which I labored to
correct his assumptions about the real estate, to distance our families
from past negotiations, and to hold firm on our current offer.

Greetings Adan,

We also do not know what the Governments have said in the
past, but now there is no one but you and I communicating.
I will speak for both Amanda and Nigel's families. Please
tell me who is Adan Madowe? And what about $800,000? I
know nothing of this and neither does Nigel's family.

Adan, I only can dream that I would have a house worth
the amount of money you speak of, so I could sell it and
bring my beautiful daughter Amanda home, and send
Nigel home to his family. How can you believe that we love
our things more than our children? Any one of us would
rather steal, or have our hands cut off, if we could bring
our children home. Amanda's father's home is 18 years old
and we have already borrowed money from the bank on his
house to pay you. This means that if we cannot pay back
the money we have borrowed, the bank will take his home.
I do not know how things work in Somalia, but that is how
they work in Canada, Australia and many countries in the
world. To buy a home we have to go to the bank to borrow
money from the bank. Until we pay the bank the money we

borrowed, our home still belongs to the bank. Because we have so much pressure, we had to sell the 2 houses quite quickly and therefore could not charge as much. It takes time but especially now with this recession.

Adan, you are an intelligent man, please go on your internet and look at what's happening in the world economy now. . . . Understand Canada's dollar is not worth as much as the US dollar currency, so that means we have to give even more money. You can look this up on the internet. We have 281,000 US dollars here in cash waiting to go to you. You will have a lot of money and we will have our children home. . . . Also on the internet you can look at the law of Canada and Australia so you will know that we are not lying about the law, please!

We love Amanda and Nigel, Adan, and we are desperate to get them home to us! . . . Please work with us to resolve this by Ramadan. . . . Kindly, Lorinda.

Adan's reply was brief:

First iam't fine, second Adan Madobe [*sic*] is the head of what is called Somali parliament's head (the president of Somali parliment) understand, and we would not trust him even if he becomes an Angel. thanks, Adan.

We had definitely not been in touch with Adan Madowe, and I was concerned that Adan now believed we'd offered the president $800,000, which of course was another fabrication, coming from where?—we did not know.

•

PIERLUIGI ROI, A JOURNALIST FOR the Toronto-based multicultural television system OMNI Television, emailed me to tell me that he had recorded a call between himself and Amanda. Besides wanting to confirm that it was Amanda's voice, he wanted to warn me that he intended to play it publicly. He had attached the audio to the email.

After Amanda made clear that she was limited in what she could say, she told Pierluigi:

My health is deteriorating very rapidly due to fever and dysentery. I need to see a doctor. They won't give me any medicine. I have a tooth that is badly broken and very infected, and abscessed. I've had severe stomach problems. I don't want to die here, and I'm afraid I will die of disease if I don't get help soon.

I have little food. Some days they don't feed me at all, and when they do it's usually just bread and oil. I'm always hungry, and I think the water is what's making me sick.

They're keeping me in a very dark room with, like, shackles on. My mental health is seriously beginning to suffer. I don't know how much longer I can bear this. I'm begging my government to please assist my family, my family that I love so much, to pay my ransom. I love my country and I want to return, so I'm begging . . .

The men who are holding me are very serious. They say that if a ransom is not paid they are going to kill me, and I'm telling you that, even if that doesn't happen, I could die of illness. And a message to my family. . . . Please offer whatever they have directly to these people. That's all I can say. I love my family very much.

Though that was awful to hear, I focused on the positive aspects: Amanda was alive, and her delivery was strong and coherent, even though I knew her words were scripted. I reminded myself of what Mellissa Fung had emphasized in one of her emails: "The kidnappers lie all the time. . . . They said I was going crazy, and that I was suicidal. None of that was true."

Maybe she was being treated better than she said, but after so long in captivity I knew she couldn't be doing well. I concentrated on her message to me and to all of her family—one of love. The two things I could count on for sure: Amanda still loved us, as we did her, and she was alive.

On August 4, Adan followed up with another brief email:

> In respection to you as the mather of Amanda, Amand's hair is be coming as some one shaved and i don't know what the reason or that disease is that is what i want to inform you!!
> an other-hand at once a morter shell thrown by Amison happened part of the residented house of Amanda an Nigel!!!

The OMNI interview disturbed us, and the email only heightened our concerns. Not only did it seem that Amanda's health was deteriorating, there were other dangers looming nearby, ones that again were beyond our control. I had stopped tracking the news in Somalia or researching other captives, but I was aware that the war was still raging and there was always a risk of misguided gunfire or mortars or even of Amanda and Nigel being kidnapped by gang rivals looking to make money.

Meanwhile, to try to clear up the mystery of the offer of $800,000 to the Somali president, John Chase emailed a colleague who was familiar with local politics. After a complicated analysis of clan interactions, the colleague reported that certain elders appeared to have sought Amanda and Nigel's release, but that the kidnappers had refused the money. This suggested to him that the kidnappers were "truly *mooryaan*, or outlaws rather than part of a somewhat organized group."

All of this to-ing and fro-ing with Adan indicated we were still mired in the perilous "Threat and Counter Offer" part of "Mechanics of a Kidnapping." The urgency of Amanda's medical situation, real or scripted, caused me to persuade the CMT to boost our offer. On August 5, I wrote to Adan offering US $319,000, explaining that the additional US $38,000 was from Amanda's and Nigel's colleagues, who had secretly collected money.

Trying to push to "Agreement," I asked in my email:

"How will we get this money to you? In just a few days, you could have all this money in your hands, and Amanda and Nigel can be home with their families. This will be a joyous day for everyone!! We do not know who the man is whom you say has offered you $800,000, but if you take his money as well as ours, you will be a very rich man—over a million dollars! Richer than any of us could hope to be!"

I told Adan that I had listened to Amanda's audio interview: "My beautiful daughter is saying that she is very sick and needs to see a doctor for her body and tooth. . . . If we cannot finish this very soon, then you must allow us to send medicine so her sickness can be treated. Please, please, Adan, let us finish this now!"

I ended by asking for two POLs:

For Amanda: "What was the name of your dive instructor in Honduras?"

For Nigel: "What was the name of the dairy cow you had as kids?"

I was so bone tired from months of stress and sleep deprivation that my brain was struggling to function clearly, and unfortunately, a draft of this letter, intended for John Chase, accidentally went to Adan with JC's UK cell number on it. That aroused Adan's suspicions, perhaps canceling any positive effects of our boosted offer. I tried to explain it away by describing Chase as a doctor I'd consulted for medicine for our children, but Adan remained deeply aggrieved: "You infidels want to cheat us!" He demanded that we send him $3,000 immediately for the medicine I had mentioned. He also used JC's UK number to leave a voice message, which was of course ignored.

Adan's next email communication was angrier and more incoherent: "If what you have still is like this $319,000 it is nothing!" He ignored our request for POLs: "i think that you and your governments imagine that Sharif's weak government, supported by the US, will do for you some thing which is to use by force but i tell you that Amanda and Nigel will not see by any one!"

He ended, rather weirdly, with a declaration of love for me, for Amanda, and for Nigel.

JC thought that Adan's incoherence, here and in other emails, might be due to his overuse of *khat*, a traditional green-leaf stimulant which drug authorities equate with amphetamines. He also wondered if Adan's refusal to provide POLs meant he was no longer in control of the kidnappers and if his request for $3,000 for medicine was intended as compensation for himself.

Four days later—on August 9—I emailed Adan to assure him that the last thing we wanted was forceful interference by the local government. "Adan, I am a simple mother, that's all. You accuse me of trickery and knowing about the military, but I know nothing about these things." I told him that we were as confused as he was by many people contacting us about the hostages who were pretending to represent the kidnappers. I requested once again that he provide answers to our POLs.

While all this was happening, I had written a fundraising letter explaining our situation. We were only days away from the one-year mark of Amanda and Nigel's kidnapping. I explained that the government had given its best shot but now it was up to us and that Amanda would die without a ransom being paid. I also explained the need for complete silence and secrecy as we worked for her freedom. As I pleaded for help, I expressed our sincerest gratitude for kindness that came in any form—financial, fundraisers, volunteer work, or prayers. We sent the letter to family and friends, and the Pink Account was opened.

Unexpectedly, Jon called me and said that Jann Arden had reached out to him on Facebook, asking, "How the hell are we going to get this girl home?" A real Canadian celebrity was reaching out to us, and I was not going to miss seizing the opportunity. I didn't know what she could do, but I contacted her via Facebook and asked if I could arrange a call with her. Between our busy lives, scheduling the call turned out to be a challenge.

Soon after, I woke up with news of another "baby alert." A reporter who had once met Amanda and had worked in Somalia himself had been asking his Somali colleagues to get information to confirm the rumors. He wrote to me, "After a long search for information, a reliable source confirmed that Amanda was indeed pregnant and had just delivered a baby boy. He could not confirm who the father would be. I'm sorry to give you this information." I was told that a journalist had just happened to be in the hospital when Amanda was brought in under the guard of several Somali men with guns.

The same garbled report claimed that Canadian prime minister Stephen Harper had been working behind the scenes to pay a ransom of $100,000. The informant was uncertain as to whether it was for Amanda alone or for both Amanda and Nigel. Apparently, the baby would not be included in the ransom. The informant also declared that the lowest sum the kidnappers were willing to accept from our government was $600,000.

Though this jumble of so-called information made little sense, the "what-if" section of my brain began spinning its web of wretched fears.

"Remember," the ever-unflappable JC said, "misinformation is a tactic favored by kidnappers. You can't mistake these reports as truth. They're meant to alarm you and prey on your fears."

His response helped quell those fears. But they would be banished only when I could see my daughter face-to-face. I followed up with a query to Ottawa. Again I was cautioned against believing these dodgy reports. Ottawa seriously denied that Prime Minister Harper or anyone else from the Canadian government was offering money to the kidnappers.

For seven long days after that, we didn't hear from Adan. We thought silence might be his new tactic. To break it, I phoned him on August 16. Over an impossibly poor connection, he insisted that the Canadian Department of Foreign Affairs *would* help with a ransom. This suggested he might also have heard the same nonsensical rumors reported to us. He now raised his demand to $2 million for "each head." He still refused to address the POL questions, strengthening our suspicion that his position within the group might have changed. Before cutting off, he said he wasn't going to email anymore because it was too difficult to get to an internet café with the constant gunfire in the streets. Besides, "I know you lying to me," he said.

I emailed him the next day, denying yet again that we would receive any government help: "They don't answer when I call!" I repeated our two POLs, then called his bluff: "When you do not answer, I wonder if you still have contact with the group holding Amanda and Nigel. We will not offer more money if we don't know they are okay."

I sent another email on the same day, pointing out to Adan how out of proportion his demands were, compared to other Somali hostage takers. "Look at your pirate friends on the coast. They take a ship that is worth $30–$40 million, and that is insured, plus 20 or 30 crew members, and after two or three months, they maybe get $1.5 million or $2 million. You are asking for more for our two children, and we are just normal families. Please answer our two questions and we will try to get more money."

I followed this up with a phone call. The Adan who greeted me that day was relaxed, though his focus was strictly on the money. He reminded us that the kidnappers had already dramatically lowered their original demand. That had been for $2.5 million *each*, not for both, as we had mistakenly thought. On this call, he was asking for only $1 million each—a total of $2 million instead of $5 million.

When I asked to speak with Amanda, he replied, "If Allah be willing." Either that, or he would get the POLs.

Three days later—on August 19—I got what I wanted. Adan allowed Amanda to call me.

Amanda was crying, obviously upset. "Mom, I love you so much. I don't know how much longer I can do this, Mom. I am sick, and I do not have food to eat. I haven't been outside. I can't see the sky."

I told her we had collected US $319,000, trying to give her hope, as well as to repeat the offer for the kidnappers on the chance that Adan was not being up front with them. I let Adan know that we needed either an answer to Nigel's POL or a phone call from Nigel to Nicky. If he arranged either one, his reward would be a new offer from us. Though he connived to know how much the offer might be, I remained steadfast in my demand of a POL for Nigel.

He said he would try.

What was supposed to be a call between Nicky and Nigel ended up being a call between Nicky and Adan only. Nicky confirmed all the points we'd previously made: our families were in complete solidarity; we were not wealthy; we did not have government support.

Adan's next testy comments flummoxed all of us: "Listen to me, if you are the brother of Nigel, did you sent any letter to Nigel before, so you remember, when you were sending the medicine? What did you wrote, you write that $1 million has been bought to the house. It has been raised as a ransom, isn't it? What changed your mind? I think that Lorinda has changed it, or somebody else."

"Adan, I don't understand what you mean," Nicky replied. "We gave Nigel letters, and my children each wrote Nigel a letter as well."

"You said, 'When we bought a house and we got 1 million dollars is ready as you ransom.' What has changed your mind?"

"Adan, I don't know what you are talking about."

This confusing conversation ended with the sound of loud knocking at Adan's end and then the voices of a Somali woman and children. It was a sober reminder that Somali domestic life continued as usual while our children's lives hung in the balance.

We all puzzled over what Adan meant by his reference to the sale of a house for $1 million. It seemed to arise out of some confusion created by one of the personal letters the Brennans had sent to Nigel, along with our pre-Christmas medicine parcel. Had a misunderstanding about a mythical $1 million led to Adan's refusal to accept our offer of US $319,000—or, for that matter, any previous offers put forth by the Nairobi team?

Upon learning all of this, JC floated an idea. "It might be time to employ an interpreter," he advised.

We agreed. We needed to crack the code.

CHAPTER FOURTEEN

DIVIDE AND CONQUER

August 23, 2009, was a grievous day, as it marked the first anniversary of Amanda and Nigel's kidnapping. A year—365 days—of extreme anxiety for Amanda, for Nigel, and for us as well. Terror, threats of deteriorating health, darkness, isolation, shackles, loneliness, despair. It was a dark anniversary.

As if that weren't enough, the media were all over the anniversary and wanted an update. The CMT decided that the best approach was to issue a simple press release from both families:

> *Together, the two families continue to work tirelessly to secure Nigel's and Amanda's safe release. With little outside support, the families, who have been united as one throughout the horrendous ordeal, continue to do everything and anything to gain the earliest possible release of their loved ones Amanda and Nigel. Our thoughts and all our love are with Amanda and Nigel, today, just as they have been for the past 365 days, and just as they will be until they are safely home with us.*
>
> *In issuing this brief joint statement, the families hope that the media will respect their wishes to be left alone during this particularly emotional time.*

Of course, we weren't left alone. Soon articles streamed forth from all kinds of media outlets, often full of misinformation. Most galling were those that sanctimoniously pretended to be helping by keeping the story in the limelight, despite my behind-the-scenes efforts to persuade editors and producers that publicity only made the hostage takers greedier and upped the ransom, delaying Amanda and Nigel's release.

My response to the frenzy was to take a hike—literally. My days were so busy now that I no longer had time to commune with nature. Living in Canmore, I was surrounded by majestic mountains that sadly I couldn't see from the windows of my basement suite. Hiking those mountains had been one of my passions in my "before" life and one that I had shared many times with Amanda. That day, I hiked a familiar mountain, Ha Ling Peak. At the summit, I sat on a rock, meditating, trying to bring myself to a peaceful place in which I was focused completely on Amanda. To me, the climb was symbolic of our current struggle, as well as a reminder of the many journeys and adventures the two of us had had together as mother and daughter.

In the fall of 2004, Amanda and I had traveled to Thailand and Malaysia. To pay for that trip, we had shared what was physically the hardest job either of us had ever had, working for a logging company owned by my youngest brother.

The previous summer, in 2003, southern British Columbia had seen the worst fires in the province's history, prompting the building of a firewall to protect the area around Canmore. Much to everyone's surprise, Amanda and I worked as loggers. From our previous work history, no one believed that we were now working ten-hour shifts, seven days a week, wearing steel-toed boots and hard hats, often covered in mud. We had to prove ourselves in an industry dominated by men, and we were determined to do so. We threw cut logs up the side of the mountain or down, depending on where the closest roads ran. One of us then drove a CAT, pulling a huge burning barrel to those log piles. We then threw the logs into the burning barrel. It was exhausting work in the heat, the rain, and the mud. We had burns and bruises all over our hands and arms. On one occasion, a guy cutting the trees felled one the wrong way, and, despite trying to outrun it, Amanda was smacked to the ground by the top, knocking the wind out of her. She was lucky to be alive, and was sore for days afterward. Despite how hard and dirty the job, the blisters and burns, the cursing and tears, we still managed to find humor and laughter almost daily. However, by the end of the job we would have to clean up our "potty mouths," which had become part of our daily communication style while working with the loggers.

•

ANOTHER TIME, I WAS WORKING at Lake Louise Ski Area, in charge of the food and beverage department for the Lodge of the Ten Peaks and Whiskey Jack Lodge. Amanda returned from one of her travels to stay with me in Canmore and decided to join me as a server in one of the bars. Every day, we would get up at 5 a.m. and make the long drive to our jobs often before the snowplows had been out, sometimes white-knuckle driving through blizzards. We made it fun despite the hours and sometimes terrifying drives.

The most fun job we had together, though, was working up in the Arctic for Plummer's Arctic Lodges. I was the cook and Amanda the housekeeper for twelve guests and a staff of nine in a remote lodge on Great Bear Lake. Much to the jealousy of the rest of the staff, we flew as the only passengers sitting directly behind the pilots on a Hercules cargo plane that had previously been used in the Vietnam War. After unloading supplies at the base lodge, we then switched to a small float plane that took us to our summer home, Neiland Bay Lodge, literally hundreds of miles from civilization. The only way in or out was by boat or float plane. Since Amanda and I were both single and the only females in the lodge, we flirted shamelessly and carefully picked our summer boyfriends, two of the fishing guides, who were proud to have scored the only women in camp. We worked hard, went out fishing in the evenings, drank and played cards with the boys, danced together in the kitchen, and laughed constantly. It was the best summer in my memory to date.

Despite the tears streaming down my face, I couldn't help but laugh aloud remembering our shenanigans as I sat on Ha Ling Peak on the first-year anniversary of Amanda's kidnapping.

Amanda, today I hiked Ha Ling, remembering when we hiked it together. I hope that you have moments when you can remember our adventures and that they make you smile. We've had so much fun and so many adventures together not only as mother/daughter but as friends. We have so many more adventures to have. We still need to take our trip to India together.

It is unthinkable that you are still in Somalia. I swear to you that we will bring you home. We're finally on the right track, and I just know that you're coming home soon. Please don't give up. I won't. Ever. I hope that you can feel all the love coming to you.

The trek down the mountain could be challenging in other ways from the ascent, but today I barely noticed. I felt buoyed by my wonderful memories and grateful for the way things were finally coming together. It was a reminder that I had a choice over my thoughts and that fear and anger could hold me down. Gratitude, on the other hand, created optimism and the belief that anything was possible. *Anything!*

•

MY DAYS NOW CONSISTED OF meeting with the CMT first thing in the morning, then speaking with Adan, referencing the speaking points I'd developed with the CMT that morning. I spent the afternoons on my computer, researching and reaching out to people whom I hoped could and would help our cause. Kelly and I invited a few of Amanda's friends to meet with us in Calgary to brainstorm fundraising ideas. Everyone was elated that they could finally do something concrete to help Amanda. We nicknamed ourselves "the Amanda Team." What heartened me the most was the optimism of the group; they were not hoping or wishing, they knew without a doubt that we were going to bring Amanda home.

The time factor was taking its toll on all of us but especially on

Mark and Nathaniel. They were at times so distraught with the thought that Amanda might die before we rescued her that they missed work. I couldn't leave my post to go see them, and my base-ment suite was too tiny to accommodate any overnight guests. Na-thaniel was especially angry at what he felt was a betrayal by Ottawa, and I could understand that he was not so quick to trust JC. The good news was that I could see that Jon's depression was lifting following our decision to work with JC. He was now fully involved, not man-aged at a distance as the RCMP had done with him. Coping, though still extremely difficult, had become easier for both him and me.

Meanwhile, the name Daniel Clayton kept popping up in the media as someone involved in Amanda's case. He was the CEO of a risk management company, Due Diligence, located in Calgary. I was shocked to see a picture of Amanda on his website, advertising his services as if she were a client. He claimed to be involved and advising the government on Amanda's case. He said he knew her location and had the cell number of the Somali bandits holding her. None of it was true. All the information he professed to have gathered while working on her case could easily be accessed through the media. As I read his grandiose self-description, I knew I smelled a rat.

The most frustrating part of it was that the media kept going to him for quotes on the progress in Amanda's case, while behind the scenes, I was trying to let them know that he had nothing to do with it. I contacted him, demanding he take Amanda's picture off his site and stop speaking to the press. His refusal came not through a reply to me but by means of continuing to use her picture and speaking to the media. Eventually I sent a lawyer's letter with the threat of legal action if he did not cease and desist.

Following Amanda's release, there were still some media touting him as a key player. In 2012, he was convicted of being part of a child pornography ring and sentenced to three years in jail. He was exposed for being a fraud on every front.

·

DURING THIS TIME, I REACHED out to a reporter who had worked with Amanda in Afghanistan and had proven his integrity. I was so frustrated with the foreign minister's seeming avoidance of me and Jon following multiple requests to speak with him that I was ready to do an interview in the hope that public pressure would spur the minister to speak with us. After discussing it in our CMT meeting, however, I was advised that bringing public attention to our work could hinder our efforts. Jon and I eventually, after reaching the point of exasperation, sent a plea to Prime Minister Harper, who personally wrote us with his condolences as well as his reassurances that Amanda was a top priority. He noted his directive to Minister Cannon to contact us. When we did hear from the minister, we didn't feel there was anything concrete he had to offer us.

On August 28, Adan allowed Nicky to speak with Nigel on the phone. This was good news, a little pinhole of light. It was the POL that we had said would be necessary before we would increase our offer. First, Adan stressed to Nicky: "What I want to tell you is that Amanda and Nigel are not in one place. What I want to tell you, the group became two because they are angry with each other."

Nicky guessed that it was an attempt to split our families. "Well, Adan," she replied, "they have to sort it out, because if they want our money, we have to have Nigel and Amanda together."

As soon as Nigel was on the line, Nicky assured him of his family's support: "I want to tell you something, mate. Mom and Dad love you beyond measure, okay? I need for you to know that, mate. We all love you."

"I know that, I know that." Then he issued a quick reminder: "I can't answer any questions."

Nicky delivered our CMT message: "You know, we're talking to the kidnappers, and we need for you and Amanda to help us get across to them that they have to be realistic because we'll never have the $2 million they're asking. It's insane. The government dropped us."

Adan interrupted the call. "You cannot talk about any money," he said.

"Okay, Adan, but can I talk to Nigel again?"

Nigel came back on line. "Nic . . . I'm going to tell you a few things, okay?" Nigel appeared to pick up from his script. "Listen, they have us in a deteriorated condition, locks and chains near on twenty-four hours a day. My health is really bad. I'm passing blood. It hurts when I go to the toilet because of dysentery and fever. I'm extremely weak, and my mental health is not very good. I know you're doing everything you can to get me out of here."

"Nige, we'll never give up. You know that, don't you?"

"I know, I know. I love you so much. I'm so sorry!"

"Nige, Nige, don't fret about that. You're making me cry, okay, don't do that."

"Tell Mom and Dad I love them and I know you're going to do everything you can. Please, please, please, please try and talk with Adan. Try and talk and negotiate with him. I don't know how much longer I can last here."

"Ah, Nige, it's incredibly unfair. We are trying extremely hard to work with Adan to get this sorted, mate."

The call ended shortly after that. But at least, at the usual nerve-racking cost, Nicky had her POL. Nigel was alive. Fortunately, she, too, had learned to overlook the scripted words by listening to Nigel's tone. As she reported to the CMT, "Nigel was upset, but he basically said word for word what was scripted last time and the same stuff as Amanda. Here's the thing: his voice sounded strong. Be it that they are in a horrible space, but I don't think it's worse."

I called Adan the next day, to make him our next offer and to attempt yet again to clarify his confusion about Australian real estate.

He could hardly wait to ask "What money is it now? How much?"

"Adan, thank you for letting Nicky speak to Nigel. That's very important. Yes, Nicky sold her house in Australia. She got $140,000. That's Australian money, which exchanges to US $115,000." I made Adan a new offer: "So, now, Adan, we have US $434,000. That's almost half a million dollars. That's a lot of money!"

His response was quick: "I fail to see it is a lot of money. What about deal, what about Mr. Roi?"

He was referring to Pierluigi Roi, the Toronto-based OMNI reporter with whom Amanda had spoken and with whom I had subsequently exchanged a few emails. It seemed that a casual remark had excited Adan into thinking the government might once again be in the picture, with an offer of big bucks. "I don't know Mr. Roi. I know that you called him and that you put Amanda on the phone with him."

"Okay, thank you, thank you. I shall call you after I pray. I want to pray now. I will call you soon, thank you."

That offer to Adan was followed by four days of silence. On September 2, I phoned him. "Adan, have you spoken to the group and told them how much money we are offering?"

"First, Nicky talk to us and tell us that $1.3 million is ready at this time."

Of course, I shot down that ridiculous statement. "No, Nicky didn't tell you that. I spoke to Nicky. We do not have $1.3 million."

"She has spoken to her brother, not me, her brother Nigel. She told him that."

Another sly obfuscation, since Adan had specifically refused to let Nicky and Nigel talk about money. Adan's next tactic was to play up what he called the split in the group of kidnappers now that Nigel and Amanda were being held separately. "I knew the group of Nigel, but the group of Amanda will not allowed to talk."

I pressed the point that always made him nervous. "Should I be speaking to someone different, then?"

"No." He insisted he still represented both groups even though he was not in control of both.

"Okay, Adan. You are the spokesperson, and we will only negotiate for Amanda and Nigel together. I know that Nicky did not say that she had $1.3 million. We have for you US $434,000. That's almost half a million dollars. That's a lot of money for us."

Adan became disdainful. "What we believe here is that this is not a lot of money. We believe that it is pocket money!"

"Well, when I look on the internet because I want to learn about

Somalia, there are not very many people in Somalia that have very much money."

"If you come here, we can show you the people who have more and much money."

He stood firm on his demand for $2 million.

JC sensed that Adan knew he was running out of options, though he was not yet ready to relent about the sum his "two gangs" would accept. Adan's insistence that Nicky told Nigel she had $1.3 million baffled us.

•

I CALLED ADAN THE NEXT day, September 3. After brief hellos, I asked, "Your friends have accepted?"

"Yes, yes, they accepted."

"Oh, Adan!" I screamed.

My joy was short-lived.

"They have not accepted the money, but they have accepted for Amanda and Nigel to be in the same place."

After claiming to have done us the great favor of healing the split in the gang, Adan then tried to create fear. "Amanda has some problem," he announced. "She is confused, and I cannot understand her English. She has an ulcer in her mouth."

When I pressed him about our latest offer, he admitted that he hadn't yet told the gang. "Okay, I shall ask, but I'm not sure they will accept. Even if, at this time, I accept, they won't accept."

I seized upon his uncertainty to ask him once again, "Is there someone else in the gang I can speak to?"

Adan shot that down: "The others do not speak English!"

As I had been instructed, I asked if he would be amenable to speaking to a Somali interpreter. Adan said he would, and then went on a bizarre info-fishing trip: "Is Amanda adopted?"

When I denied that, he responded slyly, "I think to myself that if Lorinda was the mother of Amanda, she could pay this amount of money."

"Amanda's my daughter, and I love her more than anything. If I had two million dollars, I would have paid it to you a year ago."

"You can understand, mom Lorinda—they are someplace with gunmen around them."

"I cannot believe that Allah thinks that this is okay," I said in return. "What you are doing to us and to your brother and sister."

Adan's last initiative was to talk about how much it cost to keep Amanda and Nigel. For this, he wanted us to ante up the $3,000 he had previously mentioned for medicine.

I told him bluntly, "Adan, if we send you that money, it takes away from the money we have to offer you. That is all the money we have, US $434,000."

The call ended with his son crying loudly in the background and Adan's declaration that he needed to sleep.

Though no one on the CMT was cheering, we agreed with John Chase that we were wearing down Adan's insistence on the impossible millions. Nicky felt that I spoke too nicely in my conversations with Adan, so she suggested in our CMT meeting that I push him more, be firm, show some anger, an approach reflecting her personality more than mine. JC asked me, "Can you do that? Can you speak to him more aggressively?"

I had always been very conscious when I spoke to Adan that I was a woman speaking to a man in a country where women are forced into silence; on top of that, in his mind I was an infidel. I had chosen to speak in a softer manner because my fear had always been that I would anger him if I came across as aggressive and how that could play out. My instincts were screaming, "Don't do it!" but the CMT unanimously agreed that I should try this approach, so I told JC that I would use the tactic on the next call.

CHAPTER FIFTEEN

BAD CALL

On September 4, Adan sent a text to my cell phone: Am Adan, please call me, really I love you.

After speaking with the CMT, we agreed that I should call him back, but this time I was to be firm, as I had promised the other group members. I called him back the next day, September 5. We went back and forth as I pushed for him to get the group to accept our latest offer. I talked over him again and again, forcing him to listen to me.

"If I had the money I would pay you," I said rapidly "We are not playing games, it is you who are playing games. We are trying—"

"I am playing a game?" he cut in. "You should see my game is because when I see you playing a game, you can understand, if you shall treat me like this, I will, shall treat to you."

Our call ended shortly after that.

•

I WAS SURPRISED WHEN ADAN phoned me the next morning with some good news. He suggested setting up calls with both Amanda and Nigel for the next day. "I have breakfast, then I pray, then after that is a good time."

"Oh, thank you very much, Adan," I said.

He thanked me and asked what time would be good for a call with

Amanda and told me that I would be allowed to speak with Nigel as well.

He then went on to say, "I love you really, not just to marry you, but it is not possible."

"Adan, I love you also . . . and I . . . I so hope we can work this out." I would have said anything that I thought would help him release my daughter and readily abandoned the "firm" approach from the day before.

But once I was off the phone, John Chase gave his perspective. "Just be forewarned, Adan might be staging something unpleasant." He suggested that Nicky should be the one on the call with Nigel and that both Nicky and I should be prepared to hang up if either Amanda or Nigel sounded in extreme distress during the call. Nicky had never had to take a bad call, and I felt sick just thinking about it.

Early on the morning of September 7, Adan phoned, waking me up. He was anxious to set a time for the call. I told him that Nicky should speak with Nigel instead of me, and he agreed to that. First I would have my call with Amanda at 10 a.m., and then I would tell Nicky when our call was finished so she could call and speak with Nigel.

•

THE SINGER-SONGWRITER JANN ARDEN AND I had a call scheduled for 9:30, and after all of our attempts to arrange one I was looking forward to finally speaking with her to see if there were any ways she might be interested in helping us. I didn't expect it would be a long call, so I figured that we would have lots of time before Adan called. I was pacing and watching the clock, my stomach in knots; 9:40, 9:45, finally at 9:50 Jann called. We were discussing current efforts in fundraising when I heard my phone beep. It was Adan. Jann was in midsentence and I couldn't explain why I had to go quickly, so I let her finish and then told her I had to go but would get back to her. By the time we got through our good-byes, the phone had stopped beeping.

I called Adan back, and he was perturbed. "You call late this time! No matter! I say listen!"

Then came one minute and twenty-eight seconds of garbled noise. It felt like a lifetime. I was shaking, and my heart was racing.

"Hello? Hello? Adan, are you there? Hello? Amanda? Hello?"

"Mummy."

"Amanda—"

"Mummy Mummy Mummy Mummy Mummy, Mummy Mummy Mummy, pleeease." She was sobbing, clearly in distress. She had not called me Mummy since she was a little girl.

"Amanda . . . Amanda—"

"Oh, things have changed here, Mom. You need to pay the money now, the million dollars, now, because they have started to torture me!"

I needed to stay strong, to deliver my message to the kidnappers.

"Amanda, Amanda, listen—"

"They have tied me up . . . please, pleeeease . . ."

"Amanda, Amanda—"

"My arms are tied behind my back, and I remember what they are going to do, and I'm going to be in pain."

"Amanda, listen to me. We are doing everything that we can. We will not stop until you are home. I'm sorry that this is taking so long. Adan promised us that they would take care of you."

"Noooo . . ."

My daughter was sobbing. She was terrified, her words spilling out in gasps between screams. But I knew the kidnappers were listening. "Amanda, we love you and we have offered half a million dollars. We have sold everything that we have. We are trying so hard, Amanda. We are trying so hard. Adan will not believe that we are poor families. The government will not help us, and we are selling everything we can. We are trying so hard. Amanda. Amanda?"

The call was cut off, then reinstated. I could hear other voices now in the background.

I would later learn that one of the kidnappers had punched her in the face, knocking the phone out of her hands.

"Mom, Moooom . . ."

"Amanda!"

"Mom, are you there? Listen to me."

"Amanda—"

"Please, please . . ."

"Amanda, I love you, we love you. We are doing everything we can. Adan has not kept his promise to us. He promised us he would take care of you and Nigel, as you are his sister and his brother."

Amanda's sobs continued. "Mom, they have just started today to torture me."

My heart was fracturing, but I couldn't let it show. Not now. Not yet. "Amanda—"

"I cannot handle this! You have to pay the money now."

"Amanda—"

"You cannot wait, because they are going to do this to me every day, and I can't, I can't handle it. Mom, you have to pay the money now. Where is the money?"

"Amanda, how can we pay money that we don't have? We are trying, we are trying to get all the money we can—half a million dollars we have to offer them."

"You have half a million?"

"Yes, we've been selling everything, we've been begging people every day, Amanda. I write letters and I make phone calls to big people to help us. It is illegal in Canada to raise a ransom, Amanda. I could go to jail, so I'm trying to do it so that the government doesn't know, because if I go to jail I can't help you . . . I'm trying . . . we are trying, Amanda. We have offered everything that we have."

"We need one million, and we need it now, because I can't handle what they are doing to me, Mom."

"Amanda, Amanda—"

"I can't handle it even one more day. I can't!"

"Amanda, I love, I love you. We are doing everything we can."

"It's been a year, Mom. I'm in pain."

"Amanda, I know how long you've been there. I've missed you every single day. These men are bad men. They are punishing good

people. You and Nigel are good people. We are good people. I don't
know, I don't understand why they punish us. We have half a million
dollars to give them. That is a lot of money."

"Mom, do you understand what they are doing to me?"

"Amanda, I love you."

"A million dollars. And today they had me tied up with my arms
and my legs behind my back, and I felt like my back was going to
break."

"Amanda—"

The reception was going in and out.

"You have to know, every day until you pay . . . a million."

"We love you, we love you, we love you . . ."

I remembered JC's words of advice to hang up if things were things
were going badly. I hung up.

I was shaking violently when I got off the phone. Yes, I had been
trained for this moment, and I had made it through the call, getting
my messages in with the simplest language so that the kidnappers
would understand. I needed them to hear the amount we had to offer
in case Adan wasn't being straight with them. I had talked about going
to jail, hoping they would accept what we had on the chance that if
I went to jail, they would not get the money. But I was beyond panicked. There was no solace to be found in hoping it had been a staged
distress call. There was no question this time, Amanda was genuinely
frightened and being hurt. I could hear it. She was being tortured.

My hands still shaking, I phoned Nicky and JC to let them know
what had happened on the call and to tell Nicky not to call Nigel.
I guessed that Adan had the same kind of call planned for Nicky. I
played back the recording of my call for them to hear. I hung up, ran
into the bathroom, and threw up. My knees buckled and I fell to the
floor. I cried till there was nothing left. My heart was shredded. As I
got to my feet, I yelled, "Adan, you fucker! I hope one day you'll pay
for what you've done to us!" I felt a surge of rage like I'd never felt
before. I grabbed my coat and ran outside.

When I returned home later in the afternoon, I decided that the best thing for me to do was to channel my rage into freeing Amanda. Adan didn't realize that he had only strengthened my resolve.

I had missed numerous calls from my fundraising teams and immediately began contacting everyone. No one knew about the phone call. No one could begin to imagine what my morning had been like as we discussed various upcoming events.

Later, there was an email from Nicky in my inbox: "You did the most amazing job, incredibly calm and focused. Even JC said you were the best he'd ever heard, and we know he's been in the business for years."

Had I done the right thing? My instincts had warned me that I shouldn't challenge Adan, and I had. The very thing I feared most had happened, and I couldn't help feeling that it was my fault. I had the strongest connection with Adan, and I knew him the best. I should have refused. The dark monkey of guilt was trying to get on my back again.

•

I CONTACTED JC, WHO EXPLAINED that gangs typically launch a flurry of extreme threats when negotiations are close to a settlement, just to see what more they can squeeze out. He said that Amanda's phone call might be a good sign, that even though it had been wrapped in emotional barbed wire, maybe the kidnappers were getting closer to letting her go. It helped to hear this, even though I felt sick in every possible way. It was time to tell Jon and Kelly about the call, which I did, urging them not to listen to the recording because I knew how devastating it would be. What was the point of seeding that kind of horror and anguish in all of us?

The CMT talked through the event, and we all agreed that we should not reward or recognize Adan's betrayal by following through with a call to Nigel. I also confessed that the call had done me in emotionally and I needed a break. We agreed that Nicky would take over communications with Adan for the time being. I would no longer answer his calls or emails. Nicky would explain to Adan that I didn't trust him after what he had done to Amanda. We also agreed that it was time to bring in a Somali-speaking translator, as we had previously discussed.

Nighttime was now more torturous for me, as I could hear Amanda's voice over and over in my head. "Mummy, Mummy, please help me." I was emotionally beaten down, physically and mentally tired, but I still had enough energy to feel guilty that I was taking a break from the phone.

•

I TRIED TO CHANNEL THAT energy into focusing on the fundraising. We needed more money. And we needed it fast. I had to snap back and be strong, not only for Amanda but for the rest of our family. One lesson I'd learned during this whole wretched ordeal was the power of a mother's emotions. When I appeared to be handling myself well, it was easier for Jon and my boys. Though on the inside I was falling apart on a regular basis, I kept my breakdowns to myself. Sometimes that meant driving my car on lonely roads, screaming into the wind, then pulling over so I could bang my fists against the steering wheel.

The sound of Amanda's terrified sobbing began to haunt my every waking moment. And because I couldn't sleep, I had a lot of waking moments. The truth is that on top of everything my own PTSD was being triggered. I kept revisiting a comment Amanda had made before the kidnapping, when I had tried to persuade her not to go to Pakistan. She had snapped, "How can you complain about me risking my life after all you put me through when I was a kid?" It was true that her childhood had been traumatic, and that comment hurt because she was right—my decisions had put her through a lot.

Shortly after I left Jon, when I was living on welfare in Red Deer with Mark, almost nine, Amanda, age six, and Nathaniel, age four, I fell for an abusive man. On the surface, he seemed charming and in love with me, but just when I thought things were going well, he would turn violent. Outside the house, I wore sunglasses to hide my black eyes. I lived in constant fear of leaving him, because he said he would kill my kids and my parents if I left. Once, while I was tucking Amanda into bed, she whispered, "Mommy, are you going to die?"

After he confined me for three days, with death threats and a particularly brutal beating, he was convicted of assault and spent three months in jail. It took me a while to find the courage, but eventually I left that man. Through a lot of counseling and work on myself, I learned that abusers can prey upon anyone and that my background had made me particularly susceptible to a predator's cycles of charm, abuse, guilt, and promises to change. I also learned that abusers cover up how out of control they feel in the real world, then often compensate by attempting to dominate and terrorize women and children.

With my growing self-awareness came the realization that I wasn't powerless—not against that man, not against anything. With time and the right help, I picked myself up and forged a better life for myself and for my children.

Over the years and through a lot of communication, Amanda came to understand that my own life experiences had left me with very little self-esteem or feelings of worth, which had made me an easy target for abusive men.

•

BUT AFTER THAT BAD CALL, and on those long nights when I lay awake, the specters of the past came back to haunt me in new ways. I'd ask myself tough questions, turning the answers over and over again in my mind, looking for lost clues. Which of our past experiences stick, and which roll off our backs? Is it true that what doesn't kill you makes you stronger? To what extent had my past prepared me to negotiate with criminals for my daughter's life? And if I was having such thoughts, was my beautiful, brave daughter, half a world away, wondering the same things?

CHAPTER SIXTEEN

"TO ONE PERSON,
YOU MAY BE THE WORLD"

M oney and fundraising—these two things would become a driving force in my efforts to bring Amanda home. Years before, I had been head of the fundraising committee for the women's shelter in Red Deer, but I had never done anything of this magnitude or urgency. It was hard to know the total amount we would need to raise, but we knew it would be astronomical. The cost of the ransom depended on how our negotiations went, and the cost of AKE would depend on how many days we employed them. Jon was on medical disability. I no longer had any savings and I had no paying job, but as daunting as the fundraising looked, it didn't intimidate me. I knew we could make it happen.

Our team discussed what we had. We began with Alison's gift of $125,000. That was a start. Jon and Perry remortgaged their house for an $80,000 line of credit. We had already begun our grassroots campaign by emailing the fundraising letters to trusted family and friends, who forwarded it to their trusted circles. It was risky because any one of them could have alerted the media, but we had no choice. Luckily, no one did.

Funds were flowing into the Pink Account. Dollar by dollar, we watched the amount rise. Everything seemed to be running smoothly until I got a call from the bank manager: "Lorinda, I may actually be at risk of losing my job because of the Pink Account. It's raising red flags all over our system. Everyone is asking 'What is this?' You're not going to lose your money, but the account has been frozen." I could tell that she was shaken up by the thought of losing her job, but she still wanted to help. She had been informed that using the word "ransom" could cause legal problems for everyone involved. In answer to my question of what I should do, she explained that I needed to establish a trust fund. That meant finding trustees as well as acquiring legal counsel.

A trust fund would protect me as well as the donors from fraud or accusations. This made perfect sense, but it would be a time-consuming process, and time was a luxury we didn't have. We had to do another letter campaign. Now we were asking people to make pledges until we had the trust account in place, at which time they would deposit the funds into that account. In the meantime, we had to know how much money we would have to work with until the trust was opened.

Potential donors had questions about the legalities involved and naturally wanted to protect themselves from any liabilities from donating to or holding fundraising events that might be used to pay a ransom. To avoid that, I changed the wording. The money raised was to pay AKE as well as to support "a family in crisis." My intention was never to deceive donors but to protect everyone involved and ultimately save Amanda's life.

One of Amanda's friends, Dara, worked for Blake, Cassels and Graydon, one of Canada's largest law firms. She immediately started appealing to the lawyers at the firm. We needed a lawyer who was willing to work pro bono. While we waited for their reply, we continued with the letter campaign while making plans for various other fundraisers. Amanda's closest friends lived in Calgary, where she had spent years working in the restaurant industry as a server and bartender. It was natural for us to tap into the restaurant industry because so many owners and staff knew Amanda personally.

Kelly called me one day and asked if I would come into Calgary to meet with Kaela, a friend who had worked with Amanda, and Kaela's boss, David Singleton, the VP of operations for a restaurant group in Calgary. Kaela had asked Dave if he would consider doing something at the Seven Restolounge to raise money toward bringing Amanda home. Amanda had worked there previously, but Dave had not been there at that time. He asked if I would meet with him.

I was more than happy to meet anyone who would speak with me. I had put together a binder I called my "Amanda Book," filled with pictures of her on many of her adventures as well as all the articles she had written. Besides being immensely proud of my daughter, I knew that I had to personalize Amanda, in order to reach people's hearts and prompt them to reach into their pockets. After I laid out the timeline to date and showed Dave my Amanda Book, he was silent for a few moments.

"I can see that we need to do a lot more than a dessert sale to raise over a million dollars," he said. "Fortunately, I know just the person we need on board to help us. Sarah Geddes."

Sarah, I would learn, was the founder of SASS Communications, a PR firm. Dave called her right then and scheduled a meeting for me, Dave, Sarah, and the rest of the "Amanda Team." At the time, I had no idea of the dedication and commitment that Dave and Sarah would devote to helping me bring Amanda home. Dave and Sarah, both big thinkers, got me to events and in front of wealthy people. They stood at my side, serving as my emotional pillars. Sarah was the only person in the group in whom I confided about my "secret" life as the negotiator. Everyone else was told that AKE was doing the negotiating, and they had no reason to question otherwise.

We still needed to find solid legal advice. A lawyer who was a friend of my mother's agreed to work pro bono as an advisor on many fronts. He donated many hours to helping us. He meant well, but unfortunately, he involved a Toronto lawyer, who promised he was going to help us raise millions but was also going to charge us. A lot. It didn't feel right, and there was no way we were going to take money out of the funds we had already raised. We turned him down, and shortly after that, we heard from Michael Dixon from Blake,

Cassels and Graydon, offering his services pro bono. He would advise us and help us with all legalities involved in setting up a trust account.

We needed to find volunteers who would agree to be trustees. In Canmore, a friend introduced me to Wendell Lund, a Rotarian. After touring Wendell and his wife, Beryl, through my Amanda book, I left our meeting with the thought that there was nothing they could do for me, but I did not know Wendell. He was a Rotarian, whose motto was "Service above self." He realized that due to the sensitive nature of our cause, the Rotary Club as an entity could not contribute. So instead, he introduced me to many of the members, including two eminent Calgary businessmen, Steve Allan (Rotary district governor) and Michael Going (the owner and CEO of Good Earth Coffeehouse), who agreed to be cotrustees. Still, it wasn't until October 30 that the Amanda Lindhout Trust Fund was opened.

When the Pink Account was finally unfrozen, all the money was transferred to the Amanda Lindhout Trust Fund. Then, much to our relief, all the pledges and more came flooding in. This ultimately meant we could pay our bills and fulfill our promise to pay half of the entire incurred costs.

I had learned early that it was best for me to leave most of the backstage legal and financial dealings to others. I was grateful when Sarah stepped into that role, freeing me to be the negotiator and the face of our cause. I had enough pressure with my daily CMT meetings, my calls and emails to Adan, my endless phone calls and emails about fundraising events, and my travels from Canmore to fundraisers that were popping up in Calgary, Red Deer, and Rocky Mountain. It was a juggling act, and I couldn't afford to drop a single ball.

I wanted to personally attend every fundraiser to show my Amanda Book as well as a video that Dave had put together. The video made me cry every single time as I watched the clips of Amanda. When I was introduced at the events, I would tell "Amanda stories," much as I had done at the SLOC. One of my favorite stories to illustrate who Amanda was happened on one of her trips to Calcutta, India.

She came across a little girl in a raggedy dress sitting barefoot at the roadside. The little girl was playing with a piece of plastic. It was all she had.

Amanda struck up a conversation with her, and after a little while, she said, "I have an idea. Let's go buy you some shoes."

She took the little girl to a nearby store, but the owner, seeing the dirty little girl, didn't want to let her in.

"In that case," Amanda said, "I'll take her somewhere else and you'll lose the money."

The owner quickly changed his mind.

Amanda led the girl to the shoe section, where she chose a pair of dress-up shoes. The owner intervened. "No, no," he said, "you need a pair of practical shoes, like running shoes."

Amanda bought the dress-up shoes, because, as she said to me when she first told me the story, "For this little girl, it may be the only chance in her whole life for her to feel like a princess."

•

AT THE FUNDRAISING EVENTS, WE also sold cards that my sister-in-law, Sandy, had printed. They were pictures from all over the world that Amanda had photographed on her travels. We bundled them in packages of four, with ribbons. The label included a Dr. Seuss quote: "To the world you may be one person, to one person you may be the world." Everyone loved them, and eventually we would sell the cards in a few stores as well.

Kelly and I also came up with the idea of preselling our story to raise funds, so I began another letter campaign. I wrote to publishers and to the CBC in an attempt to create interest in Amanda's kidnapping story and to see if anyone would be interested in publishing our story. Unfortunately, I couldn't speak for Amanda, and I couldn't guarantee—beyond my own conviction—that she would be released, allowing for publication or airtime. It was a desperate effort, and I understood the hesitation to front money on a gamble.

I had delegated my friend Grace to oversee events happening in the Red Deer/Rocky Mountain House area, and she worked tirelessly. She managed many fundraising events, including a Facebook sale of the newly named Pink Line, consisting of crates of items Amanda had purchased in India and Thailand. I had previously sold the goods at farmer's markets for our joint little business called Baraka, an Islamic word meaning "blessings." Now though, proceeds were going straight to the trust fund.

Our biggest fundraising event, "The Family Dinner," was held on October 8 at the Metropolitan Grill in Calgary. We sold 250 tickets at $80 for a spectacular feast prepared by four of Calgary's top chefs under the guidance of a local celebrity, Canada's first competing Iron Chef, Michael Noble. All food, wine, and work hours were donated.

Our guest speaker was Robert Draper, who had written about Amanda and Nigel in an article on Somalia for *National Geographic*'s September 2009 issue. Robert had been in Mogadishu at the Shamo Hotel at the same time as Amanda and Nigel. His car had been only about ten kilometers in front of theirs. It was highly likely that he had also been a target but had narrowly escaped. After Amanda's capture, Robert had gone into Amanda's room at the hotel and had found my phone number. He had contacted me, and after a few phone conversations and emails, I asked him if he would come to our fundraiser. When Robert's magazine editor insisted on paying his expenses to go to Calgary, Robert donated the money he would have spent out of his own pocket to the Amanda Lindhout Trust Fund.

His talk honored Amanda's and Nigel's journalistic efforts to tell the stories of the massive suffering in Somalia following two decades of war. He spoke eloquently of the majority of Somali people, whose only dream was to see their children grow up amid the chaos, deprivation, and destruction.

As I sat at the "family table" and looked around at the crowd assembled there to help us bring Amanda home, I felt overwhelming gratitude. I couldn't wait to tell Amanda about this night. I was reminded of that saying about how the stars are always there but you cannot see them until the darkness of night, and we were in the darkest of nights. All of this was happening because of the dedication, hard work, and love for Amanda. We would not let her down.

While dessert was being served, we showed a newly made video titled "A Mother's Plea." It featured me talking about our dire situation, explaining why Amanda had gone to Somalia, and pleading for help. There was barely a dry eye in the room.

We also held a silent auction with items donated by family, friends, and supporters. Mark and Nathaniel had driven from Nelson, British Columbia, with a truckload of donations from their community, as well as Mark's own paintings and handmade sculptures. Among the many incredible donations we received, Jann Arden had donated a basket of CDs and a voucher for two people to join her for lunch in Calgary. Remembering the summer Amanda and I had spent together in the Arctic, I was excited that Plummer's Arctic Lodges generously donated a fishing trip for two at Great Bear Lake Lodge.

The timing had been perfect for JC to join us as well. He had been visiting his mother in Vancouver and had flown in for the night. As everyone milled about after the event, JC made himself available for questions. His presence and expertise that night were pivotal for some of the decisions to donate.

Overall, the Family Dinner garnered $80,000, despite a colossal snowstorm that closed down highways and prevented some of our most passionate supporters from attending. I will always remember that night, October 8, 2009, as a night of miracles created by angels.

Of course, not everyone supported our cause, and sometimes we asked for help only to receive disappointing or hurtful responses. Some people, including a few family members, felt that what we were doing was morally wrong by raising ransom and that Amanda should accept the consequences of her actions. We were also told by some that they could not in good faith donate money they knew was destined to be put into the hands of criminals and extremists. I refused to argue with people who felt they were experts, who claimed to know what they would do if they were me. I realized that their judgments were made because they were not living my nightmare.

I could understand most of the reasons given, but the one I thought clearly revealed a person's character was our inability to supply a charitable tax receipt. I had spent hours on the computer and in phone calls and meetings trying to find a way we could do so, but of course we couldn't. I had been told a few times that if I could give a tax receipt, I could name the amount on the cheque. In the end, because there was no tax receipt, there was no donation. A tax receipt equals a human life. It was hard for me to swallow.

Back in Canmore, I continued my daily grind. Winter had come unusually early, and I was spending many hours on slick roads, driving through snowstorms to get to meetings and fundraisers. I was starting to have panic attacks and was experiencing an overwhelming sense of loneliness. Even though I was surrounded by people, I felt incredibly alone. If there were ever a time in my life that I wished I had a partner, it was then. When I mentioned my feelings, I was scoffed at. "Of course you're not alone!" "Look around you, Lorinda. You are surrounded by caring people." "You'll never be alone." It was true in many ways, but when I crawled into bed at night to struggle with my imagination and fears, I was very much alone. There was no one to hold me and tell me that it was going to be okay, that I was doing a good job, or wipe away my tears. It was just me, alone in the dark. I couldn't bear to think how lonely Amanda must feel after all this time.

But there was no time to wallow in self-pity, and every morning when my feet hit the floor, I said out loud, "Today is one day closer to Amanda and Nigel coming home!" The loving support surrounding me and the vision I held on to of Amanda's freedom gave me what I needed to get out of bed every morning and continue the fight.

CHAPTER SEVENTEEN

BREAKING THE CODE

Thirteen months into our hostage crisis, and the CMT was still blocked by Adan's stubborn demand for the millions of dollars our families didn't possess. Even JC, with all his experience, found the impasse unusual. The CMT had agreed that a Somali-speaking person would help us in our communications with Adan, and I had already spoken with Adan himself about it. We collectively hoped that having a Somali translator on the calls might discourage any more bad calls. JC introduced the CMT to Mohamed, a Somali-born interpreter whom he'd worked with before and whom we decided to hire. Mohamed was a teacher at a UK university. He had left Somalia thirty years earlier. JC thought his lack of a clan affiliation might be of value in speaking with Adan. Before each call, Mohamed would receive speaking points complied by the CMT.

Following the bad call, I ignored Adan's calls for six days. On September 13, I skyped Mohamed and then skype-dialed Adan for the introduction. It was not easy to get back onto the phone again, but I needed to get my daughter home. Right at the top of the call, I expressed my disappointment with his last actions and told him that I needed him to keep Amanda safe. He had no response. Then I brought up Mohamed and attempted to apply some pressure: "Can Mohamed speak to your whole group?"

I received a resounding "No!" Only Adan himself would talk to

Mohamed. I stayed on the call while they spoke to record the call, as well as to be available if Mohamed had questions for me. Even though I understood no Somali, I could tell they communicated easily. Mohamed was an elder, and as such, culturally he commanded immediate respect.

In this new phase of negotiations, each of us on the CMT received a translation from AKE the day after a call between Mohamed and Adan. We would read it, then discuss it with JC and the rest of our group to decide upon our next action.

That first translation proved an eye-opener. None of us had guessed how radically and positively having a translator would change the game. First, Mohamed restated our agenda: we were poor people; we couldn't get help from our governments; the offer we'd made was all we had. He then confirmed, "I am a friend of the family. I know very well about their situation. Really, they don't have a lot of money."

Adan confessed to Mohamed that he had previously been fired by the gang, but that he'd been reinstated when the gang had failed to make progress without him. That aligned with Ottawa's and JC's suspicion that for a time Adan had been out of touch with the kidnappers. Adan attempted to fish for Mohamed's clan association. "All Somalis know each other," he said. "If we can just have a little chat and personal conversation about our clan belongings, maybe we will recognize each other."

When Mohamed refused that bait, Adan returned to his grievous topic: our latest offer, which was now US $434,000. "The guys think it's a joke. I believe myself that what the families are saying about the money is not true."

He went on to complain about the expenses that had already piled up. "In Somalia, there is continuous untargeted shooting every day, and for a year they [the gang] have been securing the hostages' safety."

Again, Adan wished to distinguish himself from the rest of the gang. "They are illiterate people. They are gangsters who resort to violence and bloodshed." He was also emphatic about being the only one protecting the hostages. "I swear to Allah that it happened some time ago, while I was staying at my house, that I was called by the gang, saying they would kill the two hostages."

He complained about the previous negotiations with our governments. "I was having conversations for four months with people who were in Nairobi, and they were the ones who complicated things. As our negotiations were progressing, they said they were offering $25,000. The first day they called, they requested to speak to Amanda and Nigel. We have not yet recovered from the slap in the face. They were Australian spies. Those people ruined the program." No doubt the spies Adan spoke of were our government negotiators. Possibly he thought that Mike, put into play by Heather and Hamilton Brennan, was also a spy sent by the government.

Adan's frustration with the negotiations out of Nairobi was a subject he would return to over and over in his chats with Mohamed. Apparently, he had thought the US $25,000 initially offered by our joint governments was payment for the POLs he was asked to provide. When he had provided the POLs and had not been paid, he felt cheated.

By the end of the call, Adan was referring to Mohamed as "my sweet brother, Allah bless you." It amused me that whereas he had previously referred to me as Mom, or Lorinda, a woman to whom he'd professed his love and proposed marriage, now, on the call with Mohamed, he referred to me as "the old woman." Later, though I'm not Jewish I would be referred to as "the old Jewish woman," and then "the old Jewish commander." Ignoring the intended slurs, we were all thrilled with the new contact between Mohamed and Adan. We realized how important it was to have a translator on board. Now that we could see how much information we were able to get through Mohamed, it surprised me that our governments had not employed a translator between me and Adan. If there had been a translator between us from the beginning, it could have saved us months of guessing and misunderstandings. That, in addition to the Nairobi cell's failed negotiations, only aggravated my disgust with Ottawa. I tried to focus on the progress we were making now. Three days after the first

call with Mohamed and Adan, on September 16, Mohamed had another lengthy conversation with him. This time, he focused on trying
to understand why Adan believed the Brennans had $1.3 million "that
the old lady resisted not to be paid." Adan explained that the problem
went back to the personal letters we and the Brennans had included in
our medical parcel to Amanda and Nigel back in November.

As he now explained to Mohamed: "We are not fabricating lies.
From the side of Amanda, no money was mentioned. But Nigel's letter indicated that the family had sold a house for $1 million. We used
to have that document, but recently, when the war again broke out in
the country, we lost it. I was the one who read it. I swear in the name
of Allah, and I am fasting, that I am telling you the truth." He also
admitted that our personal letters to Amanda and Nigel were never
given to them. He was upset that I had stopped calling him. "Up to
recently, she didn't call me. I couldn't understand—why?" He was also
unhappy that Nicky had refused to speak to Nigel, since he had decided that the Brennans were the ones with all the money.

To demonstrate yet again that he was a "reasonable man," Adan
suggested to Mohamed a new, slightly better demand: US $1,734,000,
which he arrived at by adding our latest offer to the mythical $1.3
million he insisted that Nicky had mentioned to Nigel on the phone.
"To that, let the old lady add the amount of money she has now—US
$434,000."

Adan returned to his favorite rant, about the former negotiations
out of Nairobi. "I cannot continue talking for the sake of talking without a result. I swear in the name of Allah that during the Ramadan
month, I have decided to tell Lorinda that I will throw my SIM card
into the dustpan. The old lady earlier began her bargaining from
$25,000. They offered us $25,000, then sent elders with whom we
were familiar to force us to accept the deal. This, after we had reduced
our sum from $5 million to $2.5 million!" Our governments' decision
to freeze out Adan and work through clan elders had left Adan with a
residue of bitterness that was difficult for us to erase.

He asked once again for money for the upkeep of Amanda and

Nigel. "Look, a long time ago, I have discussed with the old lady to send $3,000 to look after her children. These captives are provided with food and fed twenty-four hours a day. If these people die from starvation in the future, don't blame me."

After our CMT received the translation, we focused on Adan's statement that one of Nigel's letters had said that the Brennans had sold a house for $1 million. He even referred to it as a document. That's when a bizarre insight finally emerged: the RCMP had dutifully combed through every one of our letters, looking for any statement that might produce negative consequences when received by the kidnappers. Apparently, the AFP had not done the same with all the correspondence sent by Nigel's family. Nicky's ten-year-old son had written a story for school, which had won him a prize. Since he was proud of it, he had wanted to include it in the family's letters to his uncle Nigel. The story was a retelling of "The Three Little Pigs," in which each pig bought a piece of property on which to build a house—one of hay, one of sticks, and one of bricks. Though the big bad wolf blew down all three, the police arrived in time to arrest him. For this, the pigs were given a $1 million reward.

It's hard to imagine how Adan, a Muslim, felt about pigs as characters in a story, but all that talk of real estate had excited him, as did the mention of a million dollars. The sale of a house was a colossal misunderstanding, one that had stymied any chance of a reasonable settlement for months. It might have been funny if the lives of our loved ones hadn't been hanging in the balance. The moment of clarity was so appalling that it was hard to comprehend. Had that innocent letter, a children's story, not been sent, Amanda and Nigel might have been free by now. Amanda might not have been tortured. It felt like I was being forced to swallow razor blades.

In the next call, before we had solved the riddle, Adan bitterly informed Mohamed that he had endured a period of mockery when the people in Nairobi had thought they would release Amanda and Nigel by force or without payment. He couldn't understand why I had stopped speaking with him. Of course he couldn't have known that Ottawa had forbidden me. In response to my silence, he said that the "boys guarding—tried to kill Amanda several times." He claimed that she would confirm that when she was released. I couldn't hear everything at once. I was overwhelmed by the horrifying statement that they "had tried to kill Amanda several times," which washed out the hopeful suggestion that she would be released.

The memory of how faithfully Jon and I had held on to the RCMP lifeline, and then how cruelly it had been cut, still had the power to rankle. Ottawa should never have cut me out of their negotiations.

So many to blame, so many stupid decisions, so much suffering, and so much time gone by. Too many absurdities to absorb at once. I had built a mental closet into which I put things to deal with later. I opened the ironclad door, threw the information in, and quickly slammed it shut before any bits of the past could topple out. It was the only way I could hold myself together so I could continue to take the epic steps ahead of me.

Adan continued to complain about the number of people who had tried to get in on the ransom negotiations, hoping for a cut of the money. He told Mohamed that our governments had attempted to use Sharif Sheikh Ahmed, the president of Somalia's transitional federal government, and other warlords to rescue the hostages by force. Since we didn't know how our governments had operated out of Nairobi, we had no answers for him, except to keep repeating that all connection had been dissolved. Though Adan's rants wasted everyone's time, it was fascinating to hear his righteous indignation over how we victims had trampled on *his* rights and those of a conscienceless gang of thugs.

Mohamed valiantly attempted to explain the misunderstanding regarding the "mockery" of our families' ransom offer: "The mention in Nicky's letter to Nigel of $1,000,000 was a story written by Nigel's young nephew, based on a tale that is very popular in the Western world. It is about three little pigs. It is not about Nigel's family selling a house. It means nothing to this situation."

Adan insisted that he had overheard Nicky telling Nigel on the phone that the family had $1.3 million: "The amount they are now offering is fruitless. Let them pay the $1.3 plus the $434,000 they have offered. I will accept that."

He then launched a diatribe about Amanda: "The so-called journalist is a camouflage name. Somalia is the third place she was captured. Amanda is a very dangerous girl and not normal." He also once again referred to me as "the old lady blocking progress."

As a counter, Mohamed suggested that Adan speak to both Nicky and me to clear up the $1.3 million misunderstanding. Though Adan still insisted that the ransom must be more than a million dollars, he had begun to sprinkle his talk with phrases such as "when they are released." Were we actually moving out of "Counter Offers and Threats" on JC's kidnapping chart to "Agreement"?

We decided to wait forty-eight hours before contacting Adan again, at which point we would offer more money. Nicky and Mohamed would take over the call, so Adan would see that he couldn't break her or "the old lady." We agreed wholeheartedly that we must not let ourselves be worn down by Adan's stubborn delay tactics. We knew our tough financial reality, whereas Adan was still living in his million-dollar fantasy world.

Around this time, I received words of encouragement from Alan Johnston, a British journalist who had been held captive by Palestinian militants for four months in 2007. I tried to take solace in Alan's words. He said that during the time he was held, his mind and body revealed strength he'd never known he had. "And that same might be true of Amanda right now," he concluded. "She is enduring something truly appalling, but she may just be finding even more strength than either you or she might have imagined she had." Alan advised me to try to manage my own reactions to uncontrollable events, and he was careful to acknowledge how difficult that was.

His words echoed what I had read in the book *Man's Search for Meaning* by Viktor Frankl. Four months into Amanda's kidnapping, I had bought the short 125-page book and had hung on to Frankl's hard-won truths. It's a book of hope and survival written by a man who survived the Holocaust, three years in four different camps. I read and reread the book and had almost as many pages underlined as not. But there were a few lines in particular that I returned to again and again: "Forces beyond your control can take away everything you possess except one thing, your freedom to choose how you will respond to the situation."

This was the wisdom—the light—that had guided so many others through dark tunnels, and I determined to keep it as my lantern.

CHAPTER EIGHTEEN

GIVE THE DEVIL HIS DUE

On September 23, I got ready for my next call with Adan. This would be a three-way call. Nicky and I would be on the line with Mohamed. We hoped to apply more pressure and show Adan that Nicky and I were aligned on all decisions; the "old lady" wasn't the obstruction.

The call was connected, and Adan immediately told Nicky that he was upset about her previous refusal to accept a call from Nigel.

"The thing you did to Lorinda was not very nice." Nicky said. Her voice was firm and direct. "She and I discussed that, and we decided I would not call."

Adan spoke to Mohamed in Somali and told him that Nicky was behaving badly.

He then offered to arrange another call with Nigel on the line, and Nicky again refused on the chance that Adan had planned a bad call. She also confirmed that our families stood together and that we were the decision makers, with Mohamed as our translator. She insisted that Adan had misunderstood the $1.3 million figure. It was nonexistent. When Adan angrily threatened to put the price back up to $3 million, she replied, "If we can't give you $1 million, we will never be able to give you $3 million. We have offered you everything we have, and we are working to get you more. However, before we can offer more, we need POLs from both Nigel and Amanda."

Adan sounded frustrated, and after the call ended John Chase warned us that we might be in for more threats.

Two days later—September 25—I received a text message from Adan: "Mom Lorinda Amanda wants to talk to you and Nigel is crying every day for his sister to speak his sister."

There was no way we were going to put Amanda or Nigel into the same position that Amanda had been in a couple of weeks before.

Nicky and Mohamed called Adan again. He was keen to hear our new offer, but Nicky and Mohamed insisted on POLs first.

For Nigel: "Who is Jumbo's wife?"

For Amanda: "What is your father's favorite color?"

Nicky asked Adan to text the answers to my cell phone.

Five days later—September 30—we had still not received our POLs.

Nicky and Mohamed called Adan again.

According to Adan, both Nigel and Amanda had refused to answer their POLs. As Adan explained, "Mr. Nigel say, 'I won't answer this because Mr. Jumbo was my kind friend, but when he married, his wife was cruel to me, and cut off the relationship.'"

This wasn't the answer we needed, and there was no answer from Amanda, either. Nicky didn't give in. Instead, she asked Adan for a new POL for Nigel: "What is a happy jack?" We didn't get much further on our attempts that day. Adan was cornered. He was not used to having to deal with us as a united front. With Mohamed, there was no more guessing for any of us, and with Nicky and me both on the phone, he couldn't try to play us against each other.

Adan tried to call my cell phone four times over the next couple of days, but we had agreed that I should not speak with him until he texted me the answers to the POL questions. Instead, he texted me that Amanda would not answer the question unless she was asked by her mother or father. After the horrific stunt he had pulled, I wondered if he really thought we were that stupid. I was desperately hoping that they were not holding to their threat of torturing Amanda every day. Our hope was that by not giving the kidnappers an audience, there wouldn't be any more bad calls.

The next day—October 1—Adan left the POL answers on my cell phone. Amanda correctly identified her father's favorite color: hunter green. Nigel's answer was right for the first POL about Jumbo's wife but not for the "happy jack" question. Regardless, Nicky accepted it as her POL.

That same day, Nicky and Mohamed phoned Adan with a significant new offer. "We had a family member die recently," Nicky explained. "After selling everything that was hers, we have an extra $130,000 Australian, which converts to US $114,000. Adan, our total offer is now US $548,000. Our sad loss through death is your gang's gain." Though it was true that a family member had died, the rest was a fabrication.

Instead of the usual outright rejection, Adan complained to Mohamed about how much he had suffered as the intermediary between our two families, "who play games," and his gang members, "who are ignorant and illiterate." He lamented to Mohamed, "It is hard to convince them with this amount when their expectations are huge."

After repeating again how important he had been in protecting the captives, he referred to the possibility of an agreement: "If Allah's willing, they will know the truth, when the captives are released, whether I was a hinderer or a helper." He was politely low key as he added, "I will go back to the group, and I will tell them the information. But I would like to suggest to you that it is better to offer them a more suitable amount." He rambled once more about his designs on Amanda: "Even though the old lady found it difficult to digest to let her daughter stay here with me, I know that I cannot marry her. The other guys will say, 'You are an infidel!' and they would automatically kill me."

Adan then got down to business: "Do you have people who are ready for the handover?" he asked. "Do you have a timetable? Do you need the matter to be resolved in a secret way?"

"It will be top secret," Mohamed assured him. "Nobody is going to leak or release information to the media or anybody else."

Could it be that, after 406 days, we might finally be reaching the "Agreement" stage? At long last, it seemed we were moving forward.

The CMT had a long conversation after this call. John Chase said, "Let the offer stand for a week, then consider adding a small amount." He also warned us that even though things were moving in the right direction, we might have to deal with more threats.

Ten long days passed before we heard from Adan. In the interim, I worried and hoped in equal measure. Then, on October 11, it was Amanda who left a number on my voice mail for me to call her. She said, "I have a solution." It was Thanksgiving Day and I was in Calgary at Sarah's house. Her voice sounded strong and upbeat, which made me tear up with relief.

Instead of waiting for our CMT call the next morning, I called JC for guidance, and together we agreed that I should call Amanda back. Considering the tone of Amanda's voice, we didn't think it would be another bad call.

I was happy to hear her voice still strong on the other end of the line. "Mom, any promises that you have made with Nigel's family, they have to be broken, like we all love Nigel, but we have been separated for nine months. It doesn't make sense to keep working together."

"Amanda, I speak with Nigel's family every day, and we are working together to get you both out."

"Now, listen to me. I am speaking to you frankly right now. Nobody's telling me what to say. If you agree to pay $500,000 for me, and $500,000 only for me, I will be released tomorrow."

It was obvious that Amanda had been told what to say. "Is there anyone coaching you?" I asked.

"Yes, I am with a few people here, with one man who is the reason we have this choice. He is the only person who has been kind to me, and I trust him, and he has persuaded the other commanders to give this chance for us and our family to pay $500,000."

"Amanda, the Brennans and I have raised this money together. We talk every day to Adan. Is he the one in charge?"

"He is one of the few people in charge, Mom. Nigel and I are not together, and I know that you guys are working together, but that commitment must finish. Nigel's family has said that they have $1.3—"

"Okay, Amanda, please listen to me." She was clearly confused about the money, and I could see where this was going, so I cut in. "That is not true. What Adan has been telling the group is not true. There isn't a separate amount from Canada and a separate amount from Australia."

I explained the misunderstanding over Nicky's son's letter and the three pigs. "It's a big misunderstanding," I repeated.

My heart was breaking. I knew I was giving her the news that she was going to have to stay in captivity longer.

"Mom, this is the only chance that I have. One kind person has convinced the other commanders to take the $1 million and to lower it to $500,000 just for me. It's just one chance, Mom."

"Amanda, Amanda, listen to me, sweetheart. I will phone you back at this same time tomorrow with a man who speaks Somali. Tell your friend I will call him back."

"I don't know what to say, Mom."

I hung up. I could tell that Amanda was desperate, and I could guess that her suffering as a woman was more severe than Nigel's. I knew that she was being manipulated by the kidnappers and the "one kind man" who had filled her with false hope. And of course, I was worried about how she was being used to drive a wedge between our two families. There was no doubt that Adan had not cleared up the misunderstanding with the other kidnappers, and my hope was that they could all listen to Mohamed explain it clearly to them. Of course, it made sense to Amanda if she thought that the Brennans had offered $1.3 million just for Nigel that she would then plea for me to pay the half-million dollars I had already told her I had offered.

Oh, Amanda, if you only knew . . . hopefully tomorrow we can clear up this absurd story.

The Brennans put on a stoic face over Amanda's plea to be rescued alone, though I later learned that it masked considerable upset. I would also learn that the kidnappers had played our taped conversation to Nigel over and over. In this way, the kidnappers were trying to seed animosity between our two families. But we didn't go there. We were focused on our common goal, and we were too close to achieving it to let others drive us apart. That next day, Mohamed was unfortunately not free to join the call, so Nicky and I spoke with Adan and Amanda. Her voice was now resigned rather than frantic with hope, as she repeated back what we had both told her. "The money that you have is US $548,000," she said. "And that's what you raised together for both Nigel and me. There is no $1.3 million."

"No, and there never was," I added.

Nicky confirmed, "And there never will be."

"Okay, Mom, thank you. I have heard what you have said, and it will be passed along. I have to get off the phone now. I love you so much. I love you both. Thank you, thank you, thank you."

Nicky and I barely had a chance to reciprocate the feelings before the phone cut off.

When we were reconnected, Nicky and I spoke with Adan. He seemed to be saying that the gang would accept our US $548,000, but before that could happen, he added a nasty condition. "You must understand," he said, "the gang is made up of good guys and bad guys. The bad guys are not satisfied, and if I try to force them, I am afraid for my life. They will kill me. There are two bad guys, and they will need to be paid off separately. They will need another $300,000 beside the $548,000, which would be $150,000 each. You understand me?"

He was quick, as always, to solidify his own position: "I am the only one who can simplify the situation. There will be no solution until you fulfill what I have said. You understand that I am the mediator, and I am not profiting from anything, but there must be two amounts."

I filtered the bitterness out of my voice as I tried to clarify what he was asking for: "You are saying that we must send two amounts, one to you and one to the group."

"I will conclude this if you increase the money by $300,000. This must be kept secret."

"Adan," Nicky insisted, "this is still more than we can pay."

"They believe that you have more money than you offer."

Adan wanted to convince us that he was actually the "hero" and repeatedly reminded us he would solve this and he was our only hope. He went as far as to say to me, "You are my mom, I tell you everything, then you see that I am, I am making you; I, I want to make you feel proud. I am not making you sick; you should know that I am the only person to want Allah allows when you will see Amanda. But I am telling you this situation will be solved by Mr. Adan only."

Nicky and I thanked him and promised to try hard to get more money.

"Even I like them very well to come to your home before Christmas to greet their friends, then, I want to work with you," Adan said. "What will you give me as a reward? Not compulsory, give me anything."

The call ended with his reminder to keep the separate amount a secret.

Nicky and I could barely believe that he was asking us to reward him. We both had a few colorful words as to how we would like to do that.

Afterward, John Chase easily deciphered Adan's cunning game: "He's likely one or both of the 'bad guys,' wanting to line his own pocket without the rest of the gang knowing. This is essentially good news. If the gang has agreed to accept the US $548,000, then they will be expecting Adan to finish the deal quickly. He has a limited time to tack on his secret payment without the others becoming impatient and suspicious." We agreed to make a separate extra offer, far lower than $300,000, in a few days' time, then promised to send more money in a few months' time, which, of course, we had no intention of doing. That would allow Adan both to make his sneaky profit and to save face when he realized he couldn't squeeze more out of us. Once again, we were grateful to JC for helping us turn an impossible situation into a workable one.

We were cautiously optimistic, but knowing that we were moving forward in our negotiations we began to contact Ottawa, asking what consular support we could expect when we flew to Nairobi to bring

Amanda home. The Brennans had done the same. We were excited to start conversations about meeting in Nairobi to bring Amanda and Nigel home.

Kelly, a flight attendant, had begun researching flights to Nairobi for herself, Jon, and me for "that day." She and I had been out shopping in Calgary and bought Amanda clothing for the return trip to Canada. We had to be tight-lipped, careful not to ignite any suspicion with our excitement among the fundraising groups. We felt so close to a resolution that we didn't want to do anything to jinx ourselves. Meanwhile, working out of my tiny basement suite, my headquarters, I was trying to manage the many fundraising events. I had become aware that there were too many people who were trying to be the boss despite my delegations. I was starting to receive daily calls with complaints, dissension, tattling, and threats of quitting. Even Mark and Nathaniel were at odds. On top of all that, the media were snooping around, suspicious that "something" was going on. I felt like a rubber band stretched to the max, hoping I could keep it all together just long enough to get Amanda home. The fatigue and exhaustion were taking a toll, and I had noticed that at times I was shaking. My head was shaky, and I had no control to stop it. Everything felt fragile, and everyone's patience was wearing thin. This had to end soon.

October 14, two days after Nicky and I had spoken to Adan, Nicky and Mohamed called Adan. He reminded us again that he was key to getting the "bad guys" to accept the additional $300,000. "I would like the hostages to be at their homes by Christmas," he added.

Nicky explained through Mohamed the difficulties caused by his extra demands. "At the moment, we are still trying to sell machinery, and Lorinda is asking people for money. This is a lot of money, and it is taking some time."

Mohamed backed Nicky by saying that he lives in Canada and he knows for a fact that "Lorinda begs people for money every day."

"I swear in the name of Allah," Adan replied. "I'll gain no interest or profit from here. If I don't have the money, how can I solve the problem here? It is said, 'Give the Devil his due!' What I need from you is to find a solution within an immediate acceptable time, within a week. So, my sweet paternal uncle, how can I resolve this without a helping hand from the other side?"

Mohamed replied, "The families phoned me after the conversation they had with you a couple of days ago. They were praising your efforts, saying every time, 'Adan is a good man. He did a very wonderful job.'"

"Listen, my friend. The others are from the bush, nomads. They are money-grubbers. And homicidal, who feel no pity for other people. They are illiterate people who want to drive new cars and chew *khat*. I just want to finish this program quickly. I want to take my mother to the pilgrimage in Mecca. Every day I lie to her, telling her at the moment, 'I am busy, but I will take you not today, but tomorrow, after tomorrow, the day after, et cetera.' She is an old lady, do you understand? So what is the solution?" Adan repeated his financial demands, then insisted on "Two sections addressed to two different names, but both for me."

Now it was clear why Adan wanted the extra money for himself: to take his mother to Mecca. I had heard that it was the dream of every Muslim to make the pilgrimage to Mecca at least once in a lifetime. It was Adan's dream.

Mohamed asked how the swap would take place.

"Understand my point," Adan said. "The whole affair is black market. No one can do the swap in a public way. It is up to you to bring a person you can trust. It will be hand to hand. We will hand the hostages safely to the designated area, without showing any suspicious acts. That is our responsibility."

"What Hawala brokers do you trust?" Mohamed asked. Hawala is a popular system used to transfer money through a network of brokers outside of the Western banking system. It is used internationally but in particular by the Islamic community.

"Dahabshiil is the most trusted." Dahabshiil, with its branches in many countries, was a broker JC had dealt with before.

Mohamed said we'd be happy to use Dahabshiil. "It is legally registered here in Western countries, and it functions in Somalia as well. It has dealt with these cases before."

Adan added, "Everyone in the streets knows which car belongs to Dahabshiil, and . . . it can pass safely through the streets."

Nicky, who had been listening in on this conversation, spoke up to stress to Adan the difficulty the families were having in raising the extra money. She and Adan agreed to talk again on Sunday, four days away.

What had been an abstract conversation, held over 419 stressful days, was turning into a reality, involving financial institutions and a process that could actually bring Amanda and Nigel home. Still, I knew better than to let my hopes run too far ahead of reality. Adan had a crafty talent for creating obstacles out of greed. But now he was impatiently talking in terms of weeks, supporting JC's intuition that he was under pressure from his gang. That, hopefully, would pressure him to accept our lesser offer for his "bad guys" side deal. As he'd said, "Give the Devil his due." With every passing day, it was clear who the Devil was.

CHAPTER NINETEEN

THE AGREEMENT

As promised, Nicky and Mohamed called Adan four days later, on October 18. Nicky spoke first, according to our plan, which was to show Adan that we were raising extra money for the secret payoff. But also she was trying to stall. The longer our negotiations went on, the more risk Adan was taking on with the gang. Soon, we hoped, he'd give in to our offerings.

Nicky told him there was a bit more farm equipment they needed to sell. "Adan, hopefully by Wednesday we'll be able to give you the extra amount. Lorinda is also trying to raise more money." She pressed ahead with details of the swap. "We are locating the Dahabshiil agent here in Sydney, Australia, so we can send the money for both families from here. Before that, Lorinda and I will need to speak with Amanda and Nigel for a POL."

Adan, as usual, told us what a big favor he was doing for our families. Then he surprised us by voluntarily lowering his "bad guys" demand. "If there is too much delay," he explained, "the gang may want more money. I am deducting US $100,000 from the extra US $300,000. I have given you my final demand. I don't want my reputation tarnished, and again tomorrow you will come up with fewer amounts than previously agreed, because I am dealing with human beings. Understand?"

It was satisfying to hear him give in a little. Finally, some of the anxiety he had caused us was being shifted onto him. We agreed to talk again in a week, at which point he closed with a demand: "Let the extra US $200,000 be ready by then."

On October 21, Nicky and I jumped the gun by calling Adan over what proved to be a very poor connection. To Nicky's alleged sale of farm machinery, I made my own false enrichment: "Adan, you know that Amanda's father is very sick. He has a special machine to keep him alive so he can stay at home, but now we have put Amanda's father in the hospital so we could sell the machine. We have raised another US $46,000. Added to what we have already offered, you will now have US $594,000, which is almost US $600,000."

Adan was indignant. "I have told you to make US $300,000 and then at least US $200,000!"

Nicky intervened. "This piece of equipment that Lorinda sold was a hugely important piece of Amanda's father's life. We're selling everything, Adan, at any possible price because we desperately want Nigel and Amanda home. To raise any more money is going to take a very long time."

"You don't know the situation here," Adan said. "And only Allah sees me, at this time, and sees in my heart, if I lie, Mom! How can I use this to tempt a solution?"

It was my turn to press a familiar strategy. "Okay, then, Adan. Can we speak to the other hostage takers?"

Click. Had Adan hung up on us, or had we lost the connection? Either way, we knew he didn't want us talking to anyone else in the gang. Despite his refusal of our offer, we believed we were moving into the homestretch—home, literally, for Amanda and Nigel.

Three days later—October 24—Nicky and Mohamed called Adan. Predictably, he complained about our puny offer and how we hadn't been returning his calls, which of course was the CMT's interim strategy. "I am not a person from the bush. I know everything that is going on around us. Even I watched a film about people who are trading with other people's organs, such as kidneys. I left a text message to Mom's mobile phone, and she didn't call me back. Again, yesterday I was giving her a call, but she didn't call back. I called her this morning, no answer."

He then issued a new threat: "There are others in Zimbabwe and Nairobi saying that they are ready to have a dialogue with us. I am in a very awkward position. What if my decision is to go to the groups and give the mobile number of Amanda's mother, and say, 'Either talk to the mother or kill Amanda if you want?'"

Mohamed attempted to calm him. "These are middlemen who want to profit from the ransom money."

"If I resign, there is a possibility that there will be a clash between the group, with unpredictable consequences."

"To resolve this matter," said Mohamed, "you have either to wait a minimum of another two weeks for the families to raise the remaining money you are demanding, or to accept what they have in their hands. . . ."

"Finish the whole affair on Wednesday, and call me," Adan shot back.

Unfazed, Mohamed replied, "Our next appointment will be next Saturday at the same hour. What do you think?"

Adan agreed, then signed off.

By this time, we were pretty certain that there was not a baby in the picture, or Adan would have used it for leverage. However, something Adan had said in that call fueled a fear that was already alive in my mind: only Amanda's name had been used in their death threats for the last few months. For whatever reason, they seemed to hold a deep contempt for her. I couldn't understand why she was the only one targeted. I discussed my concerns with JC. He felt that it was possible that the kidnappers still believed that Nigel was worth more money than Amanda. They had been told from the beginning that Nigel's family had more money than ours. And of course, there were the use of Mike and the "Three Little Pigs" fiascos.

I tried to focus on the good news. We were another step closer. We could all feel it. After the call, we spoke with JC. "He can't afford to let us talk to anyone else in the gang or to let the situation drag on much longer," JC said. He advised us to call Adan before the designated time and offer a modest additional sum. That would squeeze him into facing reality: accept the latest offer, or risk being fired by the gang and receive no payoff at all.

On Friday, October 30—434 days after Amanda and Nigel were kidnapped, Mohamed and I called Adan, prepared for the bartering game. But to our surprise, Adan quickly agreed to accept our $680,000 for both the gang and the "bad guys."

I gasped at hearing his words, the words we had all longed to hear for so very long. However displaced, I felt a surge of gratitude toward him in that moment.

"Mom Lorinda, we have battled a fight. Please forgive my part."

"Adan, you are like my son, I forgive you," I said quickly. I wasn't willing to risk tipping the scales that had finally moved in our favor.

"You happy that Mr. Adan finished this?"

"Yes, Adan, yes! Thank you. You are a good man, thank you."

I was doing my best to stifle the scream of joy rising in my throat. Mohamed and I told Adan that we would speak to Nicky and call him back with a plan for the exchange.

As soon as Adan's phone clicked off, Mohamed and I started screaming, "We did it! My God we did it! Amanda and Nigel are coming home!"

"Mohamed, thank you! Thank you so much for helping us make this happen."

"Lorinda, this situation was not right. I am ashamed of my countrymen who have behaved so badly. It puts a very bad reflection on Somalia and my people. I am happy to do such a small part. I am so very sorry for the suffering of Amanda and Nigel and for your families. It is the least I could do."

Finally, it was tears of joy that were streaming down my face. As I dialed JC with the news, my hands were shaking almost as much as they had been on that very first call with Adan so many months ago.

I called JC first, because I needed him to confirm the news by having him listen to the call. Even though I heard it with my own ears, I had to be sure that I hadn't misunderstood anything.

JC confirmed it. "But it won't be over until Amanda and Nigel are out of Somalia," he cautioned. Still, he couldn't mask the relief he felt, and I suspected that after he hung up the phone, he too let out a whoop.

It was the middle of the night in Australia, so we couldn't do a Skype call. The news would have to wait for our CMT meeting the next morning. I called Jon next, and we both cheered and cried, confessing that we were scared, knowing how tenuous our situation still was. Kelly was screaming when I called her and agreed that it was time to book our flights. "Now!" she said.

Next I called my friends Sarah, Grace, and Sue before dialing Ottawa with the news. Meanwhile, Kelly booked flights for all three of us for November 2. With the time change, that put us in Nairobi on November 4. Ottawa had already put Canada's High Commission in Nairobi on standby for us. Marion Lamothe of the RCMP would meet us in London and fly to Nairobi with us as our liaison with Ottawa. We would also be joined by John Chase and his team, as well as Heather, Geoff, and Nicky. Everything was falling into place.

There was more good news that day: our trust account was finally opened. I wanted to run out the door and hug everyone in sight. I sent out a mass email letting everyone in our fundraising circles and people who had pledged money know that, at long last, the Amanda Lindhout Trust Fund was officially open. It was a good day.

I wondered if Amanda and Nigel knew that we had reached an agreement.

Amanda, it's happening! You're going to be free soon. I promise. Come hell or high water, you are coming home!

It was hard for us to contain ourselves the next morning at our CMT meeting, but each of us also knew that as good as things looked now, everything could shift in a heartbeat. We still had a lot of work to do. After the meeting, Nicky and I called Adan. He was still anxious to finish the deal by the following Wednesday. JC agreed, joking with the group, "My ninety-day prediction expired five days ago, so we'd better hurry and finish."

Two days before my flight, I pulled out my suitcase and passport, and my heart sank as I realized that my passport had expired just ten days before. I made a frantic call to Ottawa, and it was arranged for me to pick up a new passport the next day, despite the fact that the office was closed on Sunday.

Nicky and Mohamed connected with Adan again on November 1 and explained that out of the $680,000 there were going to be extra charges to cover: bank transfers, service fees, and miscellaneous costs. We had calculated it would be close to $28,000. Adan was not happy about that and stressed that the gang would be very angry. Mohamed asked if he could speak to the gang to explain, and Adan agreed. I believed at this point Adan himself was fearful of their reaction, so he was willing to have Mohamed speak with them.

JC told Mohamed and me to call Adan back so that Mohamed could speak directly to the gang. Adan patched Mohamed through from his cell phone. From the minute Adan patched them through, they were shouting. They were angry and threatening to kill Amanda. They adamantly refused the lower amount. The call ended.

Please don't let this be happening, I thought. What happens now?

We didn't have to wait long for an answer. Immediately after they hung up, Adan texted me: "We want to solve this problem by Wednesday."

It was Sunday in our part of the world, already Monday in Somalia. We would lose two days of travel time. I had not yet told Adan that we were on our way. We didn't want to give him any wiggle room to drag things out longer in an attempt to make more money for himself. Our hope was that it would put more pressure on him if the kidnappers knew we were already in Nairobi, ready to finish the deal.

On the evening of November 2, Kelly, Jon, and I flew from Calgary to Nairobi via London, where we met up with Marion Lamothe of the RCMP. Marion gallantly exchanged his first-class ticket, which

RCMP officers are allowed for flights over eight hours, for my coach ticket. Even after we were in the clouds over Heathrow, I was gripping my seat and holding my breath. I knew many glitches could still occur between takeoff and that glorious day when I would embrace my daughter.

•

ONE OF THE CHALLENGES WE had already anticipated was getting access to the trust fund money in time. While we had been waiting for the trust fund to open, we had been using the monies from fundraising events to pay AKE, Mohamed, and all the miscellaneous expenses that we had incurred. Since the opening of the trust fund only days earlier, money had been flowing in. But it was crucial that all the money be exactly where it needed to be, exactly when we needed it to be there—which would be the minute we reached an agreement with Adan at the time of exchange. Alison had already sent her gift of $250,000 for Amanda and Nigel to Australia. Luckily an Australian benefactor had generously put up AU $700,000 to cover the ransom and any short-falls, to be reimbursed later. That gave us some breathing room. Because of this arrangement, the money would be transferred through Hawala from Sydney, Australia.

We were in the air now, one step closer to bringing Amanda and Nigel home. We could not risk the media knowing that we were in the final stages, so the handful of people who knew had to keep it secret. Not even my mom knew I had boarded a plane to Nairobi.

CHAPTER TWENTY

MISSION ABORTED

On November 4, as the plane came down through the clouds, I caught my breath at the beauty of the bright red-orange sunrise and the black silhouette of the acacia trees. It was a picture I'd seen many times in magazines and movies. It was a glorious and serene backdrop for what was taking place. Still, as I stepped off the plane, I had an overwhelming feeling of gratitude and optimism.

Canada's high commissioner, Ross Hynes, and his wife, Vanessa, were waiting to greet us. Marion Lamothe introduced us, then attended to our visas and other paperwork. We drove into Nairobi in the high commissioner's black sedan, with Canadian flags flying from the front bumpers. We felt like VIPs. At one point, Vanessa said, "We thought you might be really angry with the Canadian government and come here yelling at us."

Negative thoughts couldn't have been further from my mind at that moment. Ross Hynes had been fully involved with the previous Nairobi team working on our case. Obviously, he had been kept updated. The Hyneses graciously offered Jon and me accommodations at the high commissioner's residence, but we opted to stay at the Tribe Hotel with the Brennans and JC.

"We're rooting for you guys," Ross said. "And we're happy to help with anything we can while you're in Nairobi." Anything that is, except be party to paying the ransom.

When we got to our hotel, JC was already there with his team, and the Brennans would be arriving the next evening. While Jon and Kelly checked into their rooms, I had a quick meeting with JC, who introduced me to Shaun and Ed, two highly trained ex-military Brits whom JC had hired to go into Mogadishu to do the exchange. That moment was surreal. I felt as though I were in an action-packed thriller movie meeting with undercover agents. Except it was all real, and the life of my daughter was hanging on our ability to save her.

It was late in the day, and with the time change and jet lag we agreed that I would call Adan in the morning and let him know that I was in Nairobi and Nicky was on her way. It was time to finish this. For convenience, we would all stay in rooms on the fourth floor and meet on the third floor, which had a meeting space with couches and chairs.

The next morning, when I called Adan, he was surprised to learn I was in Nairobi and he was irritated because I had not answered his calls over the last two days. That was easily explained by travel time. I had a few objectives for the call:

- Give him my new Nairobi cell phone number.
- Get POLs—once Nicky arrived, we would need to speak with Amanda and Nigel before any money made its way into Mogadishu.
- Inform him that Noor, the agent from the money transfer system Dahabshiil in Mogadishu, did not believe Adan was who he claimed to be. In fact, Noor believed that he was part of a gang and they would not do business with him.

Adan was offended by Noor's assessment of him and told me that he would prove that "Adan is a respectable businessman."

I put the onus on him, telling him that it was his responsibility to clear it up, or no money could be transferred.

Later that same evening, Nicky and her parents arrived. Geoff and Heather turned in as soon as they got to the hotel. Nicky, JC, and I had a short meeting to catch Nicky up on my conversation with Adan. We all went to bed that night eager for the next day to arrive.

The following day, JC, Nicky, and I met in JC's room and dialed Adan. Adan again defensively accused Noor from Dahabshiil of not being fair to him but assured us that he would take care of it.

When we told him that we needed to speak with Amanda and Nigel, he became obstinate, demanding that the money must come first. There had been few moments when we felt we were in the driver's seat, but this was one of them. Adan and the gang knew that the money was so close to being in their hands, they weren't going to risk losing it now. He told us to call back in the afternoon and he would make the arrangements.

We had to make plans for our side of the arrangement, too. Early that afternoon, we all gathered to meet with Shaun and Ed. The plan was for them to fly into Mogadishu in a well-armed six-seater Cessna 210, owned and operated by an ex-military pilot with cross-border expertise.

Getting the money where it needed to go would be one of the most difficult logistical puzzles in the exchange. We needed the Dahabshiil money transfer agents to trust both Adan and us. So far, they did not trust Adan and had no intention of dealing with him. Adan promised to find a "respectable businessman" to collect the money on his behalf. Kel would have to earn the support of risk-taking Dahabshiil managers in both Sydney and Mogadishu. After extended negotiations, Kel deposited our ransom money in a Sydney Dahabshiil, with the promise that the funds would be transferred to a Dahabshiil in Mogadishu. Both Dahabshiil managers had to know the name of the person who would pick up the money in Mogadishu, along with the password the person would give the Dahabshiil agent to release the funds.

We tried to nail down as many pieces of the plan for the exchange as we could. Of course, some parts of the exchange would remain uncertain until we had a firm plan in place with Adan and the kidnappers. JC, Shaun, and Ed were incredibly patient with us as we continued to pepper them with questions. The one thing no one would mention out loud but we all knew was that the exchange would be one of the most dangerous times for the hostages.

After the meeting, Nicky and I went up to JC's room again to call Adan, hoping to hear Amanda and Nigel's voices and give them the good news. When Adan answered, he sounded drugged or half asleep, slurring his words. He insisted that the gang would not allow contact until they had the money. But when he realized that tactic wouldn't get him anywhere, he said to call at six the next morning to speak with Amanda and Nigel.

At 6 a.m. sharp, Adan instructed us that the gang would give us ten seconds each to speak with Amanda and Nigel. We would be allowed to ask only two questions: "Who are you?" and "Are you fine?"

"Mom?" Amanda's voice sounded hesitant.

"Amanda, Nicky and I are in Nairobi. We have the money to buy your and Nigel's freedom. You are coming home!"

"Are you sure, Mom?"

I had expected excitement. I repeated my good news once more, but my daughter had lived long enough with deception and uncertainty that she had developed a healthy skepticism. As I later discovered, Amanda and Nigel had been told they were being sold to Al-Shabaab, where they could expect harsher treatment. She thought the kidnappers were setting us up to steal our money and sell them again.

Adan texted me seven more times that day with a series of threats. He told us he would quit—"if you lose me, you will not get a solution"—or he would tell the gang "everything end in failure."

But I did not address any of his threats. Instead, for each threat I texted back: "When you have a safe place for the exchange, for hand to hand, we are ready"; then "When you are ready we can rent a small plane. Can you get a safe airstrip?" and "Adan, ask the group if there is a safe landing place to hand over. That is our solution now."

We decided to text the kidnappers' phone number that I had last used to speak with Amanda on the chance that Adan wasn't telling them the truth about the situation, but there was no response.

By now our group at the Tribe Hotel had grown to include two trauma psychologists from Canada and Australia and representatives from both embassies. While Nicky and I negotiated, the Canadian team, which included Ross Hynes, Marion Lamothe, and other Canadians working at the embassy, spent the day sitting on the second floor in order to remain separated from the paying of the ransom. They would be available when Amanda and Nigel were released, which would be the moment after the exchange. Then it would be their duty to protect Amanda as a Canadian citizen.

Meanwhile, Vanessa Hynes made it her responsibility to spend time with Kelly and Jon while Nicky and I were shut in JC's room, negotiating with Adan. She was equally gracious and generous to Geoff and Heather. She organized day trips, sightseeing, picnics, and shopping excursions.

After the first few days in Nairobi, I realized I had not spoken to my mom since the day we'd left, and I knew by now she would be worried, so I dialed her number. She picked up the phone. "Mom," I said, "I have something very important to tell you, and you must keep it a secret to protect Amanda." I told her I was in Nairobi and when I had arrived. I couldn't give her many details. "I am here to bring Amanda home," I continued. "Things have not gone as planned, and I will be here a while longer. Don't worry. Just keep us all in your prayers. I'll let you know when we're coming back. Just promise me that you won't say anything to anyone. Please!" It was a lot for her to digest all at once.

She was confused when I told her I was in Nairobi; for her, this came completely out of the blue. It took her a minute to accept everything I had just told her, but by the end of the call, she was on board with the plan. "I won't tell anyone, Lorinda. And of course, of course I will continue praying for you." I was relieved. That was all I needed to hear.

•

NICKY AND I CONTINUED TO spend all day, every day, holed up in JC's room, negotiating with Adan. Together, we tried to decide the quickest and safest way to exchange the money for the hostages. Talks weren't going well. Adan had become paranoid. It was clear to us that his secret side deal had put him into danger with the gang. He worried that a plot was in place to arrest him when he went to the Dahabshiil in Mogadishu to pick up the ransom. He even suspected my phone might be used to send a guided missile to exterminate him. Adan was again referring to me as "the old Jewish commander" when he spoke to Mohamed. I found it funny that Adan thought I could wield such power. We still dialed in Mohamed at times to help sort out Adan's misconceptions, but Mohamed had a job and could not be available for most of our conversations with Adan. The calls and texts between us were coming in fast and furious.

On November 8, four days into our time in Nairobi, while John Chase and I were having lunch, he received a text from an unknown person representing someone known as Musla. JC slid over beside me and said, "Now, don't panic, but read this." I looked at his phone:

Mr jon chase im friend of amanda and nigel. mr musla is tired of translator adan. Musla in charge he is waiting for you call, hurry. Mr jon, mr musla know adan want you to drop money at the market. that crazy. Waiting for call. Lorinda room 415 tribe

There was a phone number to call Musla directly. I was panicked, because that was my room. I didn't like that players in Somalia knew my room number in Nairobi. But we took it as good news that we might be able to work around Adan and his paranoia. First, though, we needed to find out who Musla was and what his connection was to the kidnappers.

After we showed the text to Marion, I was moved to a new room, with extra security personnel in the rooms around mine. Necessary precautions, as Ottawa did not want another Canadian to go missing. It had become evident there was someone in the Tribe Hotel feeding information to this Musla character. It was certainly unnerving, but the Tribe Hotel was also considered very secure, its gates and walls were patrolled at all times by guards carrying machine guns.

There was a nearby mall (also patrolled by armed guards) that was walking distance away. I loved to go to there for a short break. Today I decided I would buy lilies for my new room. They gave me a little more brightness in my day, and I could buy a huge bouquet for only three dollars. I was advised not to walk alone and to be aware of who was around me at all times. I was especially careful when I left my hotel room that day, but I was happy that I still had the freedom to make those trips.

Later, we went back up to JC's room to call Musla. A man with a high-pitched voice introduced himself as Nur Aden Nur, an MP in the transitional federal government of Somalia and translator for Musla. He spoke at a rapid clip, and his strong accent made it hard to understand him. He told us that the kidnappers were tired of Adan's delays and that Musla wanted the deal resolved quickly because the gang owed him money. The ransom figure Musla knew was US $548,000, which was consistent with the conclusion that the extra US $132,000 was Adan's secret rip-off money.

Nur told me that Musla was a soldier fighting for Al-Shabaab. This was a complete shock. I had always known that the kidnappers were a criminal gang. Now, this new information about a possible Al-Shabaab connection, whether true or not, was very worrisome. It also seemed that Nur wore many hats. Nur worked for the French Embassy in Nairobi and worked as a spy for whoever paid him top dollar. We were never entirely sure of the relationship between Musla and Nur. They came to us as a team to speed up the exchange, because they both wanted part of the money and they both had to deal with Adan to try to make that happen. Though Nur was working for Musla, they often had problems working with Adan. We would work with whoever we thought could get the exchange to happen.

We made the decision to cut out Adan for a time and see what progress we could make with Nur and Musla. We would skype Mohamed in whenever he was available, to make sure that there were no misunderstandings. Knowing that Musla was with Al-Shabaab made me feel even more that I was dealing with the Devil.

I knew that I would be judged for the possibility of handing money to Al-Shabaab, but none of that mattered as much as getting Amanda and Nigel free. It was one of many difficult decisions I was forced into, and one that no parent should have to make.

Nicky and I spoke with Musla to hammer out the safest location to do the exchange and how we would get him the money. He floated a few ideas, stressing that the exchange must happen on neutral ground between the warring sides. It was still hard to know whom to trust. Musla was adamant that he was now in charge and apologized for anything Adan might have said or done.

Now it was Musla's turn to look for a respectable businessman to pick up the money. When we disclosed how much money we would be transferring, we would also have to explain what the extra money was for. I wondered how Adan would explain that.

The next day, Nur texted my phone, saying that he was now in Nairobi and wanted to meet with us. Nicky, JC, and I met with Nur at a restaurant within the safe zone at the mall. Shaun and Ed sat incognito across the room, behind newspapers, watching the meeting, ready to jump into action on the chance that Nur had something up his sleeve. By the end of the meeting, we all felt that Nur could be the key we were looking for. We decided that Nur would fly to Mogadishu in our charter aircraft with Shaun and Ed to facilitate the exchange.

•

ON NOVEMBER 13, THREE DAYS after our meeting with Nur, Shaun and Ed were dispatched in the Cessna to land at Wajir Air Force Base in Kenya. From Wajir, Shaun and Ed planned to fly to Adan Abbe International Airport outside Mogadishu, two hours and thirty minutes away. Nur had complications, so he would fly separately on a commercial flight and meet our team at the airport in Mogadishu. We would, of course, cover all his expenses.

That night Geoff, Heather, Nicky, Kelly, Jon, JC, and I paused to celebrate. We met and shared drinks and laughter. Finally! Amanda and Nigel would be free! We had done it.

The next day, November 14, Shaun and Ed met General Mohamed Sheikh Hassan, the head of the Somali National Security Service, at Adan Abbe International Airport. So far, so good. This was according to plan.

Neither Adan nor Musla had found a respectable businessman to pick up the money on their behalf, so we were back to using Adan as the pickup person. At the last minute, the Dahabshiil manager balked because of what he considered "reputational risks"; he had identified Adan as a shady character.

We would have to move the money to a new financial agency. That would be dangerous. Shaun and Ed would have to physically take the money in an armored vehicle supplied by the MPs from the designated Dahabshiil through the tumultuous streets of Mogadishu to another financial agency called the Qaran Express. The money fit into a backpack, but it was so heavy it broke one of the straps. Nevertheless, it made it safely there.

The next day—November 15—Adan alienated everyone at the new agency, and they refused to deal with him. He tried to craft various deals in which he would have the money and the hostages at the same time, which was completely unacceptable to our team. Tensions rose. Adan and Nur couldn't agree on anything. Adan was very angry with me for getting Nur, "the biggest spy in Somalia," involved. Meanwhile, Musla tried to resolve the differences between the two. His dislike for Adan was clear, but he felt at the moment that we still needed him. Another day came to a close.

•

WE MOVED THE MONEY TO a different financial agency. But on November 16, Adan just didn't show up. That day's window of opportunity shrank, then closed. Nur and Musla were growing impatient for their cut.

The next day, Adan went to the agency three times to collect the money. After the manager refused him all three times, the gang threatened the manager, who was now fearful for his life. He firmly decided he would no longer deal with Adan. We were running out of options.

I sent Musla a text: "Mr Musla, Adan has now threatened the agency and they will no longer deal with him. You must remove Adan and take control."

He replied, "ok dear."

I sent Adan a text letting him know that we were calling our team back to Nairobi and the amount of money we were offering was going to go down to $593,000, dropping the amount by $90,000. It was time to play hardball We felt that Amanda and Nigel would remain safe because now Musla and Nur were involved and wanted a cut of the money.

While I was lying in bed that night, I thought about how Musla, an Al-Shabaab commander, might have interpreted my asking him to remove Adan. I hope he didn't think I was asking him to "remove him" permanently, as in, have him killed . . . As evil as Adan had been, I didn't want him dead. I remembered hearing his wife and two kids in the background during calls. I had no desire to send Musla the wrong message.

There were many lives at risk during those anxious days. JC checked in with Ed and Shaun at the Mogadishu airport every half hour. By now it was well known throughout Mogadishu's large criminal community that foreigners loaded with money were parked there, making our guys a target for ambush. Meanwhile, we'd moved the money through the streets several times, which was beyond risky, and we weren't any closer to rescuing our loved ones. We could no longer risk the lives of Shaun and Ed nor risk losing the money.

We had no choice but to call back our team after four days, with what remained of the money after the skim-offs. We told the kidnappers, notably Adan, that we wouldn't be jerked around any longer. The retreat was such a low point for all of us. It demonstrated how little control we had over the exchange. We had arrived in Nairobi with such high hopes, but now we began to fear that the deal, which we'd expected to conclude virtually overnight, would drag on. We couldn't begin to guess how much longer. Now we were praying that our plan wouldn't unravel completely.

After we made the decision to call back our team, Vanessa, the high commissioner's wife, knowing how hard our failure had hit us, invited all of us to their residence for an evening barbecue. I felt like a deflated tire; all I wanted to do was stay in my room and cry. But Vanessa was working hard to help everybody through those tough moments, and I decided to attend. I was grateful for the kindness she continued to show all of us.

We reconvened the next morning. We knew we had some hard decisions to make. We had no idea how long this would drag on, so Kelly, Jon, Heather, and Geoff decided to leave Nairobi and return when Amanda and Nigel were released. Nicky and I were the only family members left to continue negotiating.

•

FLYING TO NAIROBI HAD MEANT abandoning a full schedule of fundraising events at home, where I was expected to speak. At first, Sarah had told everyone I had the flu. But over time, that excuse wore thin, and she had to make up other excuses. She was even answering my emails, pretending to be me.

I wasn't sure how much longer we could keep up the charade. We could not afford for the media to find out and destroy all the hard work we'd done. But one thing was for sure: I was not leaving Nairobi without my daughter.

CHAPTER TWENTY-ONE

RELEASE

Now that most of our families had traveled back home, Nicky, JC, and I were left to decide the next moves to secure the release of Amanda and Nigel. Together with Ed and Shaun, we spent hours looking at maps and aerial photos of the area around Mogadishu, discussing various scenarios that could play out. Should we use Adan Abbe International Airport to fly Amanda and Nigel out? Or would it be safer to land in the desert for a quick exchange and fly out? Were money transfer systems still available to us, or had Adan alienated everyone involved? How were we going to get the ransom into the right hands? And finally, how were we going to get Amanda and Nigel back safely without incident?

Nur and Adan were both texting me, each trying to convince me that he, not the other, was in control. By that point, we believed Nur over Adan. Nur told me that Adan was hiding and begging for his life and that I should not communicate with him. Meanwhile, Adan was angrily texting me that the gang had now raised the ransom to $1 million again. His paranoia was still on high alert as now he claimed that "the old Jewish commander" had sent two foreign intelligence tanks and helicopters to assassinate him. Finally Musla stepped in and threatened Adan that if he did not stop interfering, he "would make him stop."

Nur texted me that the Somali MPs and the elders wanted this finished as quickly as possible. One of the MPs offered to drive Amanda and Nigel to the airport after the exchange—for a cut, of course. Musla promised to supply armed men to protect the money as well as Amanda and Nigel during the exchange.

Nur requested JC to have a phone conversation with General Hassan in Mogadishu, to ask for his blessing and assistance. The general promised both and gave permission for Nur to access the personnel he needed to make sure that no risks were taken and everyone was looked after. JC felt that everything was in order.

After much planning, on November 24, Day 459, we sent our team back into Somalia. Nur would be our key player on the ground, dealing directly with the gang during the exchange. He could maneuver through the streets of Mogadishu in a way our guys couldn't. After extensive behind-the-scenes negotiations, JC found we could still use a money system in Nairobi to send money to Mogadishu. Adan was out of the exchange, and Nur would pick up the money in Mogadishu. This meant that Shaun and Ed would have to personally drive the ransom money through Eastleigh, Nairobi's notorious Somali section, an area not much safer than Mogadishu. Once that was accomplished, JC gave Nur the receipt so he could claim the money in Mogadishu.

Even today, it makes me nervous to think about how much trust we placed in Nur. Here was a man who had all of our money in his control. And the fates of both Nigel and Amanda depended on how he acted and what he did with that money. But the bottom line was that we had no other options. We had hoped to finish the exchange that same day, but as we waited on full alert in Nairobi, nothing seemed to be happening. Shaun and Ed were stuck at the airport, where many of the Somali MPs were gathered, drinking tea and discussing how they were going to split the money. Day "one" came to a finish once again without resolution. That evening, Nur texted me that the exchange would happen the next morning. As much as we wanted to believe him, we were skeptical. Day "two" dragged on as Ed and Shaun continued to wait at the airport. We couldn't contact Nur, and we didn't know what he was doing. Somewhere on the ground, we hoped he was working toward freeing Amanda and Nigel, but we had no idea exactly how the exchange would transpire and who would be there to meet him when the moment arrived. Musla was waiting as well, as far as we knew, protecting the location where the hostage exchange was supposed to take place. It was the most dangerous time for Amanda and Nigel, and all of us knew it. So many things could go wrong; one false move, one misunderstanding, and everything could be lost. We were facing dozens of potential worst-case scenarios versus one single best-case scenario. I tried to keep my mind from wandering into the worst-case scenarios.

JC called Shaun every half hour for an update, but there still wasn't any news. It was growing darker—too dark to complete the mission. We were all thinking the same thing: there goes another wasted day. Shortly after 7 p.m., confident that nothing more was going to happen that day, Nicky left the hotel for the Australian high commissioner's home. JC and I moved from our perch on the third floor down to the second floor to sit with the Canadians, who had faithfully stayed close by, day after day. I looked at Ross, Vanessa, and the other three Canadians—Richard, Chris, and Jon—sitting with us and felt so grateful for their support. They looked as downcast as I felt. JC checked in with Shaun again. Frustration was turning into anger. Shaun and Ed were fed up with the tea-drinking MPs, the promises, and Nur, who wasn't answering his phone. After JC hung up, he said, "I'm going to try Nur's cell one more time."

This time Nur answered. "Operation in progress!" he shouted. "Can't talk now!" *Click. What?* JC and I stared at each other. Did that mean what we thought it did? Could this really be happening? What about our careful plans for the exchange to take place in daylight? Nighttime presented a whole new set of risks. We'd been told that shots were fired at anything that moved after dark. We waited on tenterhooks.

Within minutes, JC's phone rang. He answered the phone, and his eyes filled with tears as he handed the phone to me. "It's for you. It's Amanda."

"Mom?" Amanda's voice sounded small and afraid.

"Amanda!" I screamed. "You're free!"

Both of us, unable to speak, broke down and wailed. I have never heard myself cry like that before. It was like some primal noise coming out of me. I could hear men's voices yelling in the background, and then Nur told me that they had to go; Amanda could call me later.

Nicky and the Australian high commissioner were on their way. I looked around the room. Everybody was openly crying, cheering, and hugging each other, except for Chris, a CSIS agent, who was on the phone with his contacts in Somalia. CSIS, Canadian Security Intelligence Service, agents had been on-site every day as part of the Canadian team sitting on the second floor. I learned that they worked in the most secret facets of governmental security. Now that Amanda was free, it was the job of the Canadian government to keep her safe.

JC approached me. "We did it," he said. "She's free."

I threw my arms around him, still crying so hard I could hardly catch my breath. "Thank you! Thank you! We never could have done this without you."

"It was a team effort, Lorinda. We did it together."

As soon as Nicky arrived, JC called Nur's phone again to connect Nicky with Nigel. They were in a car speeding toward the airport, where our team was waiting. After a short greeting between Nicky and Nigel, Nur said Amanda and Nigel would call us later.

I called Jon, Kelly, Sarah, and my mom with the good news, cautioning everyone that Amanda and Nigel were still not out of danger. I asked them to spread the news to family, friends, and our supporters. I stressed the importance of not speaking with the media.

About twenty minutes after my call with Amanda, Chris came over and took my arm. "Lorinda, Amanda is speaking with the media. It's on the news right now. I need you to call her and tell her not to speak with any media until she is safely out of Somalia." He explained that she and Nigel were still at risk as long as they were in Mogadishu. Previous hostages had been kidnapped a second time, and we could not risk that happening to Amanda and Nigel.

I called Amanda and told her to stop giving interviews, explaining that she was not safe until she was out of Mogadishu. Her voice dropped. "What do you mean, Mom? Am I still in danger?" I was not about to share the story Chris had told me. "Amanda, until you are out of Somalia, I won't rest easy. It's safer for you and Nigel if you're not speaking with the media."

She told me that they had been taken to a hotel filled with Somali MPs. They had handed her the phone and had told her to speak. She hadn't realized that she could or should say no. She agreed to tell them that there would be no more interviews.

"I'll see you tomorrow, Amanda. I can't wait!" After all this time, after everything that had gone wrong, I said it as much to make myself believe it as Amanda.

"Okay, Mom." There was more hope than confidence in her voice.

After I got off the phone, I asked Chris how safe they were, and he told me that he had arranged for extra security around the hotel, which was already a "secure hotel," meaning gated and guarded. Still, I would be on edge until their plane landed in Nairobi.

Everyone gathered in the meeting room on the second floor, and we ordered champagne. We poured and toasted, cried and retold the moment of JC's call with Nur, our shock and subsequent relief.

The TV in the room was on, and I listened to Amanda's interviews, which were played over and over. When she was asked if she had been tortured, she said yes. I was incredulous that such a harsh question would be so insensitively asked of a woman only hours out of captivity. I started to cry again from a deep part of my being. *Why? Why had this happened to Amanda?* She was a good person, trying to help people. It wasn't fair. None of it was fair. Now those idiots on TV were using salacious details to sell news. It made me sick.

•

A COUPLE OF DAYS LATER, we would piece together the events of that night. Musla had kept his promise, and when the kidnappers' car drove up, Amanda said that armed men with machine guns came out of hiding, which terrified her. She didn't know that they had been hired to protect her, Nigel, and the money.

We learned that though the exchange had gone well, everything had not gone as planned. Nur had put Amanda and Nigel in a car, ready to take them to the airport, but as the car approached the airport, African Union peacekeeping forces protecting the vicinity opened fire. The airport was usually closed at night, and proper clearances weren't in place, so the peacekeepers assumed that Amanda and Nigel's rescue car was a threat. The driver had to turn around and return to Mogadishu. Once they arrived, Amanda and Nigel were escorted into the Sahafi Hotel and held under the protection of armed guards.

That night, as I lay in my bed, I prayed that Amanda and Nigel would be safe through the night. The dam of tears I had held back through the days of sadness, loss, hope, horror, and finally joy came in an unstoppable torrent. It was hard to fathom what we had lived through. Now I was only hours away from holding my daughter.

•

ED AND SHAUN HAD GIVEN Amanda and Nigel the packages we'd prepared for them containing toiletries and fresh clothes. Amanda's package also contained her pink teddy bear, Teeny. The team was anxious to get Amanda and Nigel out of Mogadishu as quickly as possible, but they were delayed because Prime Minister Omar Abdirashid Ali Sharmarke had requested a visit with Amanda and Nigel. By midmorning they were on their way with a short stop in Wajir to gas the plane.

Amanda called me again. "Mom, am I really coming home? Is this happening for real?"

"Yes! You're really coming home, Amanda. We'll all be home for Christmas. It's going to be the best Christmas ever." I could tell she was still nervous and looking for reassurance. It would be "real" only when she arrived in Nairobi.

I waited at the Tribe Hotel until the Nairobi airport radioed that their plane was coming in. Ross Hynes had arranged a car to pick me up and take me to the Aga Khan University Hospital to await their arrival. Prince Shah Karim Al Hussaini, Aga Khan IV himself, had arranged for Amanda and Nigel's care at his hospital. The media was anxiously trolling the airport as well as the hospital. Careful arrangements would be made to stay out of sight. We would be taken through a private entrance into the hospital once Amanda and Nigel arrived. Nicky and Heather, who had flown back, were with me as well.

That moment in time is forever etched in my memory. The blue sky, the warm sun on my face, and a breeze blowing my hair as I listened to the sirens of their cars approaching the hospital. Four black SUVs came screeching to a halt in front of me. Chaos ensued as men jumped out of the cars, yelling and speaking into walkie-talkies. I was frantically trying to see through the darkened windows of the cars.

Then a back door opened, and there she was. She got out slowly, holding on to the car for support. As I walked toward her, someone asked her if she needed a wheelchair, and she said yes. We embraced each other and cried until the wheelchair showed up. I could see Nigel nearby with Nicky. He, too, was frighteningly thin, his face hidden in a thick dark beard. Amanda and I tightly held on to each other's hands as we were whisked into the private entrance and taken up to the second floor of the hospital to the Princess Zahra Pavilion, a private wing usually reserved for VIPs. When the elevator door opened, a soldier was sitting there with a machine gun on his lap. He had been hired for our security should we need it.

I am often asked what that moment was like, when I first saw Amanda. I know that people are picturing a "movie" moment, the same one that I myself had pictured for 460 days. Amanda and I running into each other's arms screaming with joy. But it was not like that. I was shocked by the skeletal girl standing before me. Though she had her hair in braids, there were bald spots showing through. Evidence of malnutrition and abuse. Some of her back teeth had been smashed out. When I hugged her, I could feel her ribs, shoulders, and hip bones jutting out. But hardest to bear was her eyes, surrounded by dark circles. They were haunted with experiences of pain and sadness that no one else could comprehend. Any fantasies I had held about

Amanda's release and our return to our "before" life were shattered. We had a very long journey still ahead of us.

Amanda's hospital room was huge and included a cot that had been made up for me.

"I can't believe it," she said, getting up from the chair and looking around.

"I know," I said. "I know."

She pulled up her pant leg. "Mom, look."

I could see the bruises around her ankles where she had worn chains for more than ten months.

A nurse came into the room, handed Amanda a hospital gown, and told us that a doctor would be in soon to check on Amanda. While we waited, an attendant came in to bring us tea and a menu for Amanda. She told her to order whatever she wanted. Amanda started to cry. "Mom, it's been so long since anyone has been nice to me."

As she excitedly perused the menu, she couldn't decide, so she ordered four different entrees, but when the food arrived, she could force down only a couple of bites. Staring at the plates, she said, "I can't . . . I can't eat. I want to, but I just can't, Mom."

We weren't alone for long. Doctors soon began coming and going, but the hospital staff didn't know who Nigel and Amanda were. For their protection, their identities were being kept secret. Amanda was treated for malnutrition and dehydration. Some of her broken teeth had become abscessed, so she was sent immediately to an in-house dentist.

That night, even though we were exhausted, we both sat on her bed. She sat cross-legged and excitedly asked how her family was doing. She wanted an update on everyone. I kept the conversation light and told her some funny stories. In those precious moments between us we even had a few giggles. It was as if for a few minutes we had a magic bubble shielding us from all the badness.

There would be plenty of time to cover the heavy subjects later.

I tucked her in and kissed her forehead.

"Mom, you're not going anywhere, right? Please don't leave me."

She sounded like my little girl from years ago, when she had been afraid of the dark.

"Not a chance, Amanda. I'm going to be sleeping right there on that cot."

As I lay on my little cot, looking at my daughter in the big hospital bed, I cried for the miracle of her being safe beside me. I woke up many times throughout the night just to look at her. To make sure that she was really there. All through that night—and for months to come—she would wake up suddenly, gasping and screaming, and then gaze around in abject terror.

"Shh, it's okay," I said. "You're in the hospital in Nairobi. You're safe now, Amanda. I'm right here."

The next morning, when Amanda woke up, she climbed out of bed and went straight to the window. She opened the curtains and let the light stream in. Then she stood with her hands held up toward the sun, tears streaming down her face.

"Mama, I didn't see the sky for so long."

Throughout that day, and for days to come, I'd notice that she was pinching herself. "What are you doing?" I asked.

"I still don't know, Mom. Is this real? When I was in captivity, my dreams of being free were so vivid, and then I would wake up, still a prisoner. I can hear what you're telling me. I know you keep saying I'm safe, but I'm so scared that I'm going to wake up and still be there." There was nothing I could say to make those fears go away.

A couple days into our hospital stay, I found Amanda lying on the bathroom floor, crying. Instead of asking her what was wrong, I lay down beside her and wrapped my arms around her. She said, "Mama, they did such terrible things to me."

"Amanda, you can tell me as much or as little as you want to."

We continued to cry in silence. Details were slow to come over the years as Amanda felt ready to share them.

Amanda knew that Jon and Kelly were flying back to Nairobi, but she didn't feel that she was ready to see anyone else. They would have to wait until she was ready. Amanda would sometimes panic. "I need

Nigel!" she'd say. By then Nigel had rid himself of his beard. No one else in the world could understand what they'd been through, and they gave each other great comfort in those first few days. They reveled in the freedoms that they now had to enjoy the simplest things in life. To speak to each other, to go wherever they wanted without permission and supervision. To eat whenever and as much as they wanted. To live through the day without fearing for their lives.

While Nigel and Amanda talked, I sometimes went to the elegant hospitality suite where those involved with our case gathered daily. We thanked our lucky stars that Amanda and Nigel were just down the hall rather than hidden away in the hands of dangerous men.

One day, when I got to the hospitality suite, I slumped down onto a couch. Amanda and I had just talked about the worst "bad call." In the same conversation, I compared notes on information we had been given by Ottawa. I came to realize that she and Nigel had been kept hundreds of miles away from where Ottawa had told us they were. I was feeling distraught and angry.

Marion came in, carrying his backpack, all cheery. "Well, hi! How are you today?"

In that moment I snapped. All the tension, all the months of believing that Ottawa was so close to getting Amanda released, all the shock of now knowing what had happened to Amanda while we waited, it all came pouring out.

Marion was quiet for a minute. "I'm really sorry," he said.

By then I was crying hysterically. JC had witnessed the whole conversation and sat on the chair across from me. "Remember that call?" I asked. "That really bad one, when the line dropped, then Amanda came back on line? One of the kidnappers had punched her in the head, knocking her over. She really was being beaten and tortured."

The Canadian trauma psychologist, Joy, came over and sat beside me. "Stop crying, Lorinda. Be strong."

I lost it again. "I *am* fucking strong. Just because I'm crying doesn't mean I'm not strong. Fuck you!"

Apart from the calls I had not been allowed to answer at the SLOC and my subsequent meltdowns, very rarely had anybody ever seen me behave like this. But in that moment, my empathy evaporated and I was on a tear. Everyone in the room was uncomfortable, their eyes downcast. No one wanted to observe the scene I was making. I kept on going until I finally exhausted myself.

.

THREE DAYS INTO AMANDA'S HOSPITAL stay, Jon and Kelly arrived in Nairobi. They were so excited to see Amanda, but she still didn't feel ready to see them.

"I can't," she said. "I just can't face any more people right now."

"Of course," I said. "I understand."

Jon accepted this and decided he was happy just to be there, just to know he was in the same place as his daughter and that she was safe at long last. But Kelly didn't understand right away.

"She's in shock," I explained. "Please don't take it personally. She just needs a bit of time."

A couple of days later Amanda did feel ready to see Kelly, and the two spent some quality time together. After that, Amanda was ready to see her father as well. They both looked nervous as Jon came into her room. I left to give them privacy.

After six days spent recovering, Amanda was finally strong enough to leave the hospital, but she was not yet well enough to make the flight home. She and I stayed at the high commissioner's residence for another week. Jon was booked into the Tribe Hotel again. Amanda slept in the Trudeau Room, where Prime Minister Pierre Trudeau had once slept.

During that time Amanda also needed to be debriefed by Joy, the psychologist. It would be beneficial for Amanda as well as the government. It would give the government the chance to see from the inside, through Amanda's experience, at how it might have made different decisions, for reference in the future. It also allowed it to collect data on the chance that down the road they would have an opportunity to prosecute one or more of the kidnappers.

On December 7, Amanda, Jon, and I flew together from Nairobi to Canada in a Challenger jet sent by the federal government. We stopped overnight in Greece, then in Ireland to refuel. When we flew into Nova Scotia, our moment of touchdown onto Canadian soil felt so significant. I was so proud and grateful to be a Canadian, to be free and safe. From there we flew to Calgary, where we landed in a private part of the airport, enabling us to avoid the media. A van whisked us to a hotel in downtown Calgary, where Perry joined us. We rested for a couple of days. Jon and Perry went back to Sylvan Lake, while Amanda and I headed to my tiny two-room basement suite in Canmore.

We were home!

PART III

CHAPTER TWENTY-TWO

HEALING

For months I'd harbored dreams of welcoming Amanda home with a lovingly planned Pink Party, featuring banners and balloons and cupcakes, with everybody toasting our Pink Princess. But Amanda wasn't well. She was sick, really sick. She had crawled out of a deep, dark hole, and she wasn't ready for fanfare and celebrations. She needed time to process and to heal. And the truth was: so did I.

The planning of the Pink Party, I now understood, had been for me—to give me hope that would sustain me through the very long ordeal of Amanda's kidnapping. Now, though, reality was anything but pink. I let all of Amanda's supporters and friends know that the Pink Party was not going to happen, at least not now. The reaction I received in response was quite a shock. Some people who had been so selfless in supporting the cause of bringing Amanda home now felt that they had a right to see her and tell her how much they had done for her and even how much *they* had suffered. On one level, I understood their reaction. All of us had wanted, hoped, sometimes even expected that the Amanda who went to Somalia would be the Amanda who came back. But she wasn't. And how could she be? That was too much to ask. After Amanda's return, I sometimes became angry at well-intentioned people. And I definitely became upset at those who did not understand boundaries and what Amanda needed to begin her long journey of recovery.

At home, Amanda tried to carry on and acclimate to life. She felt obligated to see her family and friends, but 460 days held in captivity under the worst possible conditions made it difficult. Above and beyond what she herself had endured, life had gone on for her friends. Three of her closest friends had become engaged. Amanda was happy for them, but she didn't feel that she fit in anymore. She also needed to talk, to express some of what she'd been through. One of her friends lashed out at her, "Everything is not about you!" Amanda was so hurt that she stopped talking about herself. It seemed that an underlying anger, which had been invisible before, was coming out in shocking ways. It was a confusing and difficult time. Amanda would often express how guilty she felt, as if she owed everybody. She was pushing herself to please everyone, but it never seemed to be enough.

This estrangement reached deep into our family. Amanda was eager to see her brothers, but they were hesitant and conflicted. Now that she was back, their anger about her going to Somalia in the first place surfaced. They had lived the nightmare on this side, and had helplessly watched the hell that Jon and I had gone through. They were also afraid that Amanda might share details of what she had endured, and they weren't sure how they could possibly bear the pain and anger of hearing it.

"Amanda," I said to her, "they don't understand what happened to you, not really."

"I'm not going to tell them—not that part." She had decided not to reveal to any of her family the worst of what the kidnappers had done to her. That was her right, and we all respected that.

I had hoped for a fresh start for our family, a new unity, to emerge after the crisis, but instead it seemed as though our family was fractured in new ways. Nothing was what I had expected after Amanda's return. Every one of us had been traumatized at different levels, and not one of us knew how to process it. I felt bitter toward some of my relatives who had discouraged my efforts to raise money for a ransom on the grounds that it was preferable to let Amanda die there because it had been her choice to go to Somalia. Jealousy also reared its ugly head among some of Amanda's family and friends, what had *she* done to deserve all the attention except get herself kidnapped? What about us and what we did to save her?

Without question, far more people were kind. We arrived home in Canmore to a big WELCOME sign and a full refrigerator. Then, just a few days before Christmas, Amanda and I were sitting on my couch, with a yule log burning on the TV channel, listening to Christmas songs, when there was a knock on the door.

I opened the door and found a little Christmas tree with twinkling lights. My upstairs landlady, Shirley, and her son, Chris, had placed it at our door, then ran back upstairs. We were both deeply touched by that simple gesture. As we sat on the couch, staring in awe at the Christmas tree, "Hands" from Jewel Kilcher's *Spirit* album played and Amanda started to cry. "Mom, this song used to play in my head when I was in captivity. It gave me something to hang on to." I immediately googled the lyrics. Then it was my turn to cry. The words reflected the strength and courage of my daughter and her determination to stay positive no matter how dire her circumstances.

Our immediate family gathered at Jon and Perry's house for Christmas that year. We celebrated with the full turkey dinner that both of us had dreamed about while she was gone. Amanda's freedom and our family safely reunited were the most precious gifts we could have ever received.

In those early days, Amanda still felt the need to reach out to Nigel. She would often go into the bedroom, shut the door, and skype with him. The two remained closely bonded for a couple of months, then slowly they went their own ways, trying to leave their shared nightmare behind. Even as captives of the same gang, Amanda and Nigel had lived through very different experiences because of the kidnappers' contempt for women, especially Amanda. After their release, they became reintegrated into families that were thousands of miles apart, families who had joined forces for a common cause but didn't share much beyond that.

With time, Amanda began to grasp that she was free, and she

started to become excited about life's possibilities. I watched that shift, as she turned into a more mature version of her old self. What drove her now was her desire to pay forward her gratitude by establishing what she called the Global Enrichment Foundation. This was an organization with the mission to empower Somali girls through education and through addressing gender-based stigma and abuse. Six months after returning home, she had the foundation up and running.

There are two moments during that time that stand out like beautiful jewels:

On the first Mother's Day after Amanda came home, she gave me a Celine Dion CD, and played the song "Because You Loved Me." When the song came to an end, she said, "Mom, I thought about you and this song in my darkest times. I just knew it would be you, Mom. I knew you would find a way to bring me home."

The other time, Amanda and I were in the living room listening to some upbeat music, and Amanda slowly started to dance. With tears streaming down her cheeks she said, "Mom, I didn't know if I could ever dance again." I felt as though I had witnessed a miracle.

●

As AMANDA STARTED TO FIND her footing, my biggest surprise—what I had never expected—was how Amanda's homecoming would come crashing down on me. I had survived, day by day, by blocking out what Amanda might be suffering and focusing on the singular goal of bringing Amanda home. Now I could no longer ignore what had happened to her—the horrific abuse. The closet in my head where I had been stuffing everything to "deal with later" burst open. It was now "later," and all its terrible contents came tumbling down on me.

The joy I felt about getting Amanda back was fleeting. Joy was followed by rage, which escalated until it consumed me. I raged at Ottawa for the time I'd wasted believing in them. I raged at the AFP over their idiocy with the tactless "Three Little Pigs" debacle. I raged at Heather and Hamilton for hiring Mike to get Nigel out. If that had actually worked, I was certain that the kidnappers would have followed through on their threats of murdering my daughter. But especially, I raged against her kidnappers. That rage grew exponentially until it materialized into a maniacal plan. I still had phone numbers connecting me to dangerous people in Somalia. Why not hire them to track down Amanda's kidnappers to castrate or kill them? I felt justified in my thoughts even as I knew that rage was consuming me in the most unhealthy of ways.

I had a pivotal moment of clarity while indulging in my dark fantasies about how I would punish the kidnappers. I looked at myself in the mirror one day and thought, Who are you? I was becoming someone I didn't recognize. I was a child of the 1960s and '70s, singing along with John Lennon, "All we are saying is give peace a chance." My worldview had been based on the idea that love had the power to heal the world. I had marched in peace rallies and sat in silent protest against the testing of nuclear weapons. I could not fathom how anyone could intentionally hurt another human being. But suddenly, now I could, and I had to ask myself what was I going to do with that. I could perpetuate the madness of violence and war—"You hurt me, so now I will hurt you," and on it goes. If I continued feeding my rage, I could become "one of them." It frightened and shocked me. I had to find a way to release the rage before it ate away my own humanity.

I plummeted from my fiery peak of fury into a deep valley of despair. Now I had a different target for revenge. The person I most wanted to kill was myself. I blamed myself for the length of time Amanda had suffered because of my unwavering faith in Ottawa. I should have known better. But what really took me down to the darkest depths was the worst bad call. If only I hadn't challenged Adan by being aggressive with him, Amanda would not have been tortured. It was my fault. The pain and guilt were so overwhelming, I didn't know what to do.

I was a walking open wound, but I was supposed to be happy. My daughter was free. I couldn't understand what was wrong with me. Everyone around me expected me to be happy, too. When my friends would excitedly ask how we were doing, I would break down crying. I was hanging on by a thread that could snap at any moment.

In the beginning, in front of Amanda, I pretended to feel what I thought I was supposed to feel for as long as I could. But then there came a time when I could no longer hide my darkness.

"Mom," Amanda said, "promise me you will never do anything to hurt yourself."

I couldn't answer her because I couldn't make that promise. Suicide consumed my thoughts.

Amanda took matters into her own hands then, and in an incredible reversal of roles, she did everything she could to help me. She phoned a big donor, who had helped us with fundraising, and she told him, "I'm really worried about my mom." He flew me in his private jet to a naturopath at an American clinic for the day. Then, on the same day, he flew me to Vancouver Island, where I spent a week at the Biocybernaut Institute, working with its founder, Dr. James Hardt, who specializes in trauma.

I had always been a strong, healthy, energetic person. I didn't realize how depleted I had become. I was fatigued and stressed, my body and mind weakened. I had been running for so long on adrenaline that I had nothing left. My own doctor in Canmore diagnosed me with severe adrenal fatigue, Hashimoto's disease, and hyperthyroidism, all of which were contributing to my severe depression. After months of treatment, I would start to feel better and more optimistic.

Amanda and I both had trouble finding professionals trained to deal with PTSD for the depth of our trauma and for how long it had gone on. Amanda would eventually find the perfect trauma therapist for her needs. I continued being introduced to a collage of different healers and healing techniques. No single option provided an instant cure, but each contributed a piece to the puzzle of healing.

We started to repair our lives in more ways. After a couple of months living in my tiny basement suite, we found a larger home to live in. By that time, I had given up almost all my furniture through the many moves and the limited space of the basement suite. Our new friend and neighbor Wendell Lund, who had already done so much for us while I was fund-raising, made it his mission to fill our new home with furniture. A few months later, Amanda and I both felt secure enough to exercise our independence again. I found a house on the same road, a two-minute walk away. It couldn't have been more perfect, giving us each our own space but close enough proximity to visit as often as we wanted. Sadly, we lost Wendell to cancer that same year.

.

THROUGHOUT MY LIFE, I'VE TURNED to the inspiration of books written by people who have suffered and not only survived but learned how to thrive. I returned to my well-used and underlined copy of *Man's Search for Meaning*, by Viktor Frankl. While he was imprisoned in Auschwitz during World War II, Frankl learned that meaning could exist in every moment, no matter how intense our suffering. Though we may have no control over what is done to us, we have a choice about how we react.

Frankl wrote about the moment when the gates of his camp were opened and the prisoners cautiously walked through them to freedom. They did not run through with excitement, as everyone had expected; they walked through slowly and fearfully. When I read this months before, it was the first time I had any inkling that things might not be as I had envisioned when Amanda came home. Although the idea stayed in the back of my mind, I hadn't believed that this would be our experience.

Frankl's book, which I read over and over, not only sustained me throughout Amanda's kidnapping, it then helped me to understand Amanda's feelings, my feelings, and the feelings and judgments of others upon her release. It inspired me to turn my negative emotions, reactions, and impulses into recognizable rescue stations along a path to recovery. What astonishes me is the number of times Frankl used the word "opportunity." He chose to see prolonged suffering as a teacher. I was determined to grab the opportunity to learn and grow from my experience.

•

It's been eight years since Amanda's release. I'm still a work in progress, but I have made great strides. I've learned that suffering has the potential to be one of the greatest opportunities for spiritual awakening and evolution. It can teach us who we are and how we can become better people. I no longer feel imprisoned by rage, and I take great joy in the world around me. That doesn't mean it has been easy. Five years ago, the shaking that had visited me off and on toward the end of our negotiations turned into constant shaking, so much so I could barely function through my day. The tremor was now affecting my voice, and for a time I almost completely lost my ability to speak. I also had a seizure. It was as if my nervous system had reached overload. Despite a multitude of tests—MRIs, CT scans, cameras down my throat—no physical reason could be found. Today I'm still shaky and my voice still sounds choppy, though I refuse to accept it as a lifelong sentence. I believe that through nurturing myself mentally, physically, emotionally, and spiritually, I will heal completely.

Anxiety has become a formidable nemesis, an unpredictable beast that can be triggered by seemingly innocent things: sight, sound, smell, comments, movies, the news, or no reason at all. PTSD shows up unexpectedly and unwelcomed, challenging me to find ways to transcend its mire.

What helps me deal with PTSD and anxiety is acknowledging that fear is real only in the moment that something is actually happening. Otherwise, it's an illusion. Nothing that happened in the past can hurt me or my family now, and worrying about what "could" happen in the future is a waste of time.

Sleep continued to elude me for years following Amanda's release. Nightmares and panic attacks plagued me, but with a medical prescription for marijuana, I can now enjoy a good night's sleep. Sleep itself is one of the ways the body heals and resets itself.

I don't handle stress as well as I did in the days when I felt I was made of Teflon and nothing could stick to me. I try to keep my life as peaceful as I can. Doctors tell me that the adrenals are like a gas tank: when they're depleted, you're not going anywhere, no matter how hard you press the gas pedal. Though you can build them up again, a stressful incident might slide the gauge back down to empty. I've been cautioned that it could take years to fill up my tank to the level I used to consider normal. Since I don't have the energy to work full days yet, I work part-time instead. And I prioritize my health and well-being.

I also regularly take stock of the many blessings around me, especially the amazing people who came into my life because of Amanda's kidnapping. I continue my daily gratitude practice because it brings me joy. Recognizing beauty in its many forms, despite the circumstances, is a healing salve for a wounded heart. I realized through our experience that gratitude is a powerful force and can exist independent of our circumstances. Gratitude brings transcendence, raising us above whatever is happening, inviting the flow of grace.

My extraordinary daughter came home carrying the message of forgiveness, whereas it took me a while to get there. Any parent knows that it's easier to forgive someone who has hurt you than it is to forgive someone who has hurt your child. I always understood, in my heart as well as in my head, that not all Somalis were responsible for making my family suffer. It was a handful of criminals. Most were teenagers, a product of more than two decades of poverty, starvation, and civil war. I doubt they've ever lived one day free of trauma. In Canada, we cannot comprehend that kind of daily desperation. Amanda was a victim of victims, which doesn't mean that those who tortured and imprisoned her are innocent. They are not. They committed heinous crimes and should be held accountable if possible. There is a difference between justice and revenge.

Again and again, I practice forgiveness as memories arise. Forgiveness has been the key to reclaiming my life and moving forward. I know that forgiveness really has nothing to do with the person or persons responsible for my suffering. They may not know that I have chosen to forgive them. It's equally important to remember that forgiveness never obligates me to have that person in my life again, especially if he or she is toxic or dangerous. Ultimately, forgiveness has been a gift of freedom to myself.

Can forgiveness change what has happened? No, but it can change our present and our future. All of us have to live with ourselves and our actions, including Amanda's kidnappers. Marianne Williamson, the author of *A Course in Miracles*, wrote that "the practice of forgiveness is our most important contribution to healing the world."

No one gets through life unscathed; suffering is a part of our human experience. We can use it to enhance or diminish our lives. We choose what to do with it. That's the one freedom that can never be taken from us.

At the heart of forgiveness is love. Love for myself and for the world around me. It's a choice that makes the world beautiful again.

For the past few years, I've spoken to groups about my experience as the mother of a daughter whose health, life, and spirit were put at risk for 460 excruciating days. I have tried to help other families who have had a loved one taken from them and will make myself available in the future to anyone else who finds themselves in the same situation. Without choice, I belong to a small, elite group now that no one hopes to ever find themselves included in.

Sometimes I'm asked, "Why don't you just forget about it and lead a normal life?"

This is my "normal life." My hardships have made me stronger and more compassionate. Just as I have learned from the experiences of others, I believe it's my turn to pay it forward. I still believe that love is the answer to healing the world, though I'm no longer naive enough to believe that's it's as simple as I thought in my teenage years.

Peace starts with each of us choosing to forgive whatever we hold against others and against the world. Each of us has the potential to heal or to hurt, which is why it's so important to cultivate kindness as well as forgiveness. There is no power greater than love and no place so dark that light cannot shine. Hope is one of those lights that radiates in the darkness. As Victor Frankl wrote, "More people died from lack of hope than lack of food or medicine."

It's still hard for me to face the fact that I can never take away the pain and trauma my daughter suffered, but both Amanda and I are moving forward with immense appreciation, gratitude, and hope for the future. I know there are many more good people than bad in this world. My experiences have made me better appreciate the beauty that surrounds us every day. Forgiving myself has perhaps been my biggest challenge, but giving up self-judgment and acknowledging that I did the best I could under the circumstances has given me peace and freedom. In fact, I have come to feel great compassion and admiration for "that woman" who never gave up and ultimately saved her daughter's life.

Before and after, I choose compassion and joy, and the freedom that comes through forgiveness. I choose love, because love brings us home.

EPILOGUE

On June 12, 2015, coincidentally Amanda's birthday, an RCMP investigator called Amanda and me with some news concerning the RCMP's ongoing investigation. We had known that police continued investigations after Amanda was released, so we were curious what the investigator had to tell us.

To our surprise, they had arrested a man called Ali Omar Ader after luring him to Canada with the promise of a publishing contract to write a book about Somalia's history. We were stunned.

In October 2017, Amanda and I both traveled to Ottawa to testify at his trial at the Ontario Superior Court. The trial was a challenging process in which Amanda and I had to revisit the trauma of her captivity, with her captor sitting just a few meters away. It was terrifying to face him, but the minute I took the stand and looked him in the eye, my fear subsided. The control he once held over us was gone.

On December 6, 2017, Ali Omar Ader was found guilty of kidnapping Amanda. By the time this book is published, Ali will have been sentenced. This is justice. I find no joy in his suffering. I will pray for his wife and five children, who are innocent victims of his crimes. They have been left to fend for themselves in the midst of war and famine.

"Adam" stole so much from our lives, but I am no longer consumed by that. At a certain point I realized that through post-traumatic growth I can choose to become unstuck. I am stronger, and I can grow from an experience in new and healthy ways. Amanda, myself, and our family continue to focus on healing and the future, living and enjoying our lives to the fullest.

A NOTE TO READERS

This memoir is my personal recollection of events that took place during the time that Amanda Lindhout, my daughter, was kidnapped and held as a hostage in Somalia. At times, I also delve into our family's history and backstory, using my memory as my guide. There are moments in my story that were particularly traumatic for me; despite the emotional and psychological trauma I have endured, I have done my best to accurately reflect my experiences in these pages.

In regards to phone calls that took place between me and Adam over the course of Amanda's 460 days in captivity, I have faithfully re-created conversations as much as possible. I have taken liberties only in the following ways: to change punctuation in certain transcripts for the purpose of clarity; to condense conversations to avoid the repetition of ideas; and to omit indiscernible moments in the dialogue due to poor phone connections or miscommunications.

Regarding other dialogues that appear in these pages, I have re-created conversations based on my memory of the experiences; while no doubt imperfect, what I have written represents my best efforts at honest disclosure about a very trying time.

—LORINDA STEWART

ACKNOWLEDGMENTS

First and foremost, I want to thank my family, all survivors of trauma. Without their love and support, I would never have made it through 460 days of hell and the following years of breakdowns, illnesses, recovery, and growth.

My mother, Jean Stewart, you taught me love and modeled strength by your example. When the going got tough, you got going. You taught me that love was not meant to keep but to share. Thank you for the significant financial debt you incurred through your generosity in helping to bring Amanda home.

Mark, you were my first child and thus my guinea pig. Every day I give thanks that you still speak to me. Your love, strength, and kindness are a gift to all who have the privilege to know you.

Amanda, thank you for choosing to live when life handed you its worst. You are the embodiment of strength, beauty, and grace. You continue to inspire us. I am so very proud of the woman you've chosen to be.

Nathaniel, my loyal, compassionate, loving, gentle giant. Your strength is your gentleness and your unwillingness to tolerate what you see as "bullshit." You bless my life every day.

Janet, you taught us all from the day you were born what it means to fight for your life. You suffered endlessly, and yet you smiled and allowed your suffering to make you a more compassionate person. Love is eternal even in your physical absence.

Tiffany, my youngest daughter, you are a bright and shining light. Your determination to break the cycle is a beacon of hope to others. People told me that you and Jan were lucky to have me, but the truth is, I was lucky to have you.

Jon and Perry, we brought Amanda home together. Thank you for being the amazing human beings that you are. Together, we set a unique example of a mixed-up crazy family that continues to forgive and love each other without end.

Thank you to my extended family. Many of you held my family up in any way you could with prayers, phone calls, donations, and fundraisers. Special thanks to Angie, Christy, Alana, Dan, Terra, Chris, Trisha, Danny, and Nicole.

To Jon's extended family, Oma and Opa, Tony and Sharon, Jack and Sjanie, Corrinne and Stu, thank you.

I am forever grateful to all the RCMP members who trained me and held me up in the most unbearable of circumstances. You tried to make my bizarre life manageable. Many of you are named in the book, but for all who are not, you are not forgotten and no less important to the story. Heidi, Jim, and JM. Robert T., lead investigator, thank you for more than I can express, but mostly for your gentle patience and understanding for Amanda and me.

Kelly Barker/Cox, thank you for being there for Amanda and me. You gave me a little piece of Amanda whenever I saw you. You held up as a loyal friend under circumstances that could have crushed a weaker person.

Grace Baxter, your loyalty and dedication as a friend are second to none. You literally put your life on hold to work tirelessly to help me save my daughter's life. Thank you could never adequately express what is in my heart.

Sue Robinson, thank you for bearing the burden of the truth and trying to "normalize" my life as much as you possibly could. Your friendship is a treasure.

Sarah Geddes and David Singleton, you two became my pillars. You both worked relentlessly on our behalf, even to your own detriment. You welcomed me into your homes and families and never once cowered at the immensity of the goal ahead of us. You will forever hold a special place in my heart. Thank you.

Immeasurable gratitude to the "Amanda Team": Kelly, Jelara, Dara, Brenna, and Kaela for all the hours of planning and executing. Everyone dedicated an enormous amount of time, and you ultimately saved the life of your friend.

Michael Dixon of Blake, Cassels and Graydon LLP, thank you stepping in pro bono to give us the key to opening the Amanda Lindhout Trust Fund.

Thank you to Linda Wolfe, Caroline Allard, Michael Going, and Steve Allan for diligently taking care of all the monies.

Aunt Alison, there are no words to express our gratitude for your gift of love and the emotional support you gave us. There is so much said about a person's character when they give without expectation for anything in return.

Allan Markin, not only were you one of our big donors helping to bring Amanda home, but you continued to care for us in so many ways afterward as well. Your altruism is truly inspiring.

On the other side of the world in Australia, my deepest appreciation to the Brennan family for our partnership in bringing Amanda and Nigel home. It was a heart-wrenching time for all of us, but we never gave up. I wish you nothing but prosperity and joy as you move forward.

Dick Smith, you were an important key when we needed help, available at a moment's notice. Thank you.

John Chase, you brought two desperate families together and guided us through the most difficult time of our lives. You always kept your cool and never once lost your compassion for the human beings in the story. You are one of the most extraordinary people I know. Thank you.

Shaun, Ed, and Derrick, you guys willingly risked your lives by going into Somalia to bring Amanda and Nigel back to their families. You are heroes!

Mohamed, thanks for stepping in to translate for us. Another key to making it work.

Enormous gratitude to former High Commissioner Ross Hynes and wife, Vanessa, for taking such good care of us while in Nairobi. And to the entire Canadian team for sitting close to us throughout and stepping in after Amanda was released. Richard, Jon, and Chris.

There are countless people to thank, most notably from Canada and Australia, who stepped forward to help us raise the money we needed to free Amanda and Nigel. There is no way to repay them, so I will continue to pay forward the acts of love, generosity, and kindness. I hope the knowledge that you saved two lives will inspire you to continue to be kind and help others in need. You were the stars shining in my darkest night.

I owe a debt of gratitude to the many healers who have come into my life to help me put my life and health together again. Thank you to Dr. Lourens, my family practitioner and friend, for properly diagnosing me and assuring me that I was not going crazy.

Thanks to Heather Cummings and João Teixeira de Faria (John of God) in Brazil and the generous sponsors of the St. Ignatius Fund. *Obrigada!*

Thanks also to Dr. James Hardt and the staff at the Biocybernaut Institute.

I wish to thank my *ayahuasquero* Ronin Nai for safely guiding me through my healing journeys with the Amazonian plant medicine *ayahuasca*. And to Dr. Gabor Maté for helping me process my journey. It was profoundly enlightening and healing.

Thank you to the generosity and intuitive healing initiatives of Rita Bozi at Brilliant Healing Systems.

And last but certainly not least, thank you to Simon & Schuster Canada for giving me the opportunity to share my part of our story. My editor, Nita Pronovost, you patiently kept me on track and encouraged my belief in this book. Erin Bartnett, thank you for your expertise and editing. Sylvia Fraser, for your added touches. My book agent, Dean Cooke, thank you.